Julia Feyrer

and

Tamara Henderson

Bottles Under the Influence

Consider the Belvedere

The Last Waves

This publication marks the culmination of Julia Feyrer and Tamara Henderson's three-part exhibition project:

Bottles Under the Influence at Walter Phillips Gallery, Banff Centre May 4–June 23, 2013

Julia Feyrer and Tamara Henderson: Consider the Belvedere at the Institute of Contemporary Art, University of Pennsylvania April 22–August 16, 2015

Julia Feyrer and Tamara Henderson: The Last Waves at the Morris and Helen Belkin Art Gallery, University of British Columbia September 6–December 4, 2016

Julia Feyrer and Tamara Henderson documents the project viewed through the artists' films from the perspective of the exhibition installations at Banff Centre, ICA and the Belkin Art Gallery that served as the sets for their films, as well as from the artists' process archives, which include the writing, poetry, drawing and painting that form the backbone of the artists' respective practices. We are pleased to print two texts that illuminate the artists' collaborative practice. ICA curator Alex Klein contributes a perceptive essay focusing on hypnosis and the nocturnal in Julia and Tamara's collaborations. Jesse McKee, who played a catalytic role in the project at Banff, considers the artists' work through the lens of René Daumal's early twentieth-century surrealist group, *Le Grand Jeu* (*The Great Game*). Our sincere thanks are due to Mark Owens for his remarkable design of this publication, which honours the spirit of Julia and Tamara's project.

The ambitious exhibitions at ICA and the Belkin would not have been possible without the heroic efforts of our committed staff who worked closely and diligently with the artists throughout the process. We thank them for their tireless and resourceful contributions.

We are enormously grateful to all the individuals who worked behind the scenes with Julia and Tamara on the many details and components that contributed to the success of the exhibitions: At ICA, to the crew, led by Paul Swenbeck, who went above and beyond; to Jeannine Han and Daniel Riley who provided expert help

     Directors' Foreword

with sound, fabrication and technology; to Jim Hopper, the dream stenographer; to Tony Solitro who composed the drinking song; and to the wonderful opera singer Lauren Pearl Eberwein who performed it with such aplomb. At the Belkin, to Vivienne Bessette for creating the very effective and delicious NRG drinks; to Kallie Clayton and Scott Rumble for their rousing performance of the drinking song; and to Brian Ditchburn from UBC's Department of Chemistry glassblowing studio, who created the *Communicating Vessels* with Julia and Tamara. Our thanks, too, go to Catriona Jeffries, Catriona Jeffries Gallery, Vancouver and Sylvia Kouvali, Rodeo Gallery, London for their support through the exhibition and publication process.

We extend our deepest gratitude to all those who have funded this project, whose generous and long-term support have enabled our galleries to realize these ambitious and innovative exhibitions and publication. *Julia Feyrer and Tamara Henderson: The Last Waves* at the Morris and Helen Belkin Art Gallery was made possible with the generous support of the Canada Council for the Arts and our Belkin Curator's Forum members: Audain Foundation, Christopher Foundation, Nicola Flossbach, Henning and Brigitte Freybe, Jane Irwin and Ross Hill, Michael O'Brian Family Foundation, Phil Lind Foundation, and Scott Watson and Hassan El Sherbiny. We gratefully acknowledge the support of K.T. Aydin Law Corporation, the UBC Department of Art History, Visual Art and Theory, the Beaty Biodiversity Museum, the Department of Theatre and Film, the Faculty of Arts, the Alma Mater Society and the Department of Chemistry.

Julia Feyrer and Tamara Henderson: Consider the Belvedere at the Institute of Contemporary Art, University of Pennsylvania (ICA), was supported by Wendy Fisher, Cheri S. and Steven M. Friedman, Christina Weiss Lurie, Norma and Lawrence S. Reichlin and Lori W. and John R. Reinsberg. Related programming was supported by the Christian R. and Mary F. Lindback Foundation.

And of course, most importantly, we would like to thank the artists, Julia Feyrer and Tamara Henderson, whose imaginative spirit and dedication to their practice are exemplary in the art world today. It has been our sincere pleasure to work with them.

Scott Watson
Director
Morris and Helen Belkin Art Gallery
University of British Columbia

Amy Sadao
Daniel W. Dietrich, II Director
Institute of Contemporary Art
University of Pennsylvania

Directors' Foreword   5

past
Chance

hers

blind

Hag

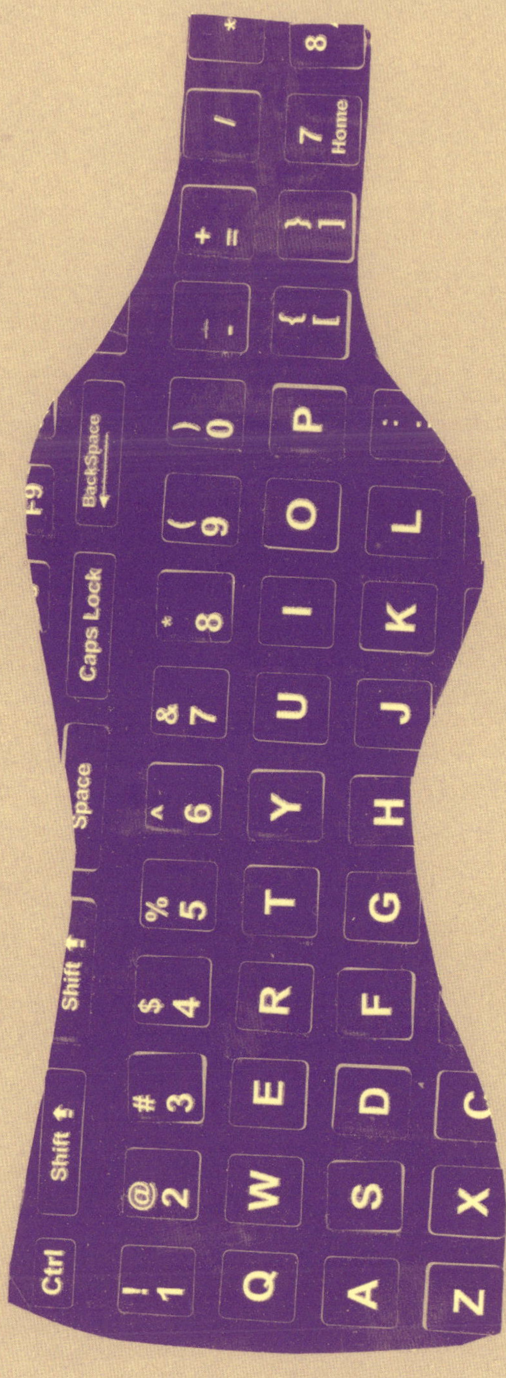

Some ten thousand bottles
we've killed in our time
beer, gin, cider, whiskey,
mead, cocktails and wine

Is it any wonder why
we've gone to pieces again
punctured, severed, dismembered

Ah hey oh what the hell if
we drink enough we can't tell
ladies of virtue turned to vice

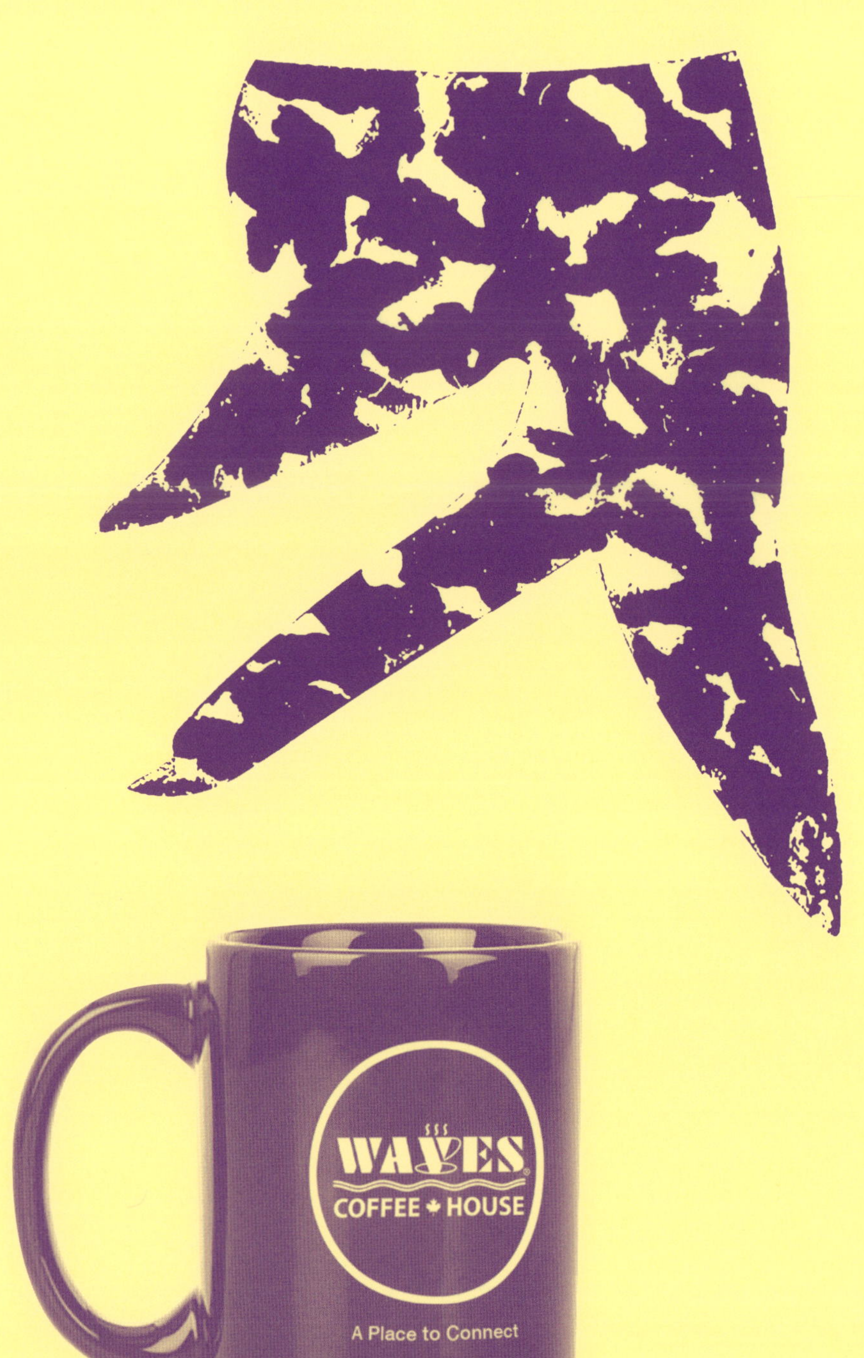

WAVES
COFFEE ★ HOUSE
A Place to Connect

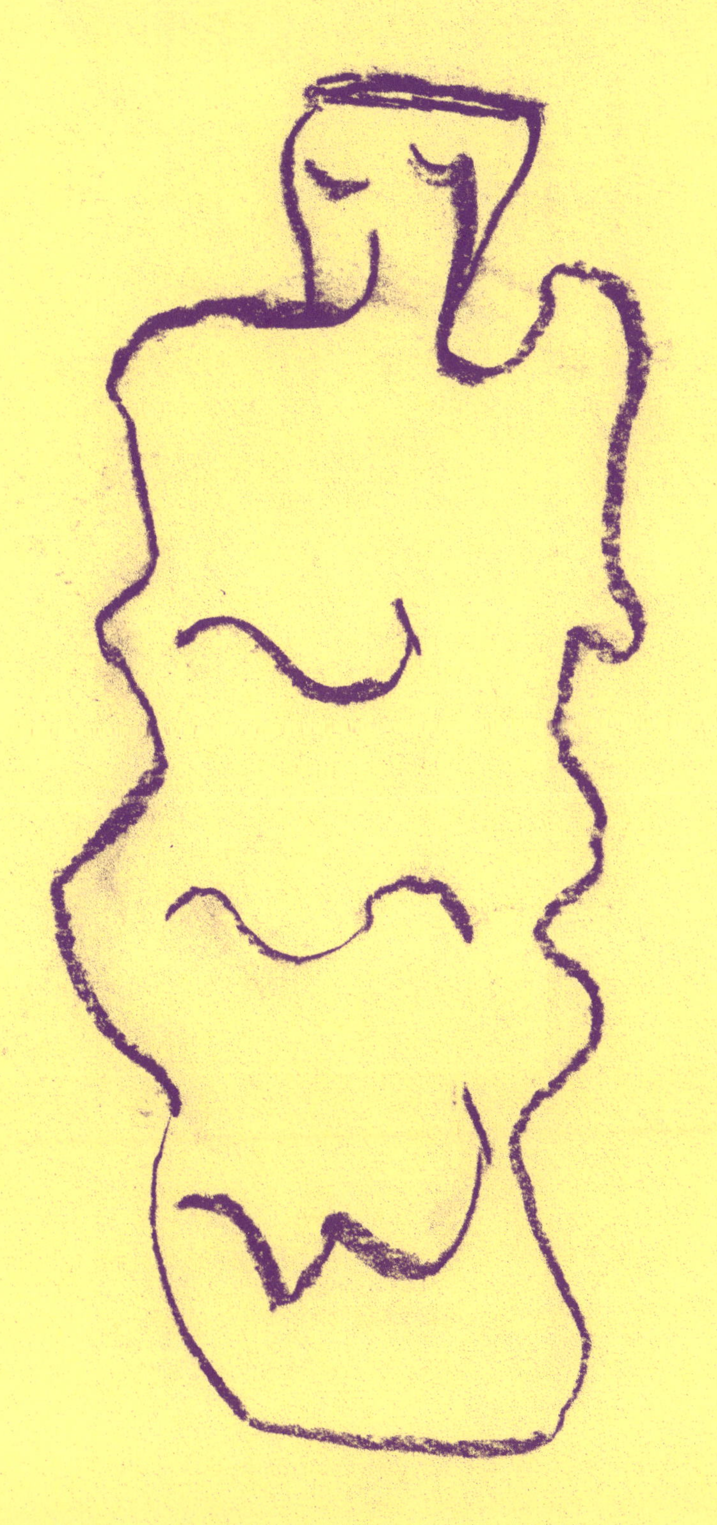

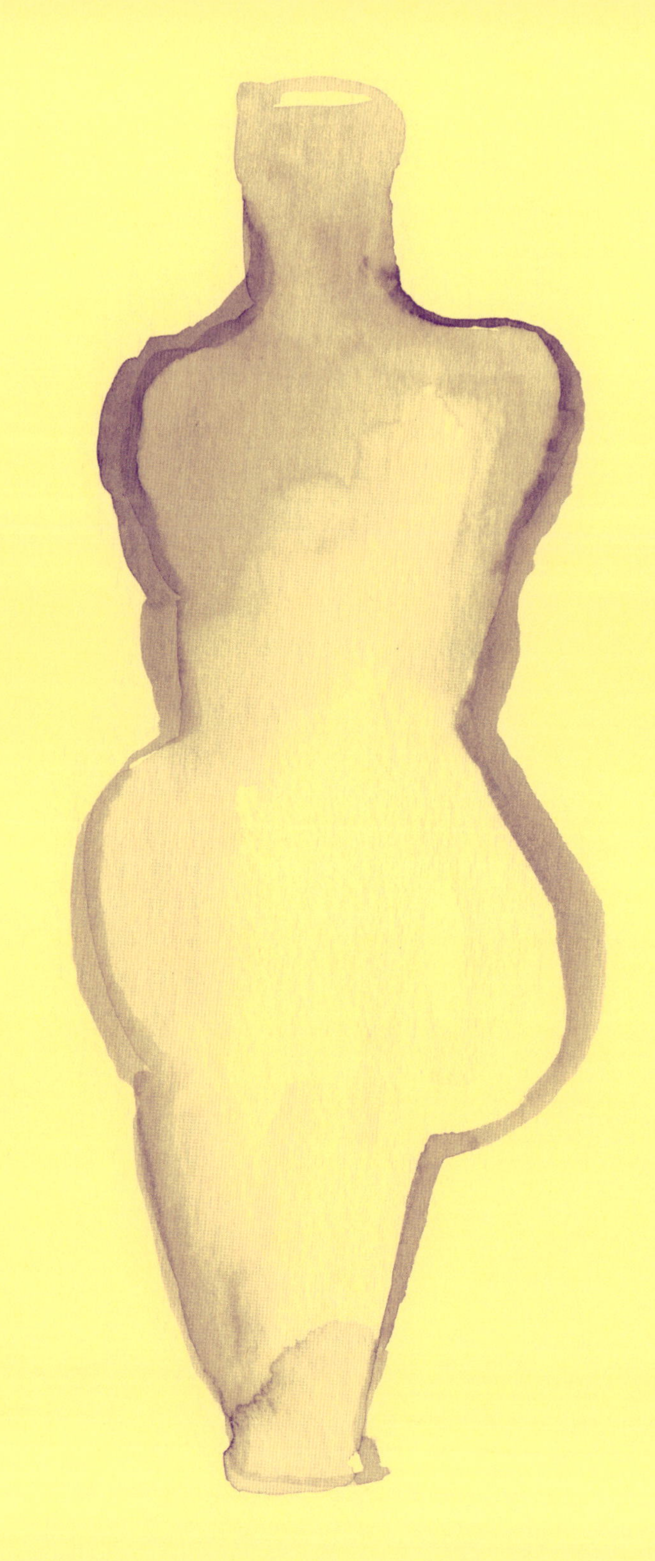

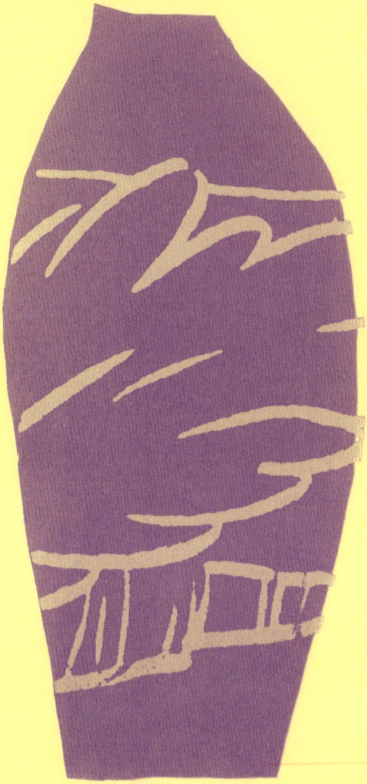

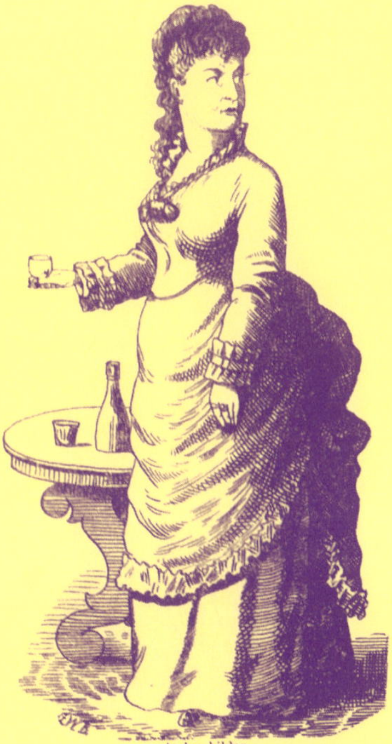

Andra bilden.

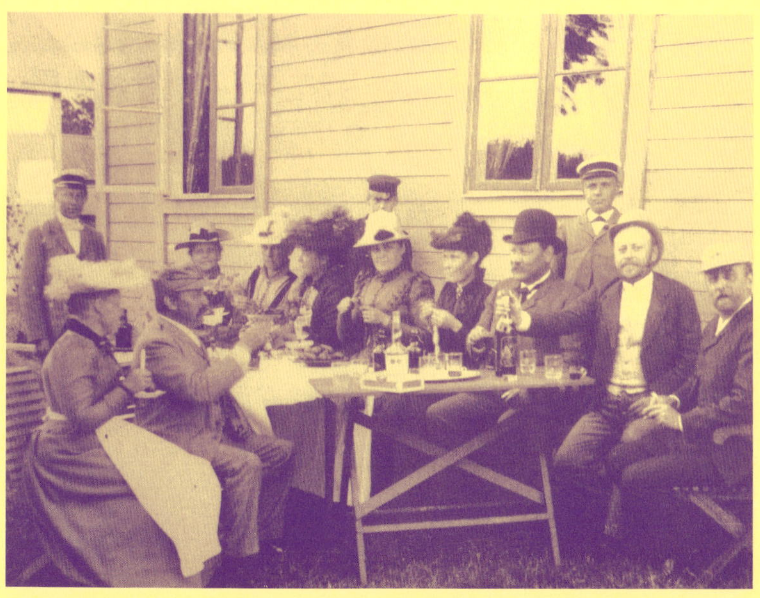

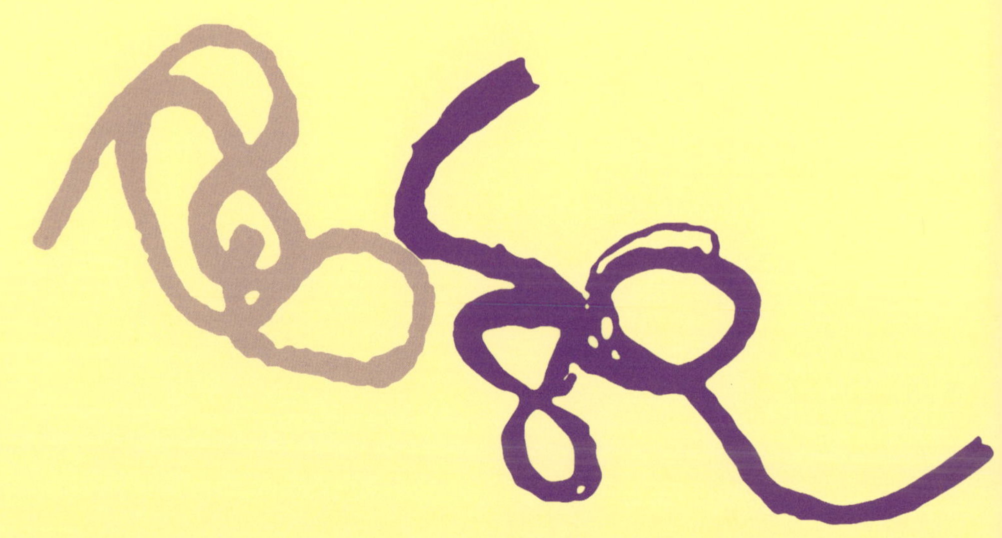

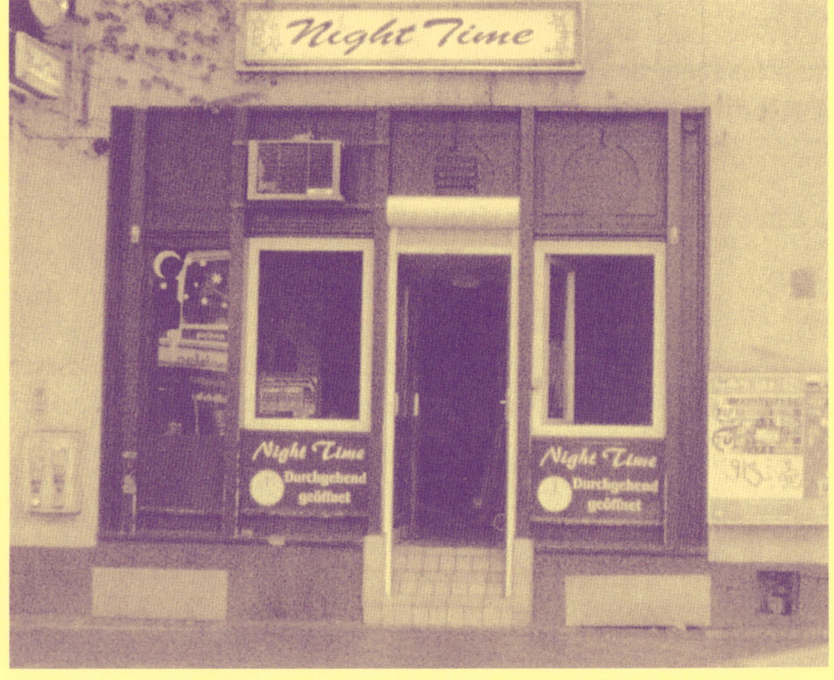
Night Time
Night Time
Durchgehend
geöffnet
Night Time
Durchgehend
geöffnet

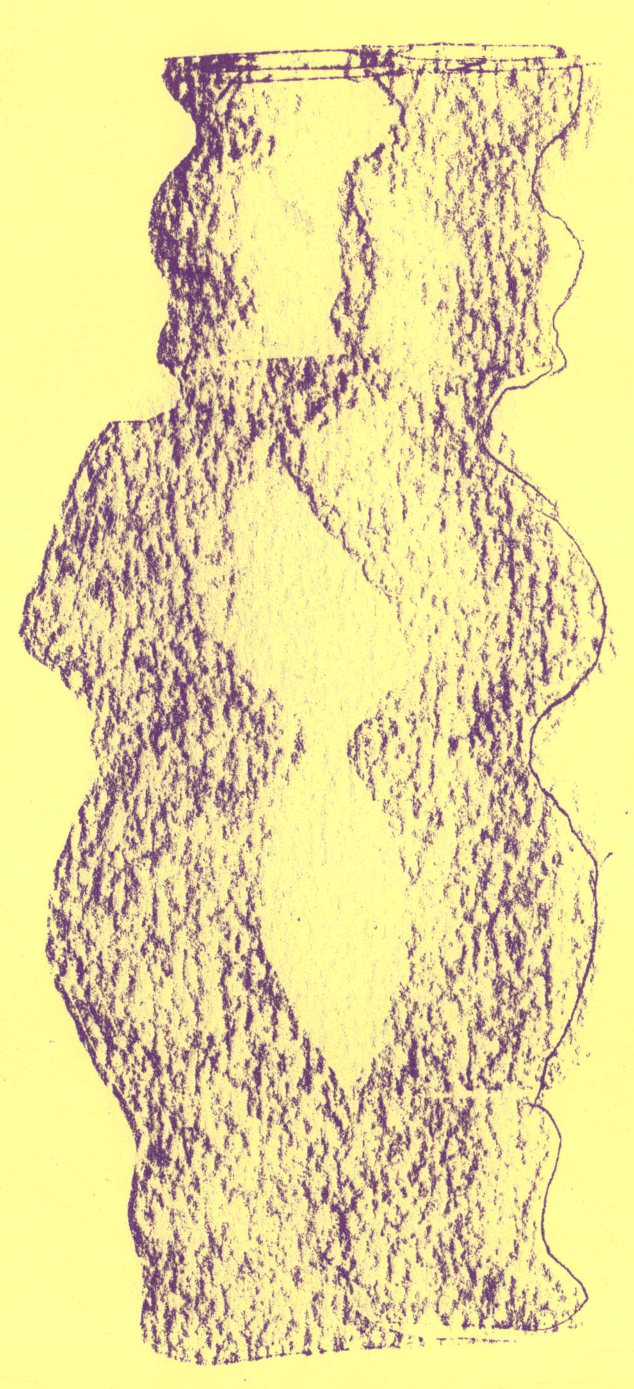

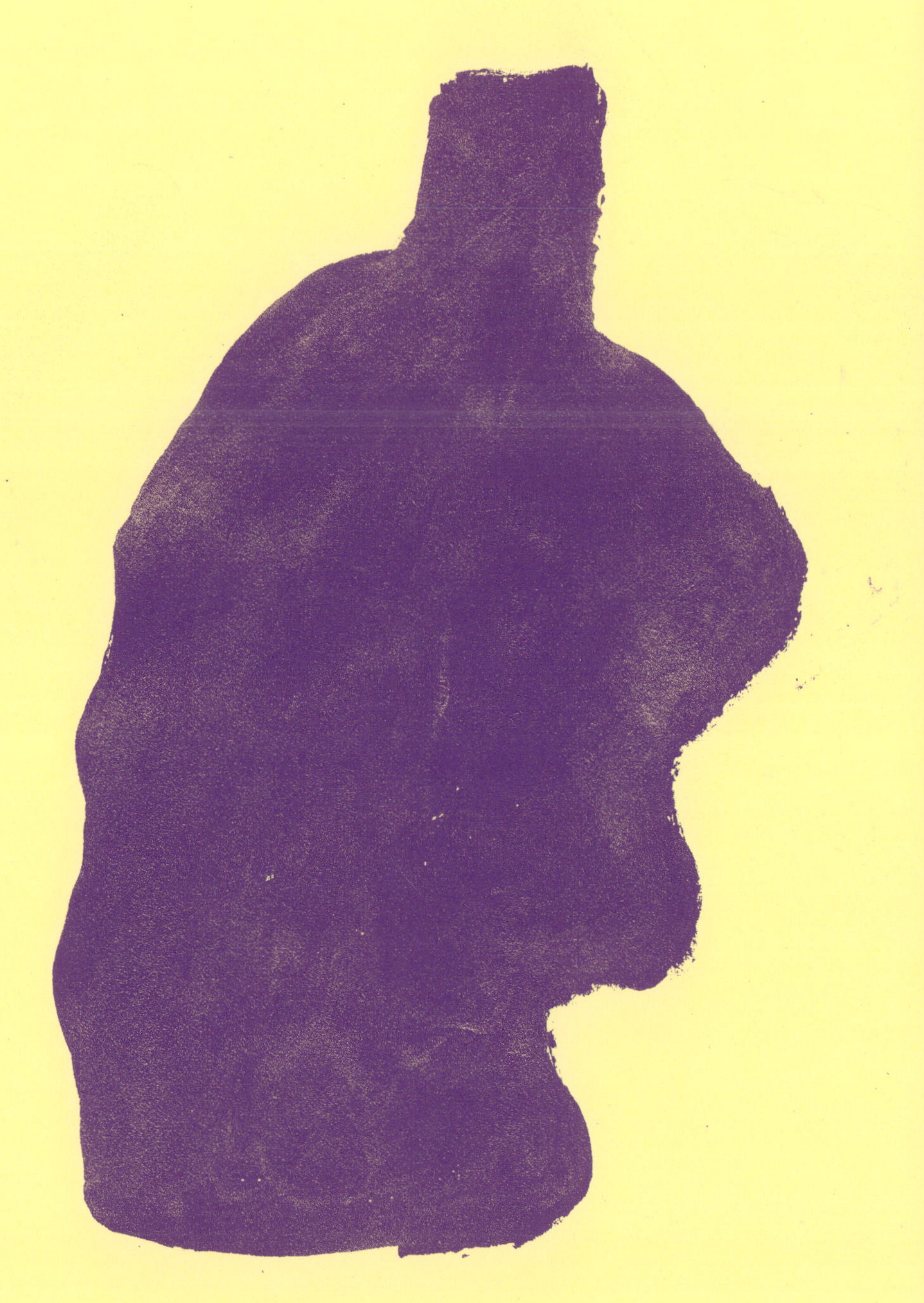

Bottles Under the Influence

Banff Centre

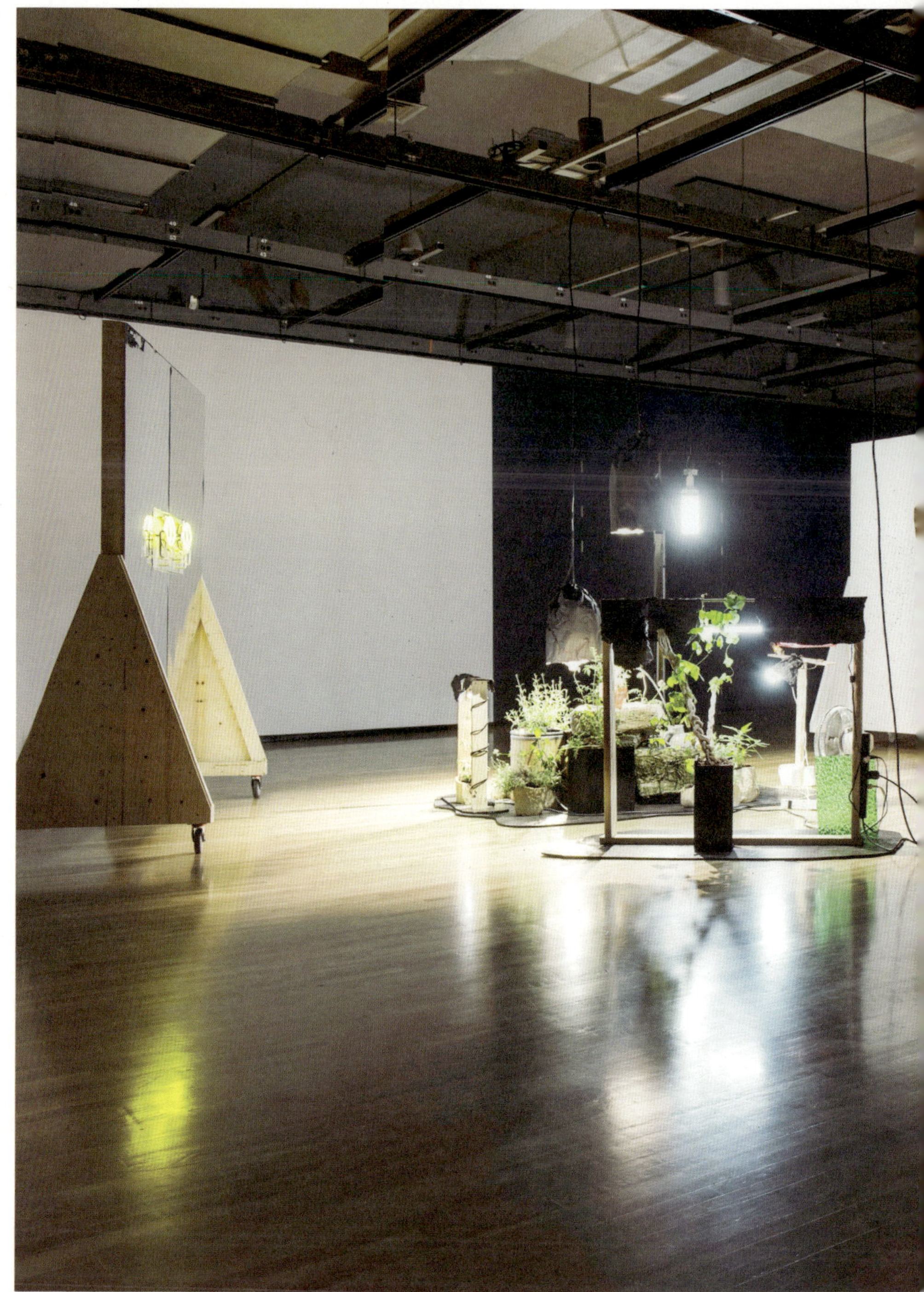

Installation view, Walter Phillips Gallery, 2013

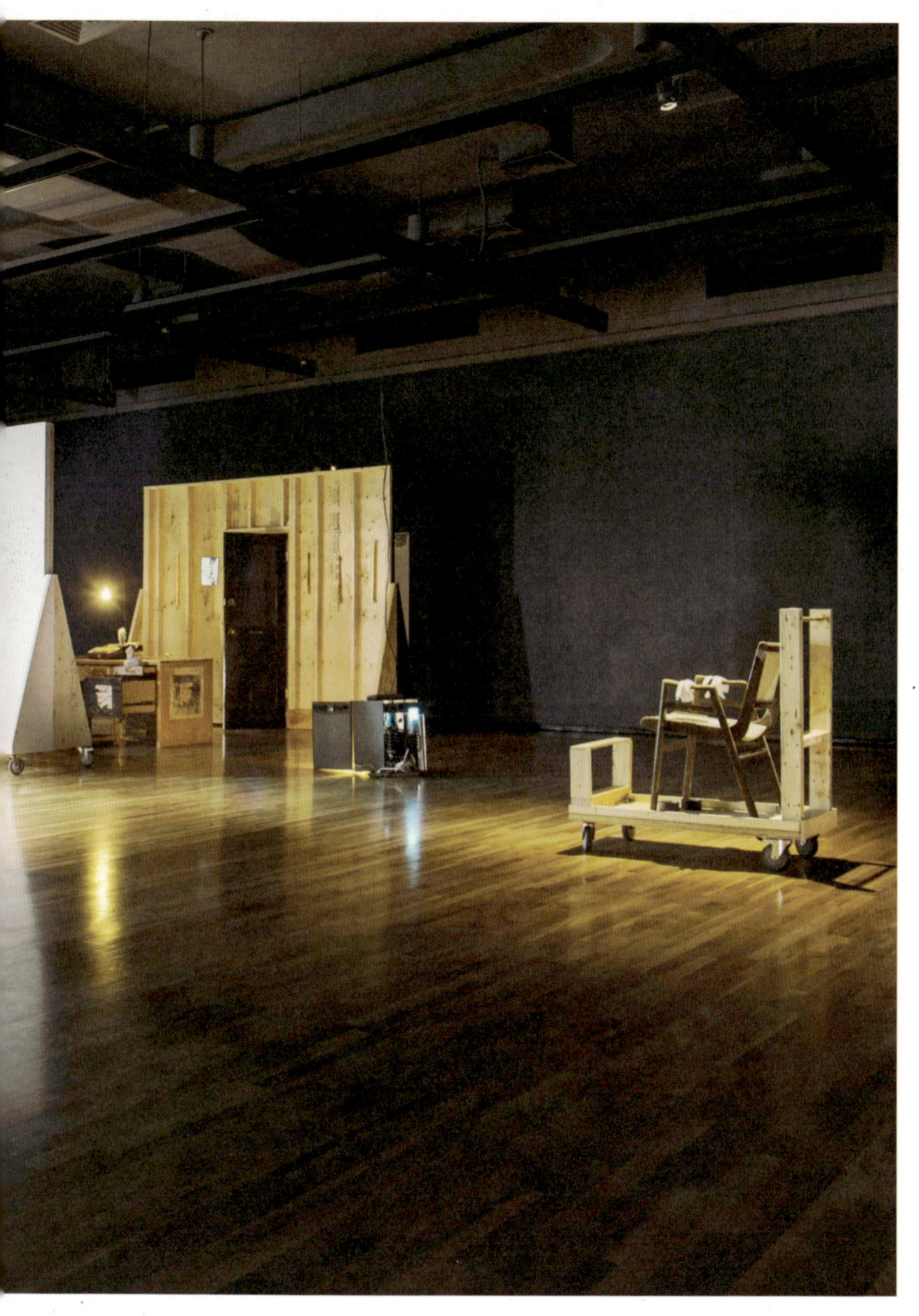

Banff

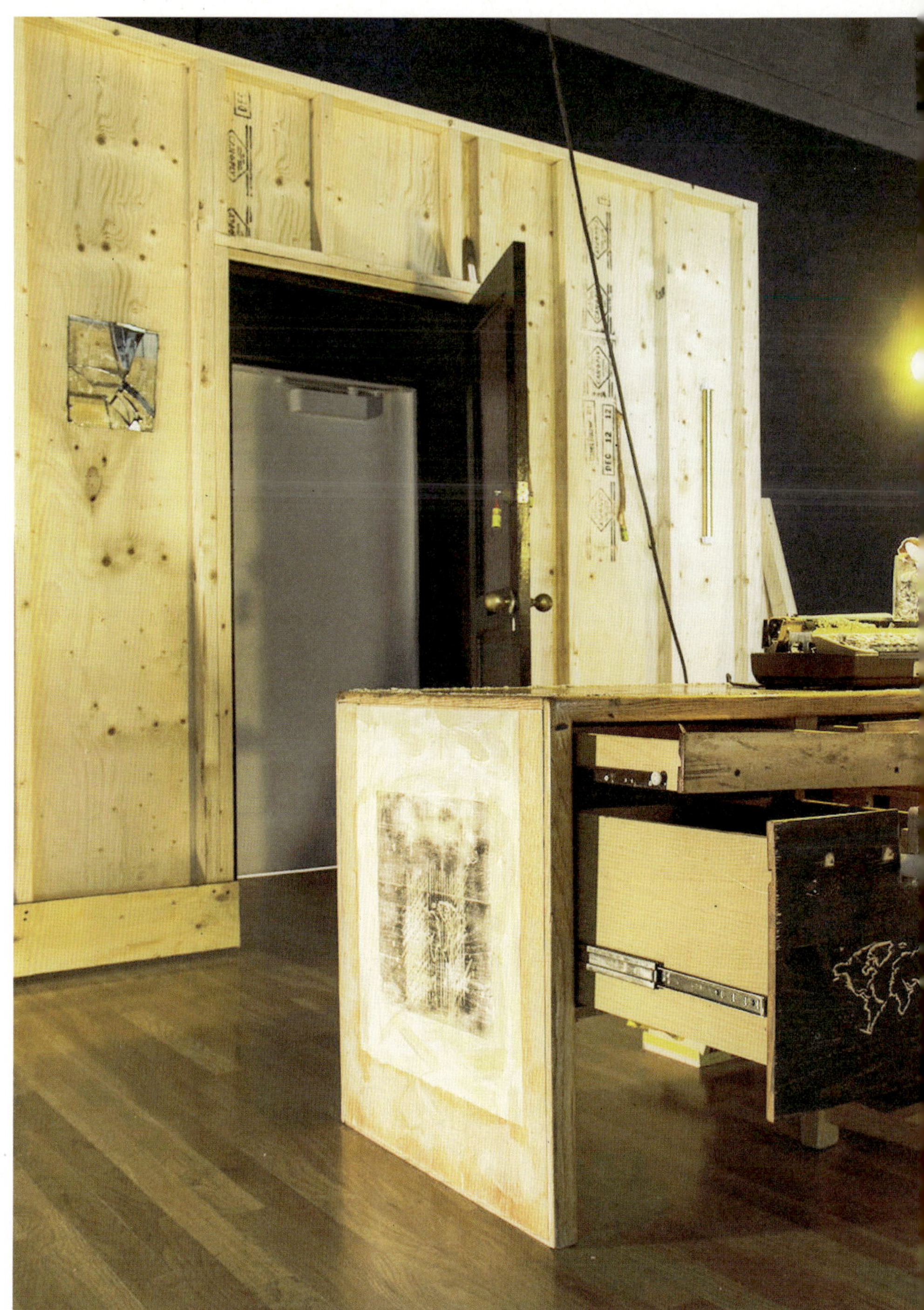

Installation view, Walter Phillips Gallery, 2013

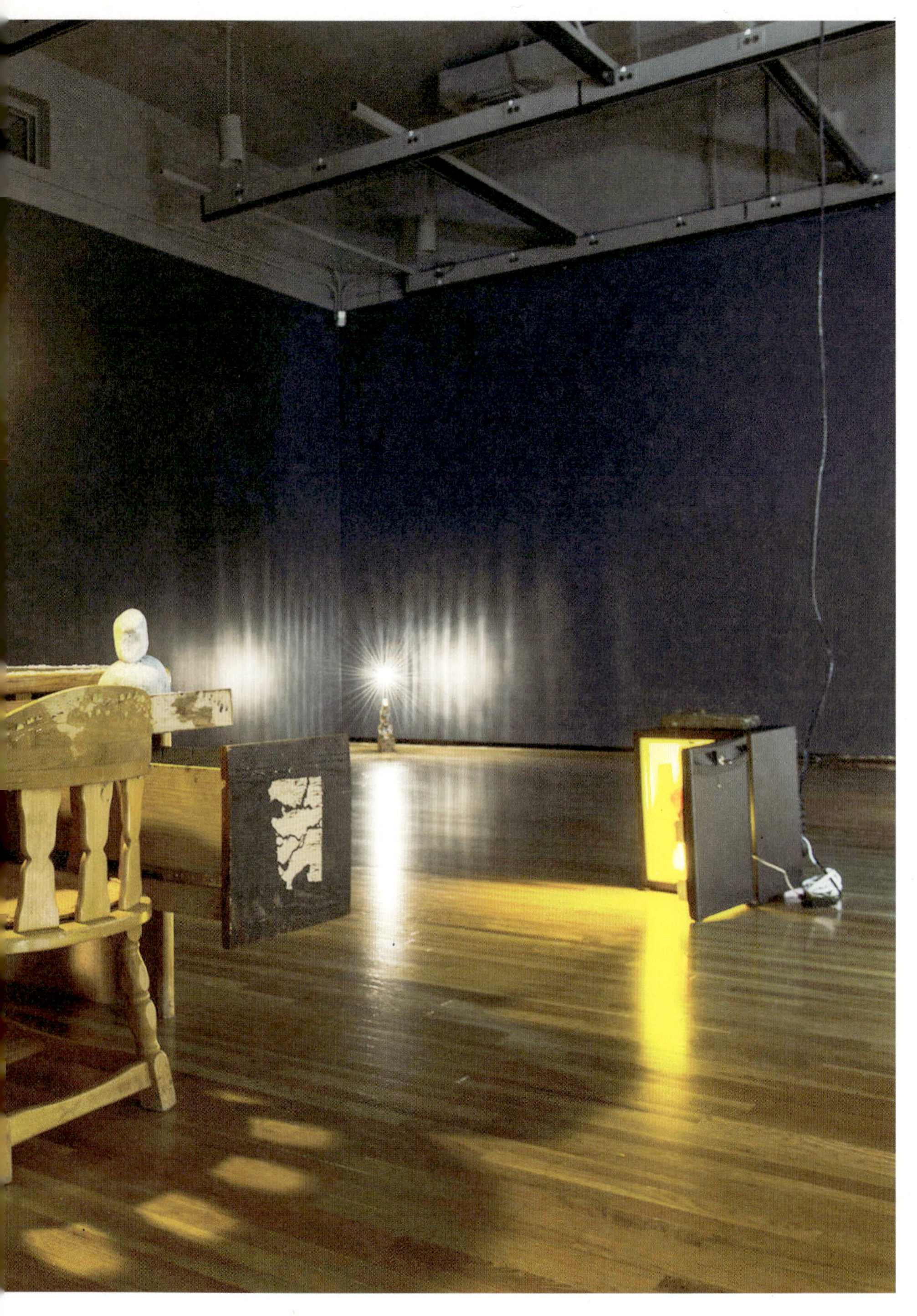

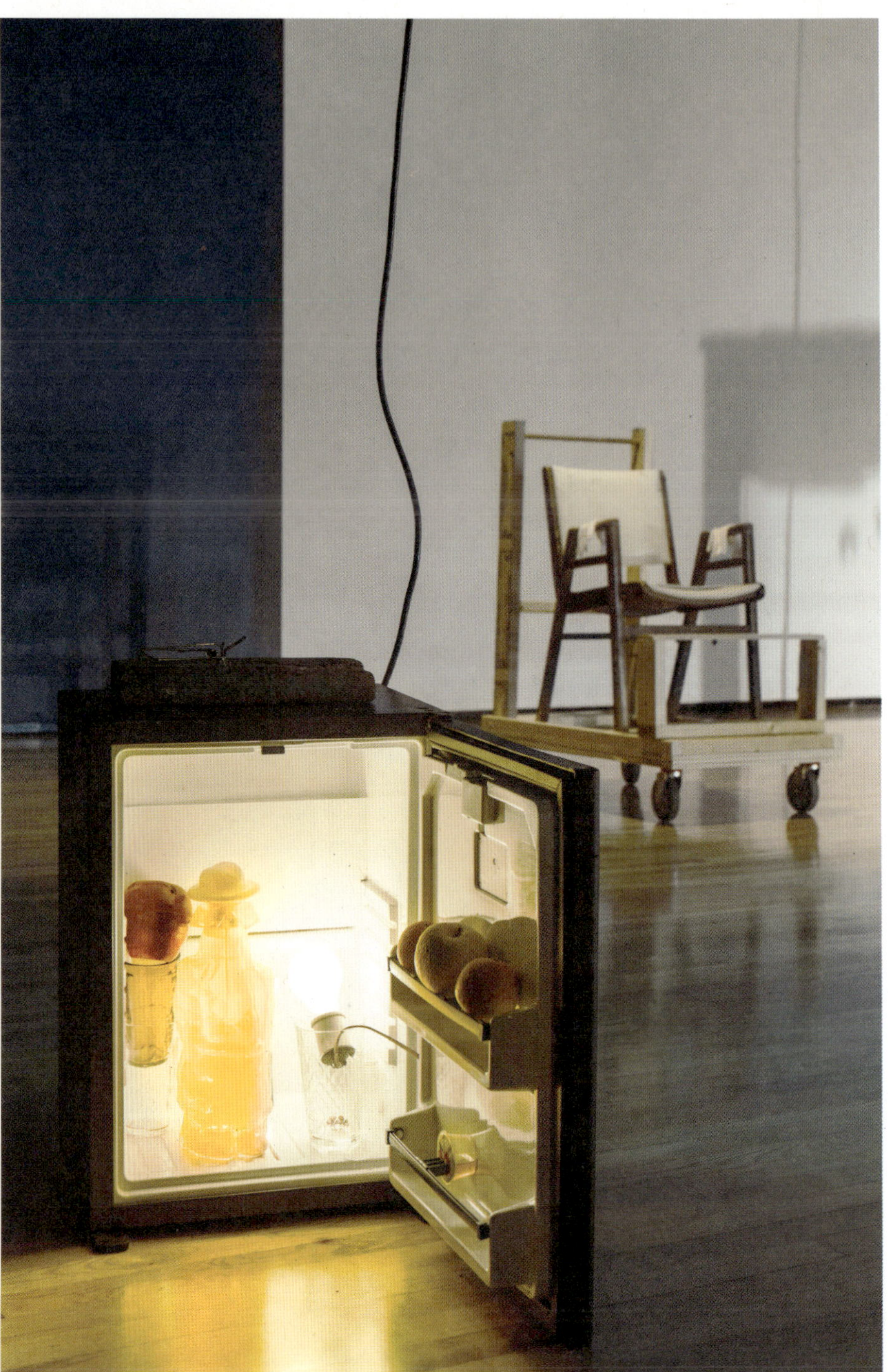

Installation view, Walter Phillips Gallery, 2013

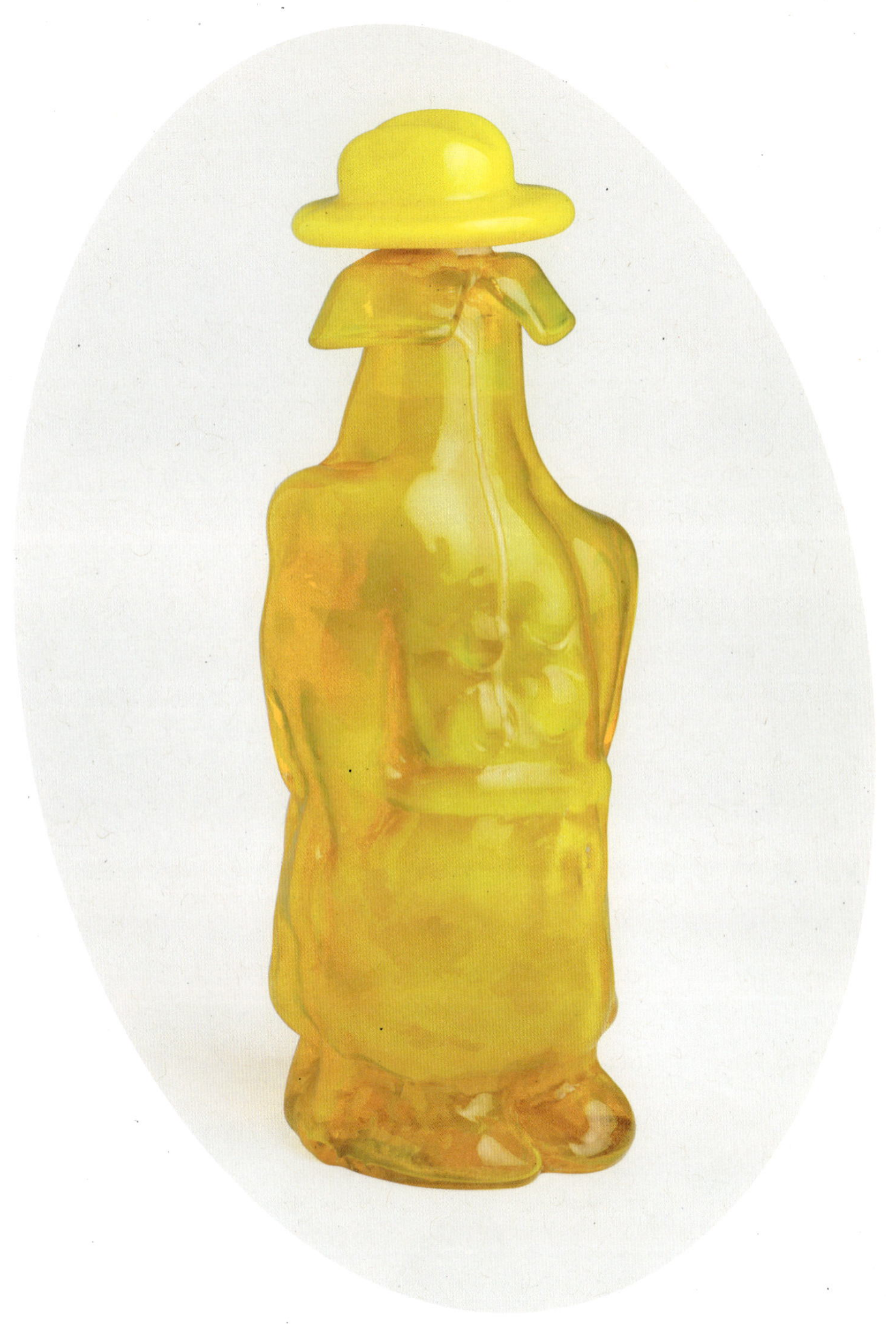

Yellow Apfelwein Bottle (Pest Detective Bottle), 2013

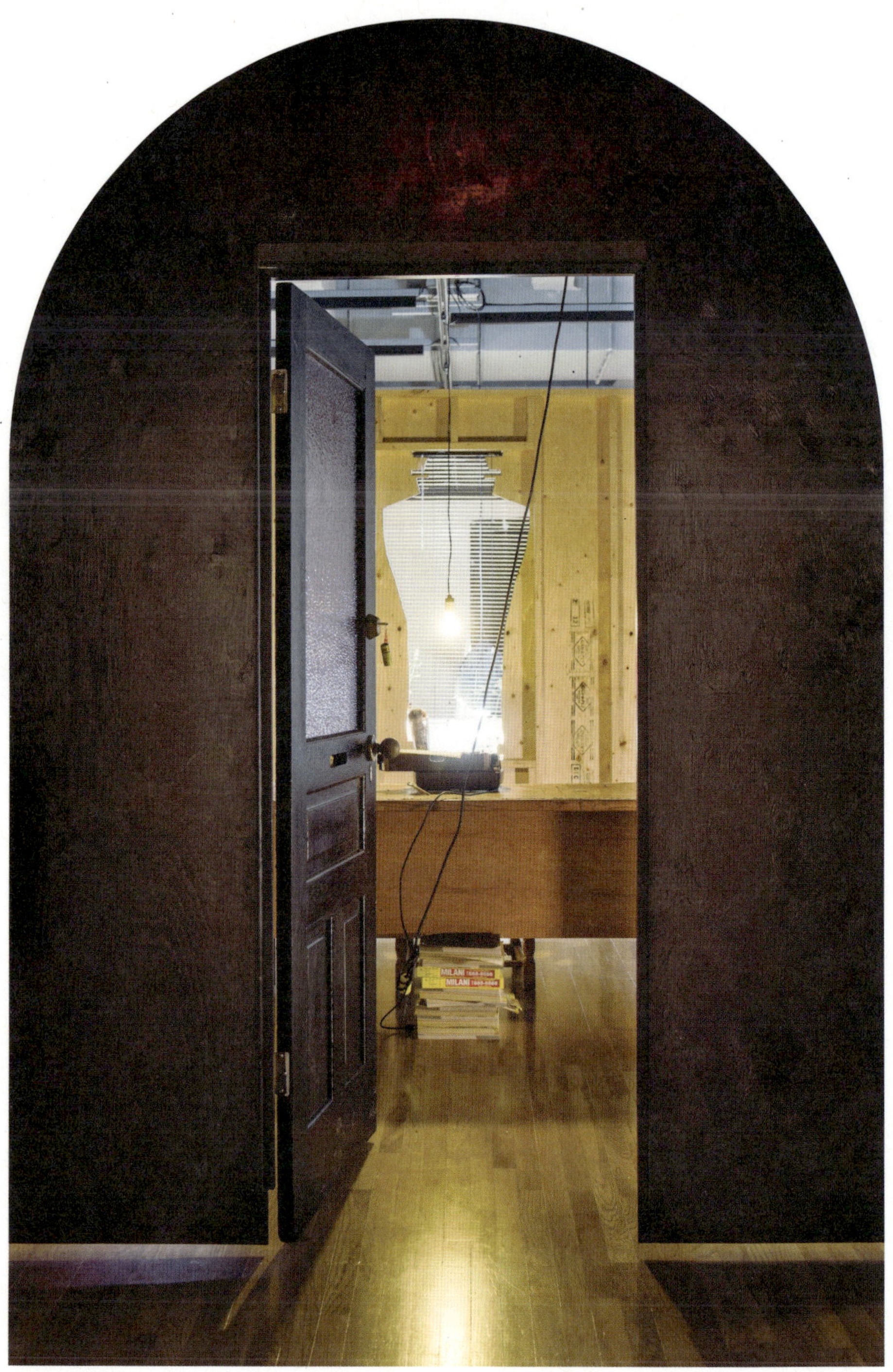

 Installation views, Walter Phillips Gallery, 2013

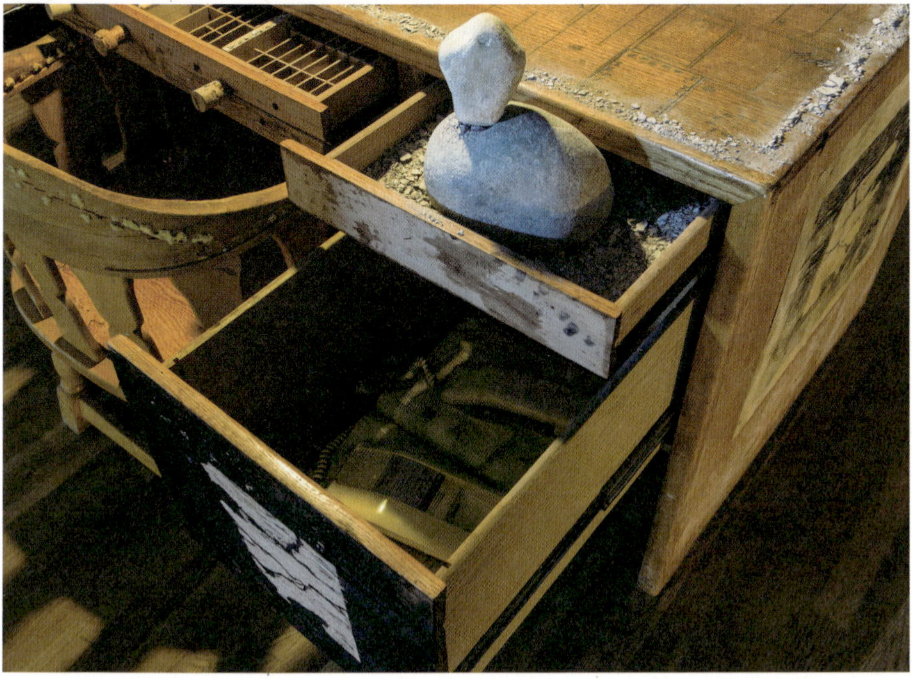

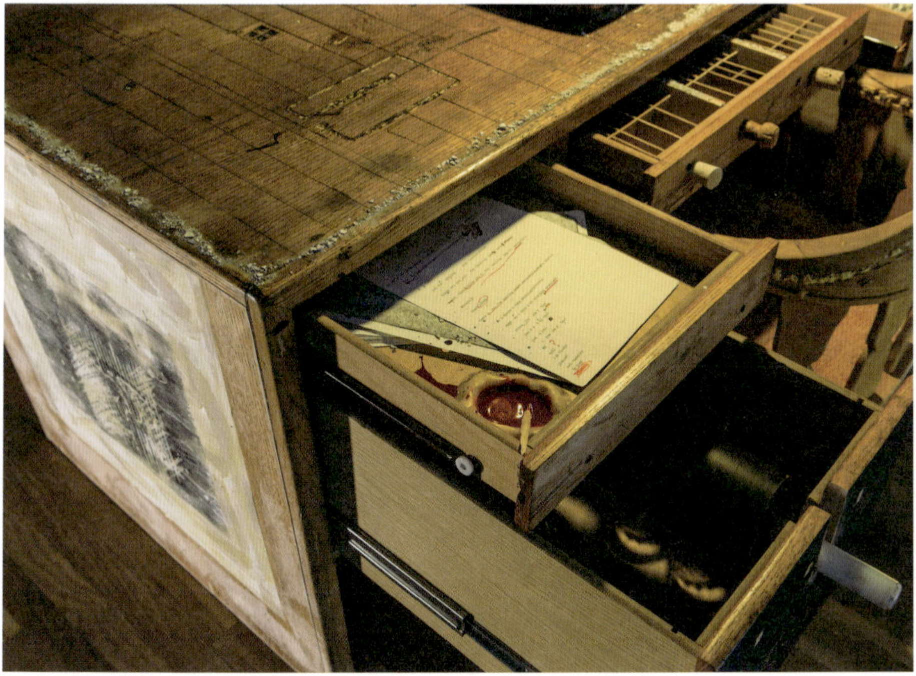

Banff

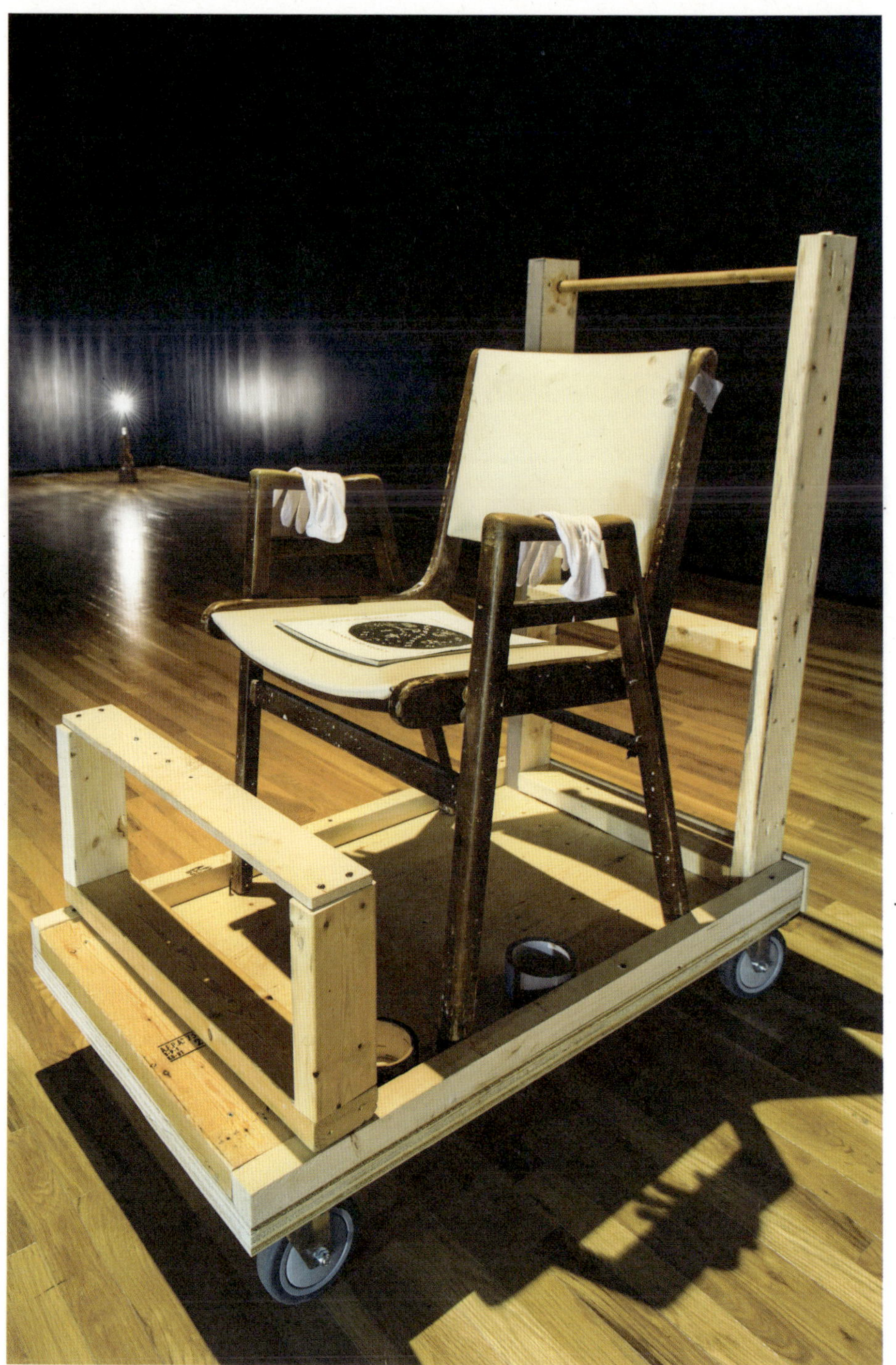

Installation view, Walter Phillips Gallery, 2013

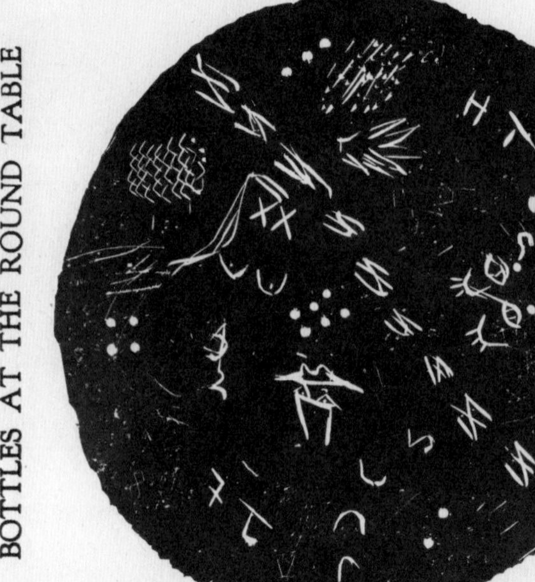

Banff

Bottles at the Round Table, 2013, artist book

27

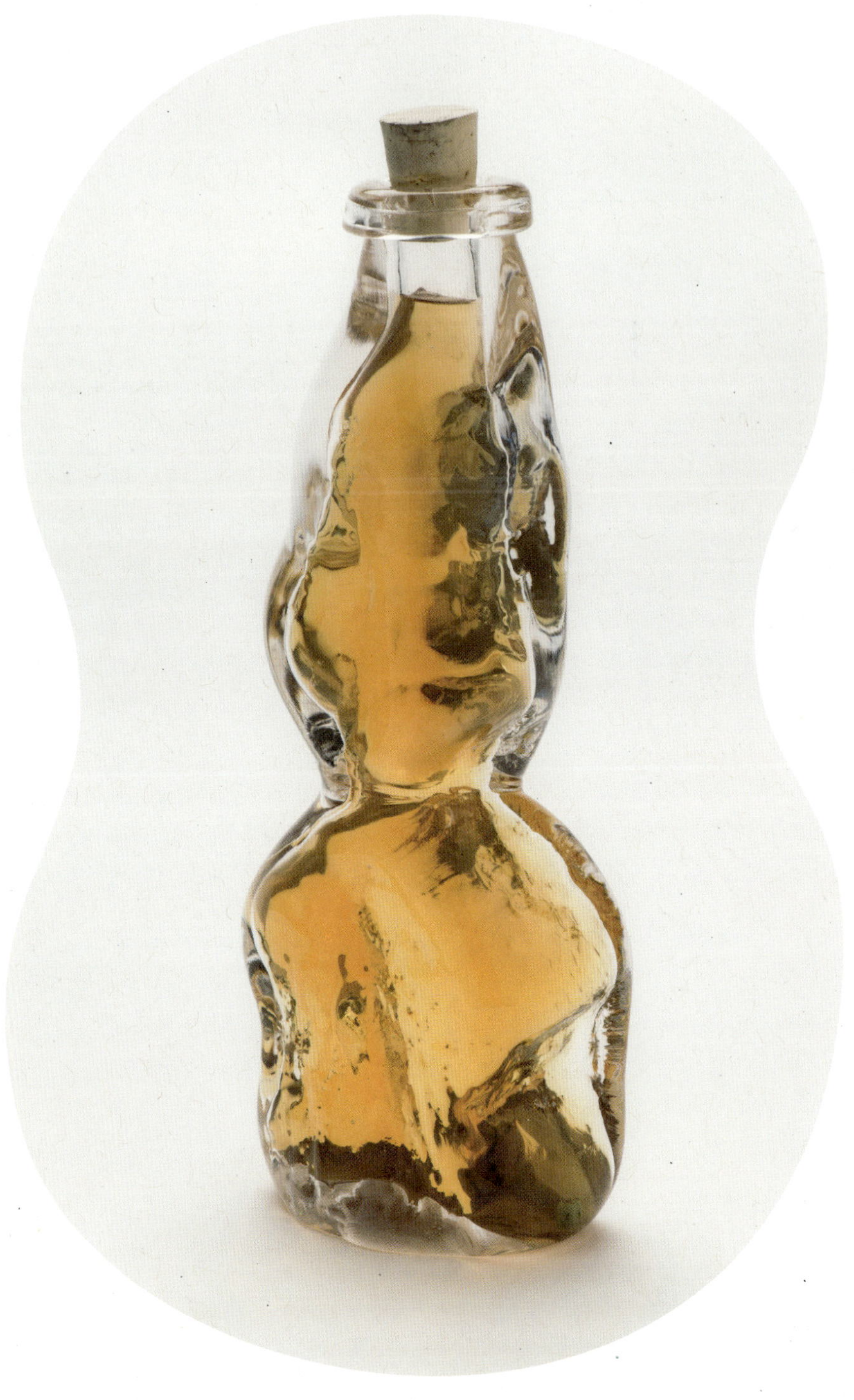

Clear Chance Mixed-Alcohol Bottle (Chance Bottle), 2013

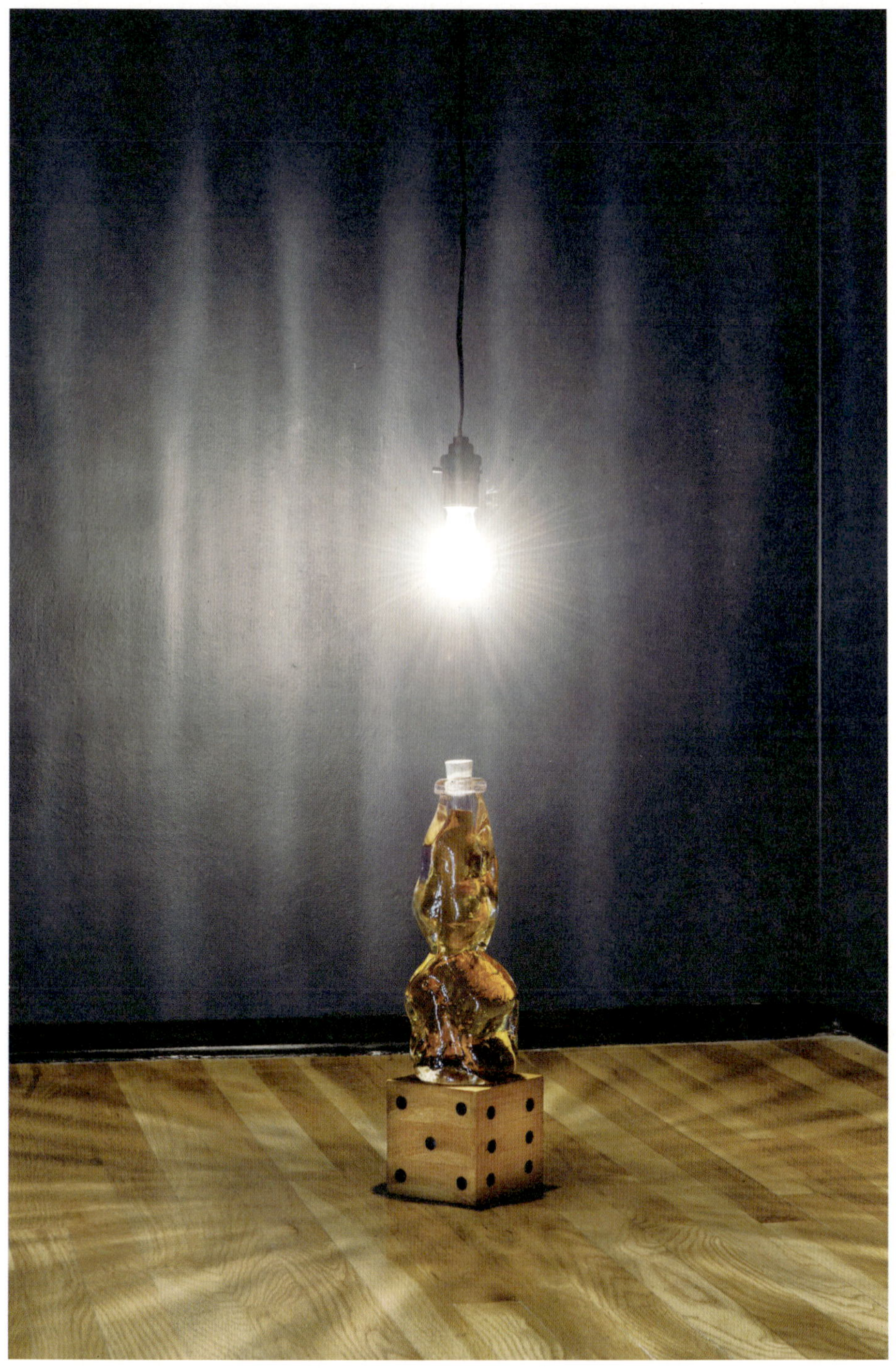

Banff

Installation view, Walter Phillips Gallery, 2013

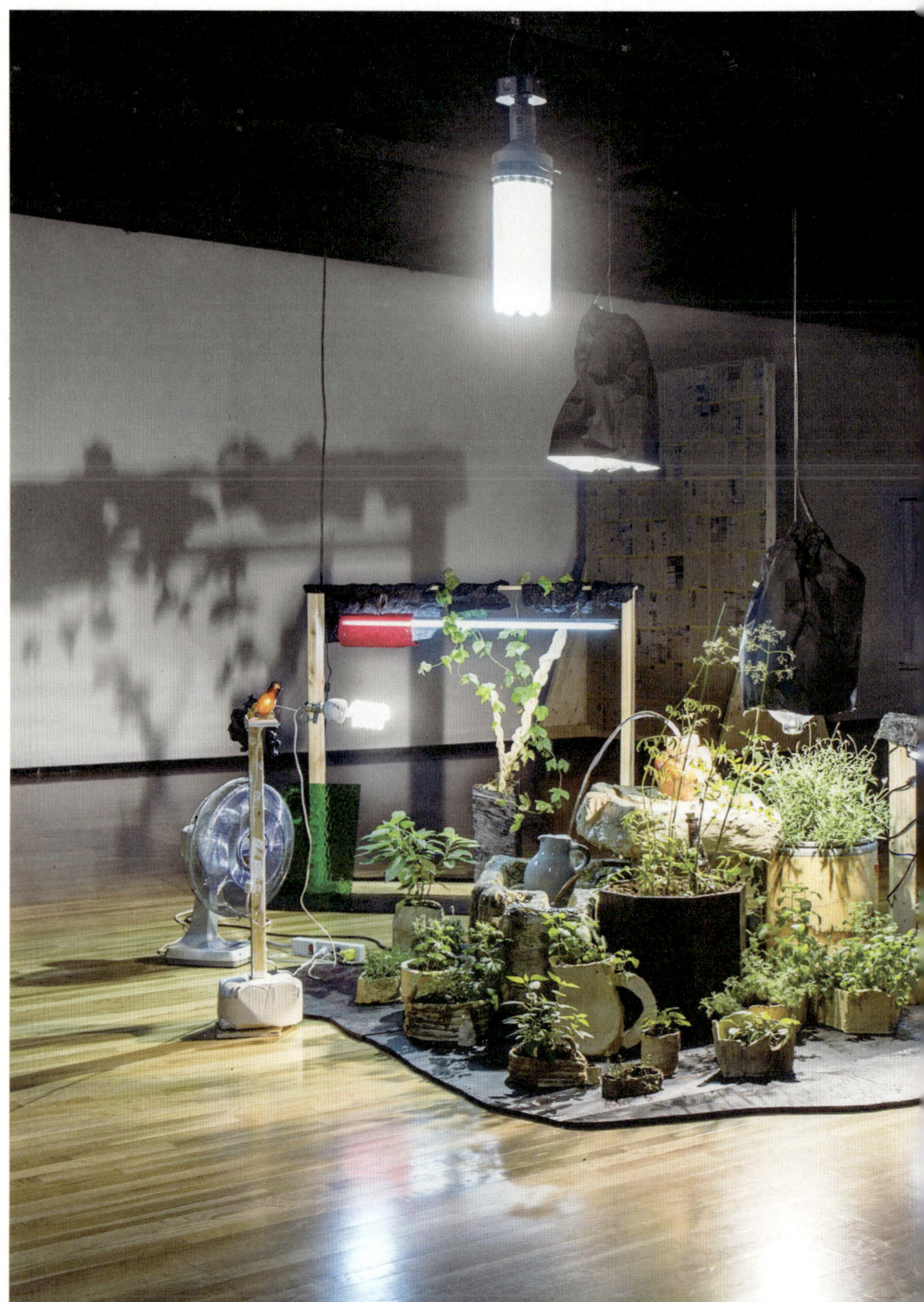

Installation view, Walter Phillips Gallery, 2013

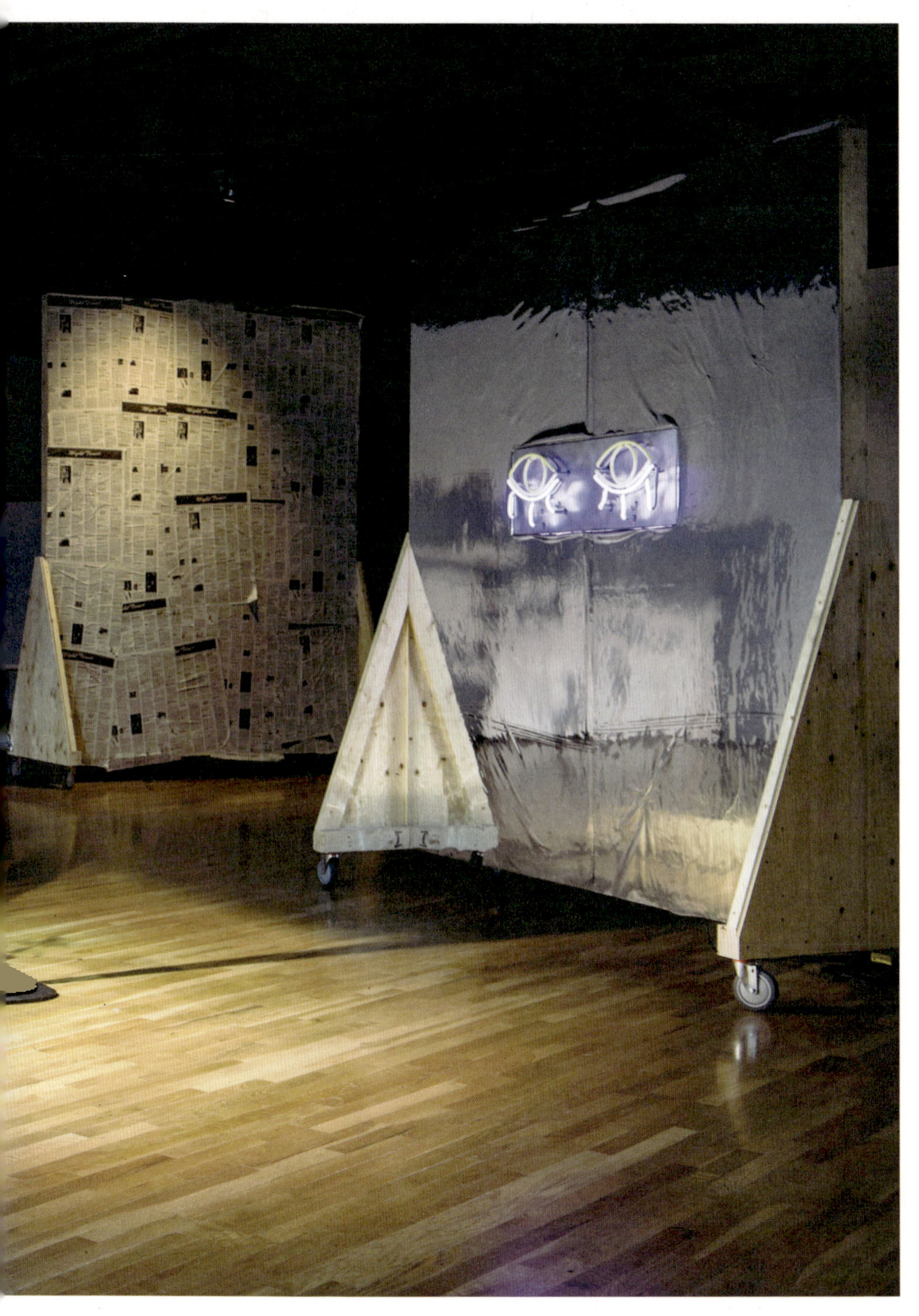

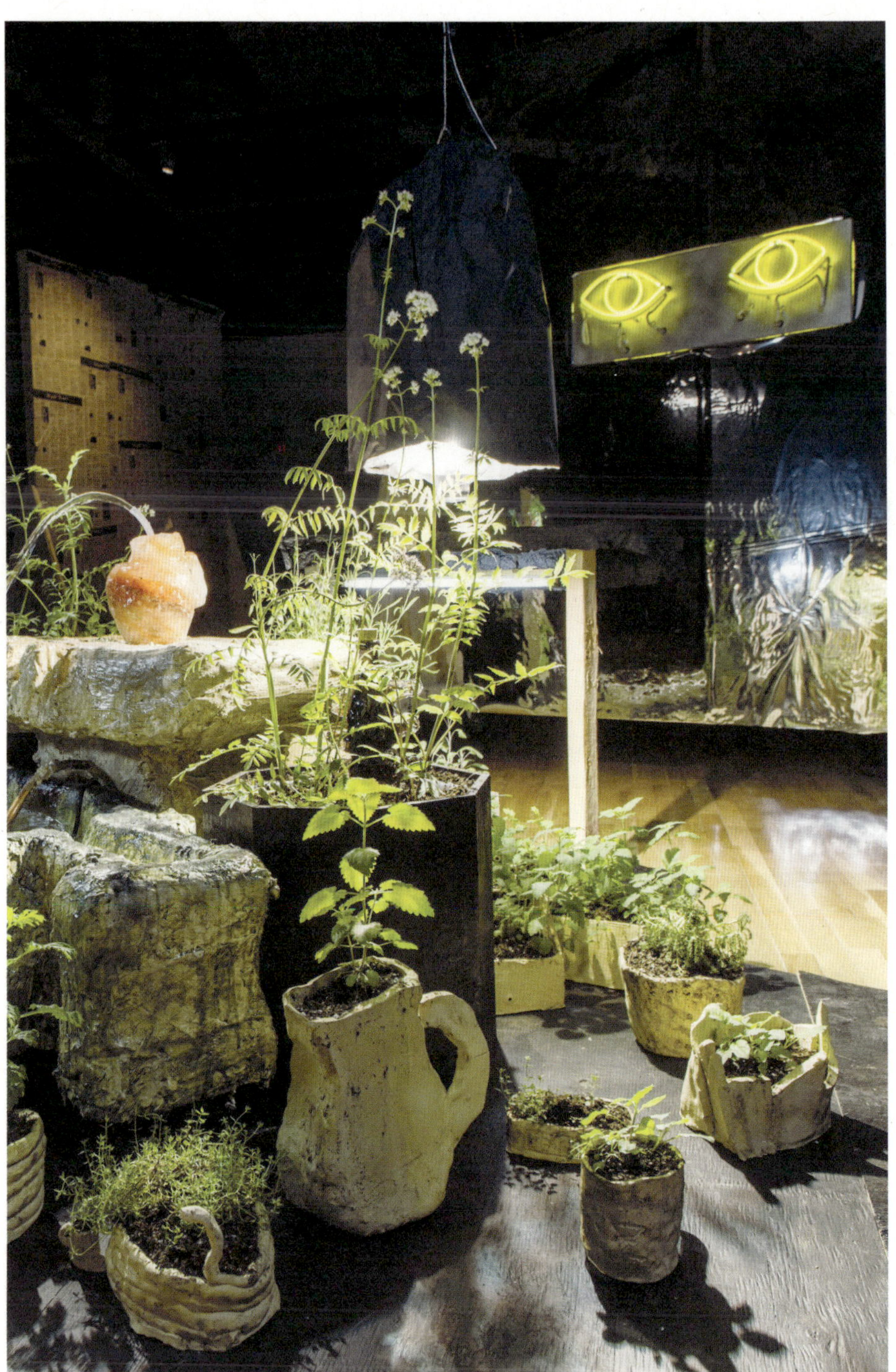

Installation view, Walter Phillips Gallery, 2013

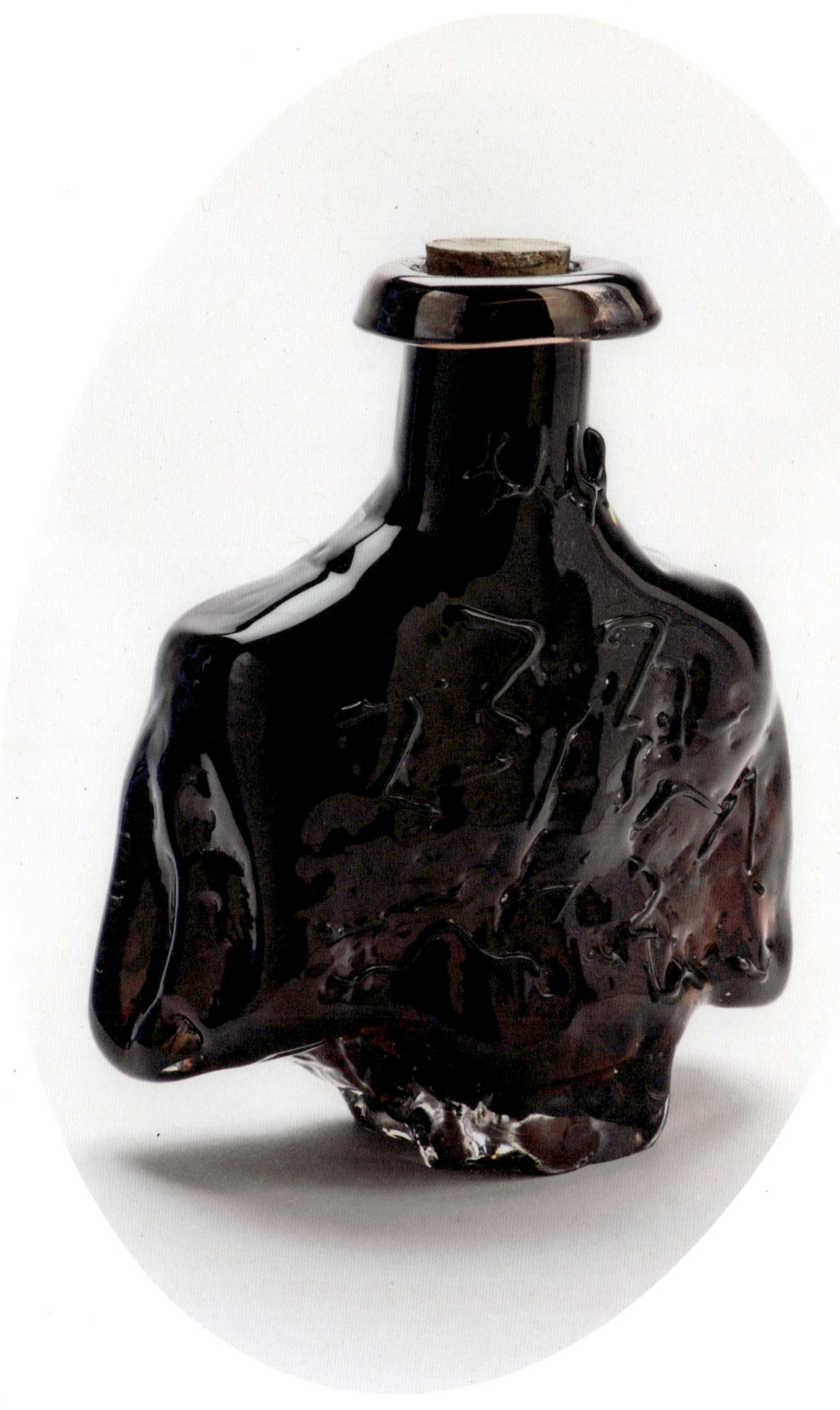

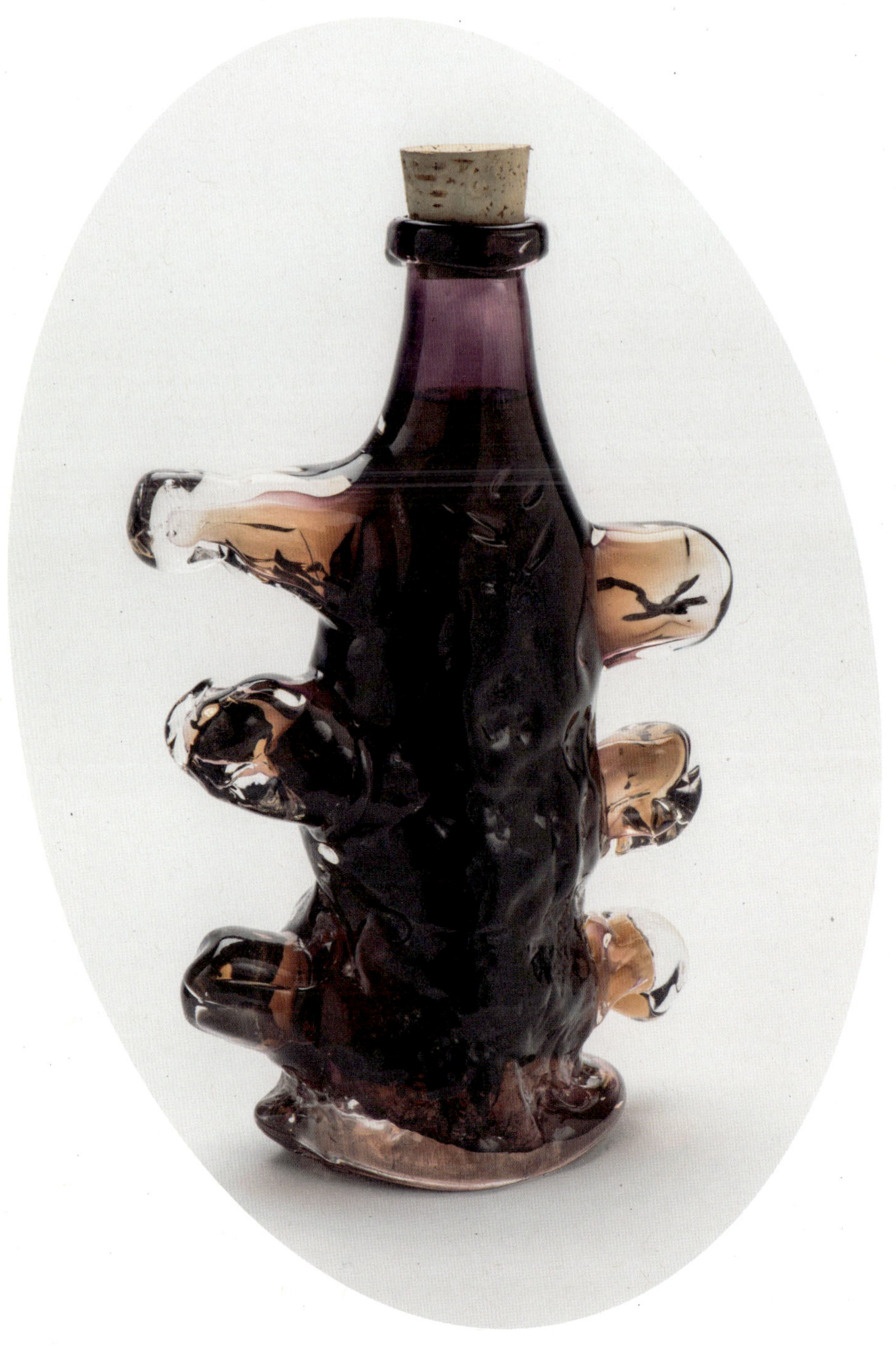

Purple Valerian Bottle (Old Hag Bottle), 2013

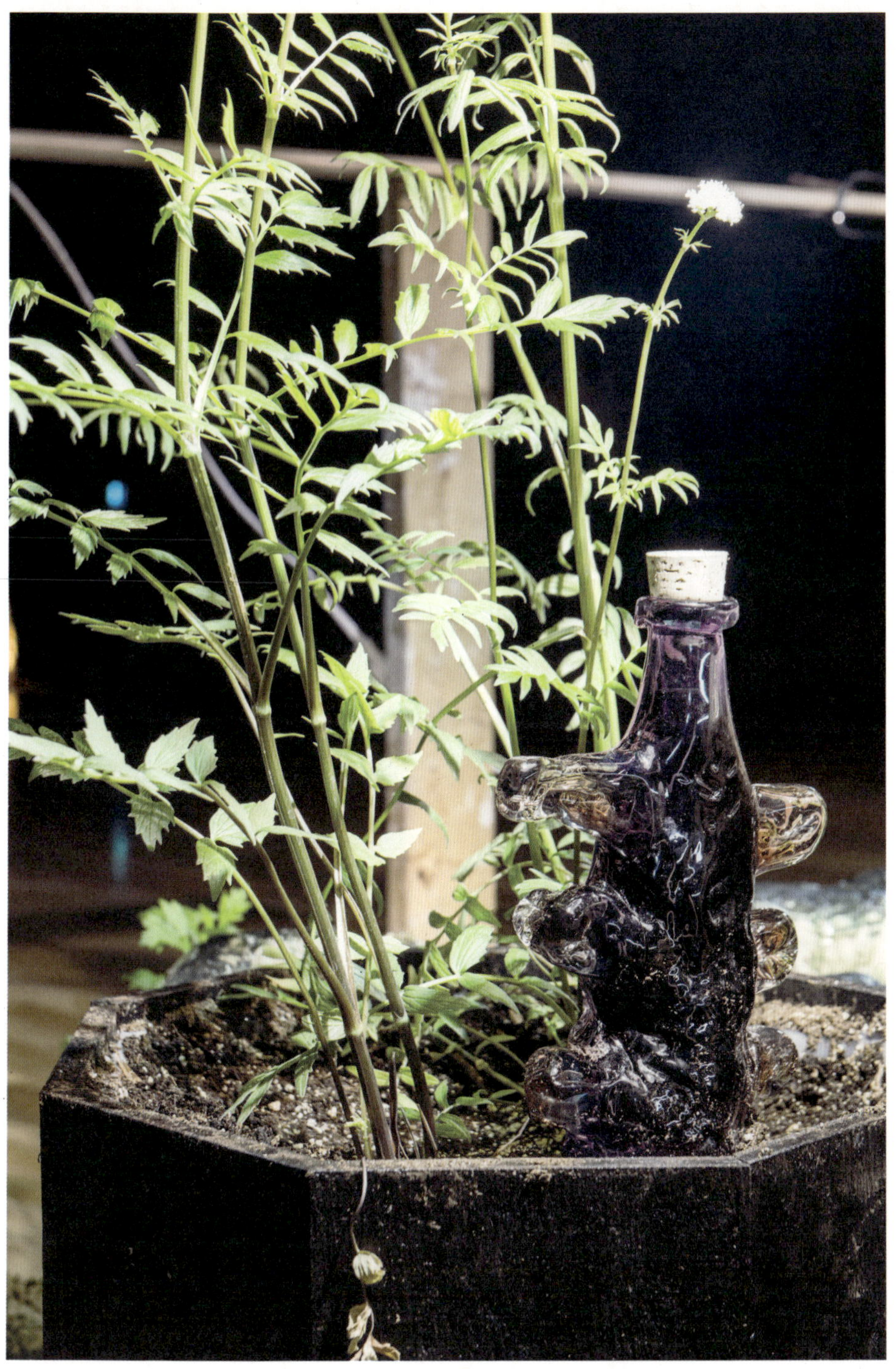

Installation view, Walter Phillips Gallery, 2013

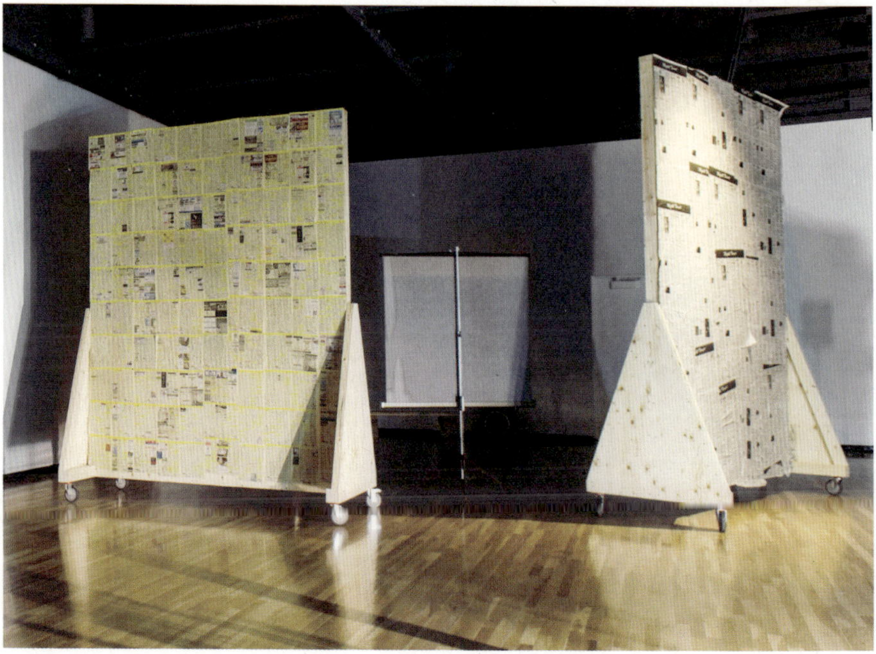

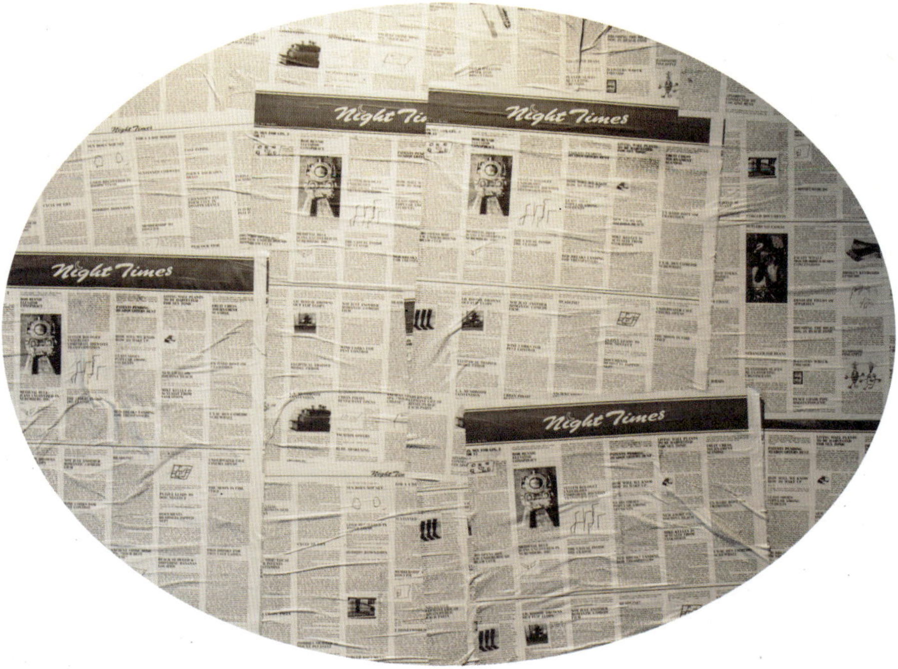

Installation views, Walter Phillips Gallery, 2013

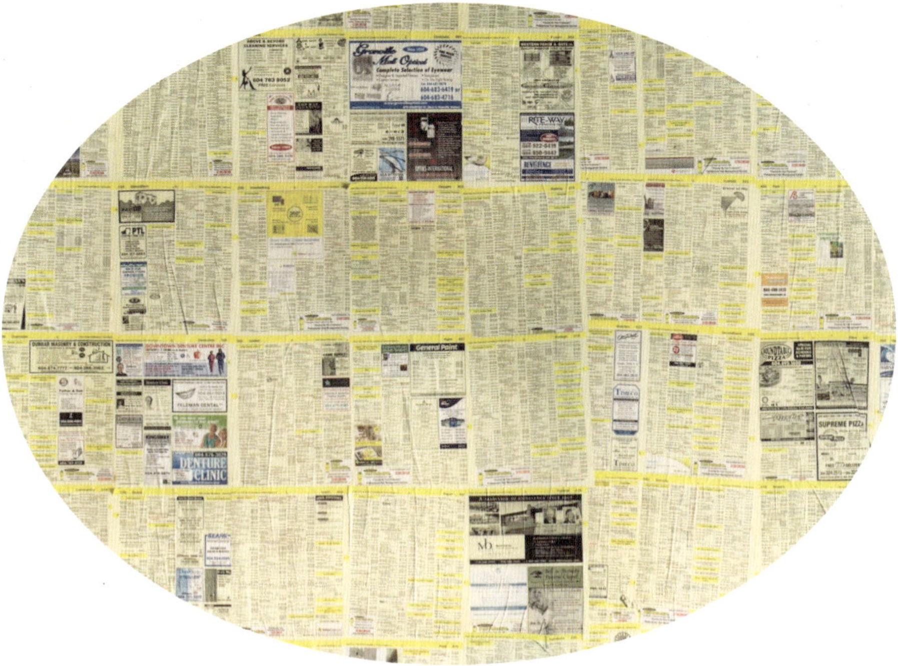

Banff

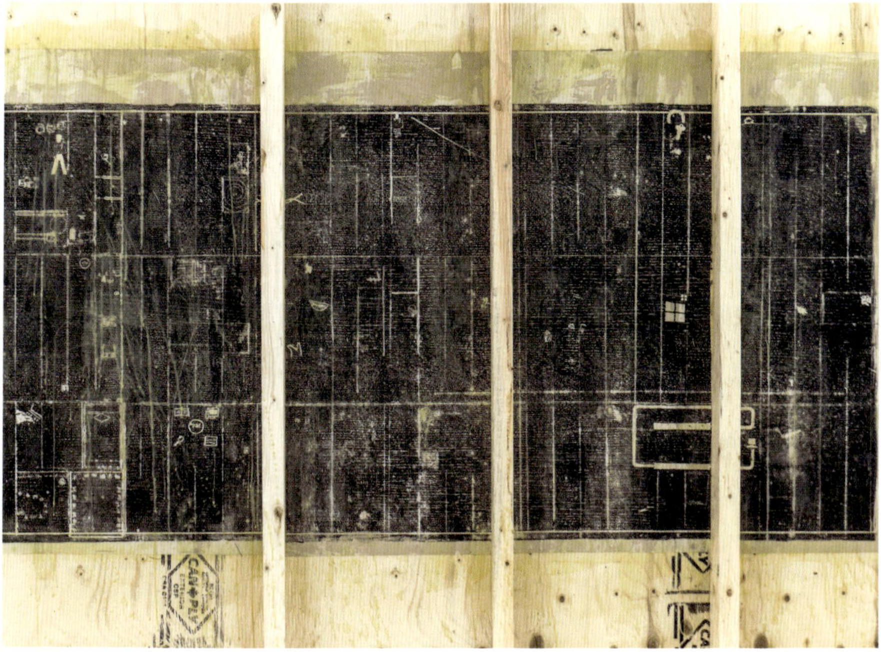

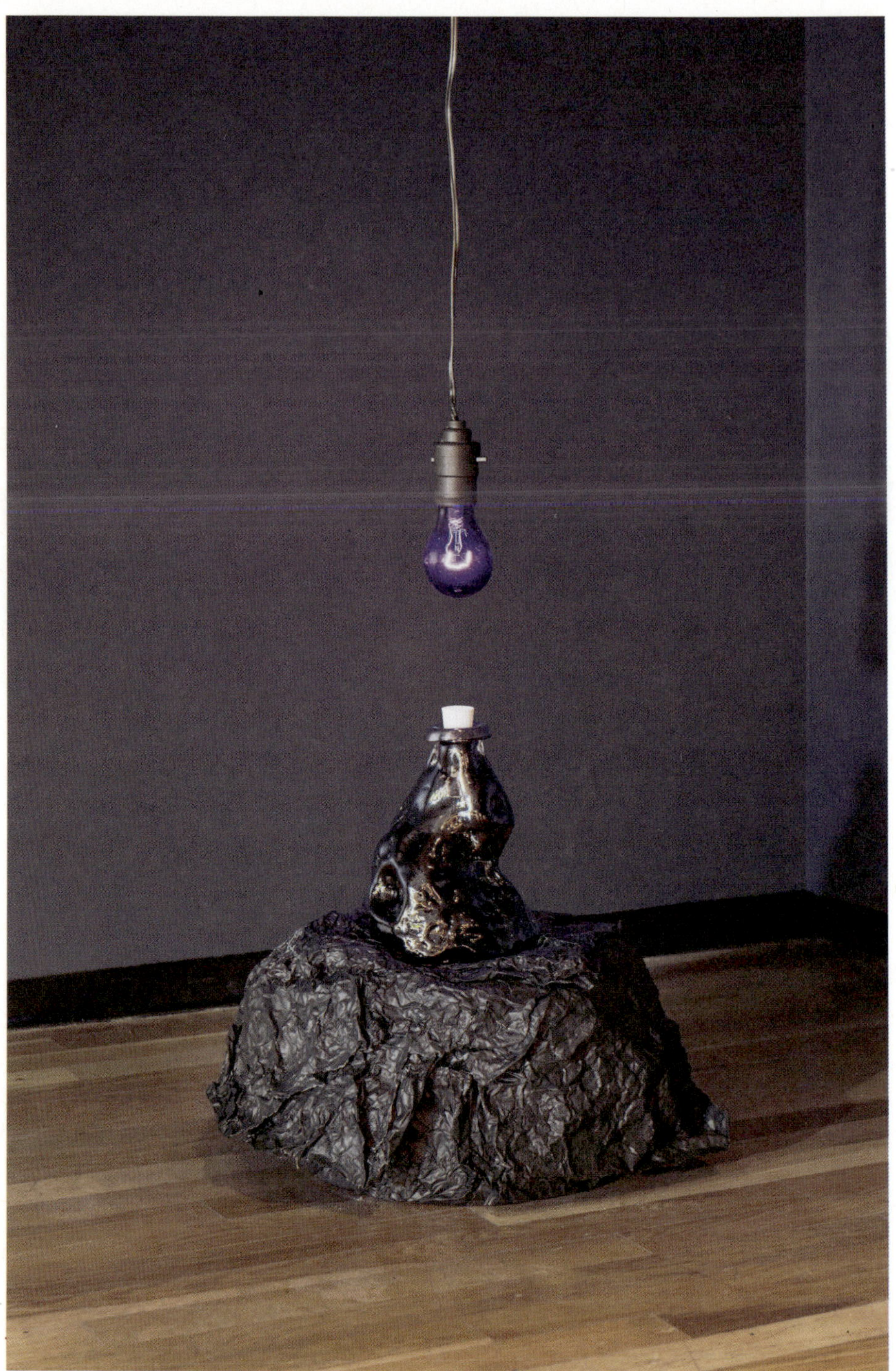

Installation view, Walter Phillips Gallery, 2013

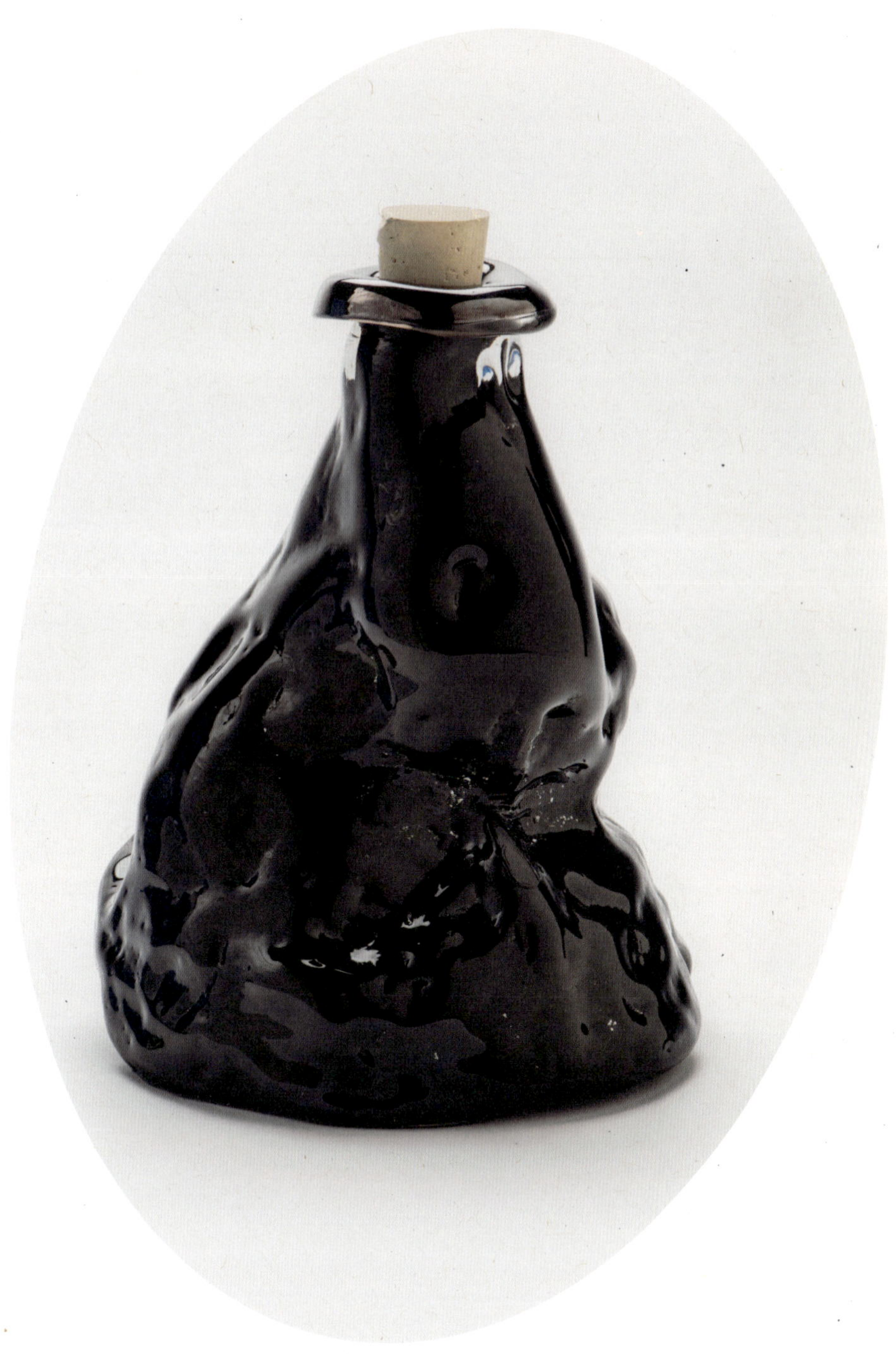

Moonshine Bottle (Blind Bottle), 2013

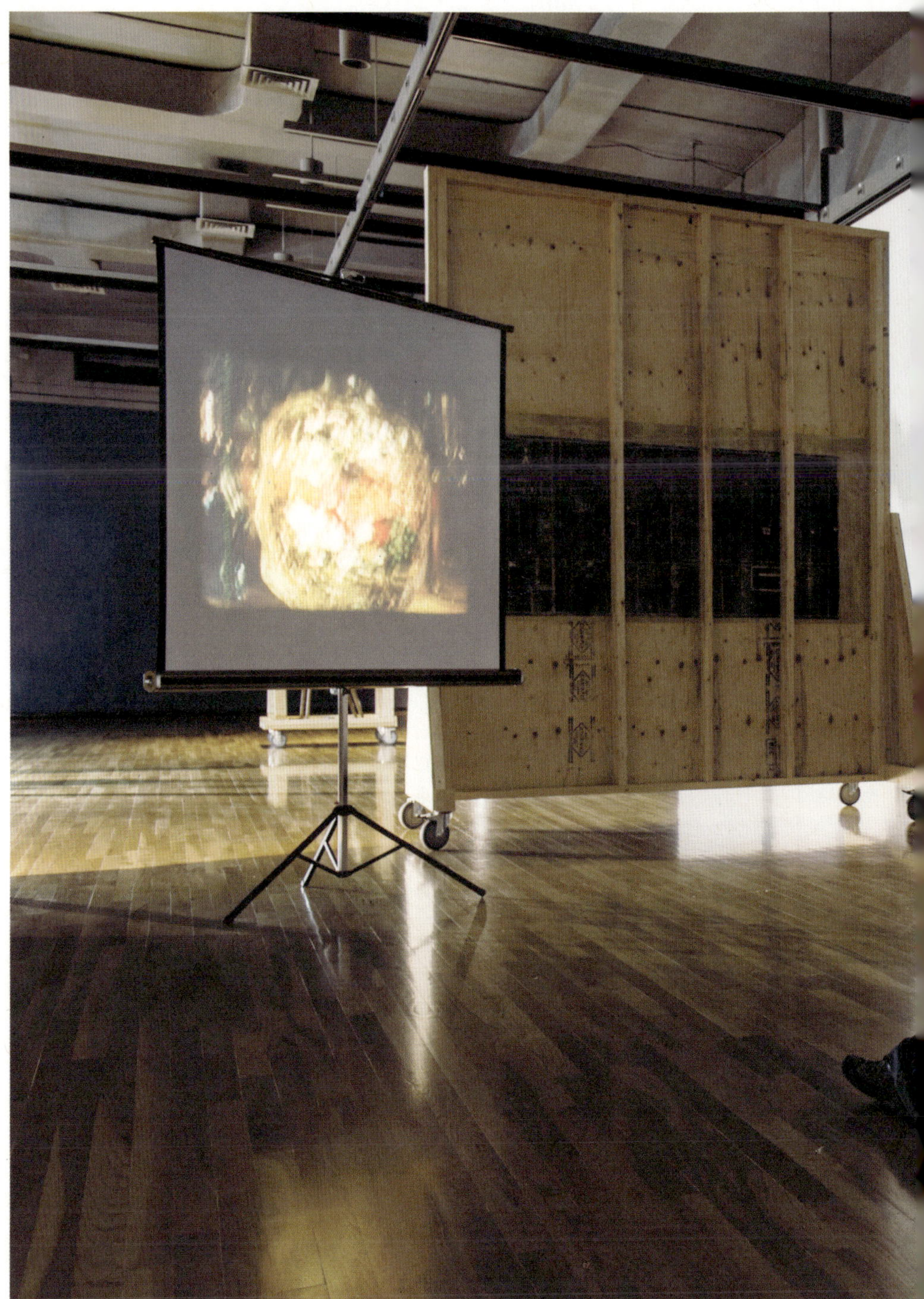

Installation view, Walter Phillips Gallery, 2013

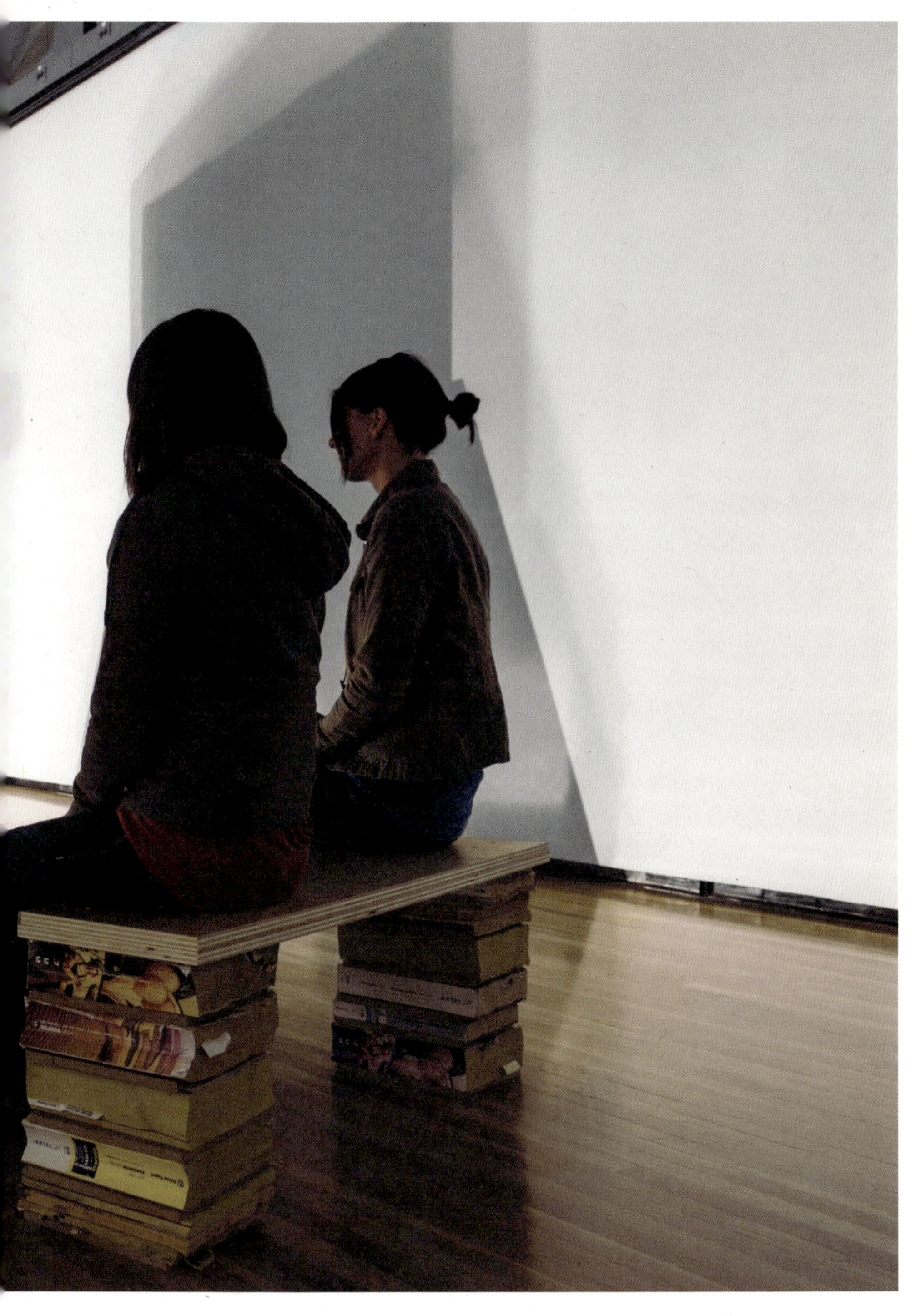

Banff

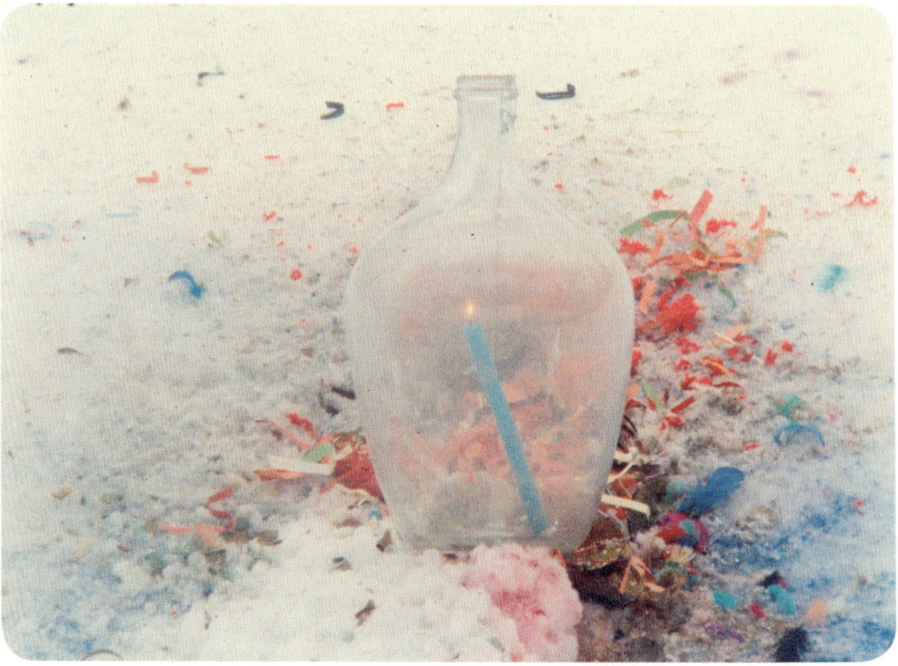

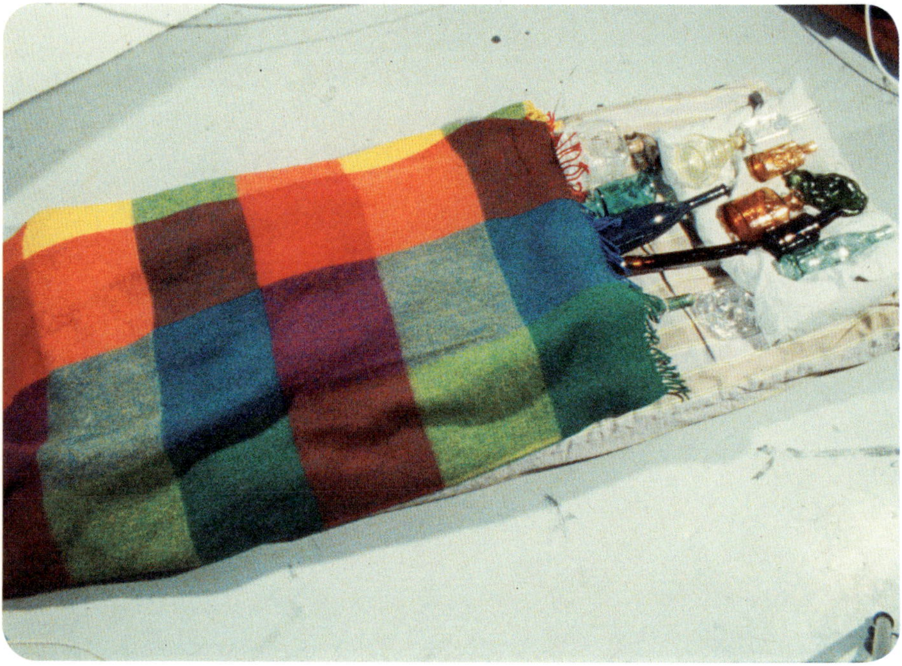

Bottles Under the Influence (film stills), 2012

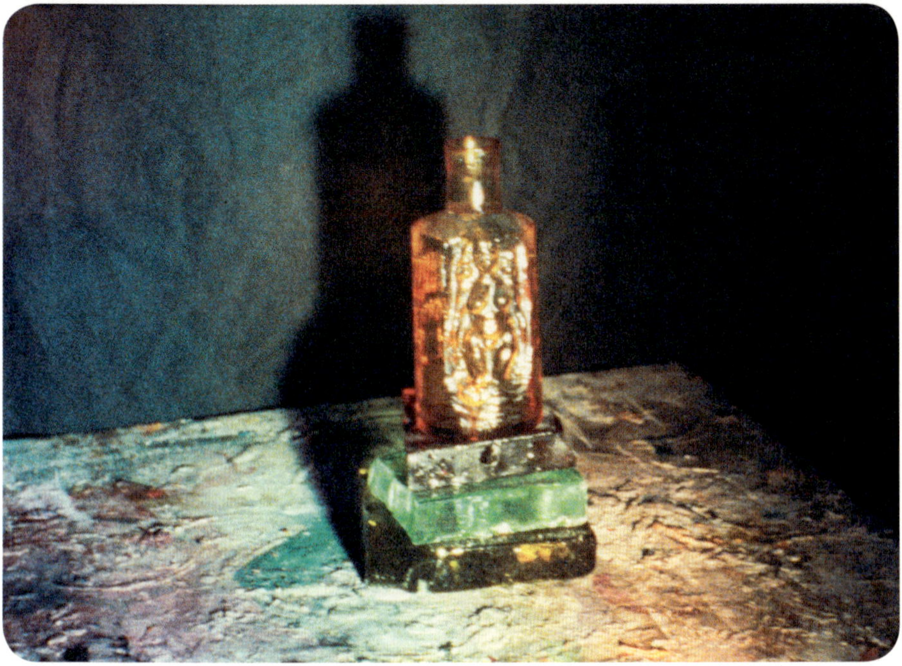

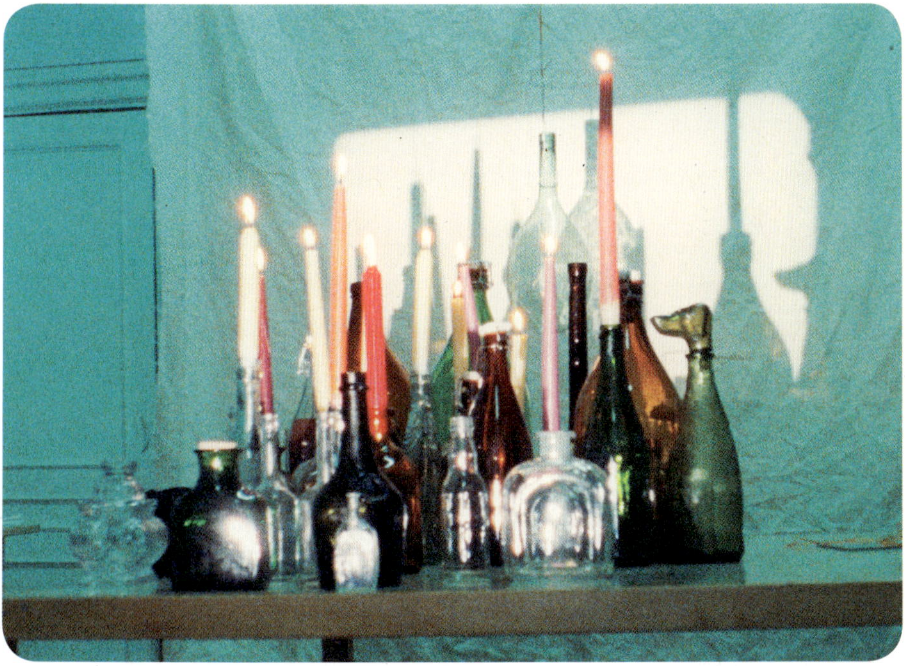

Banff

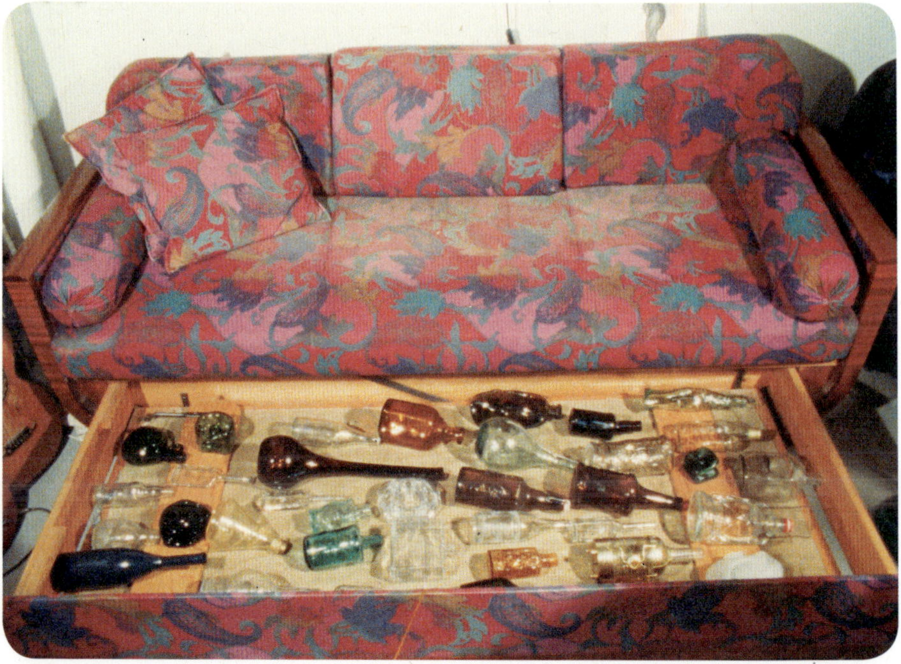

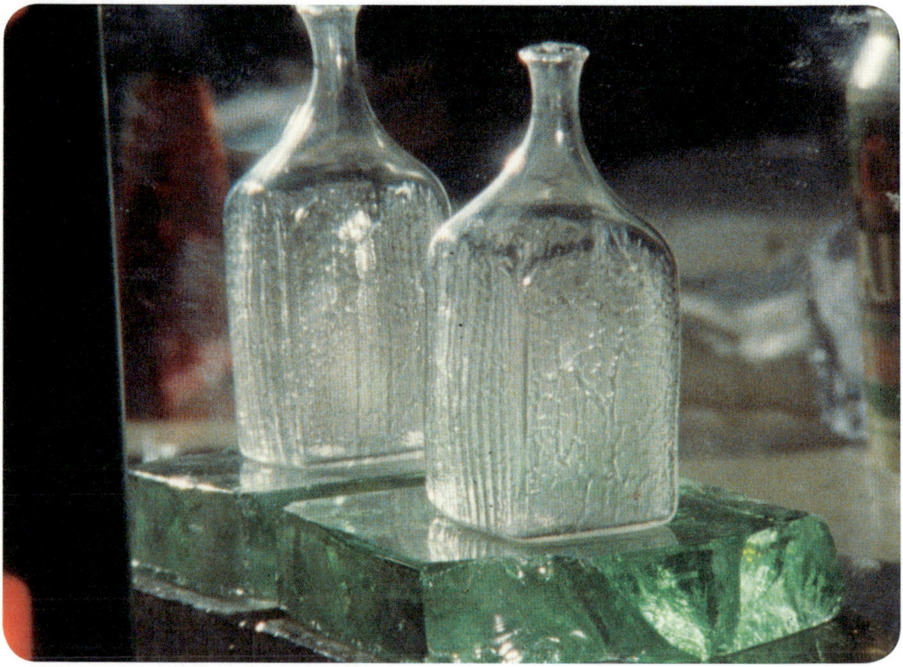

Bottles Under the Influence (film stills), 2012

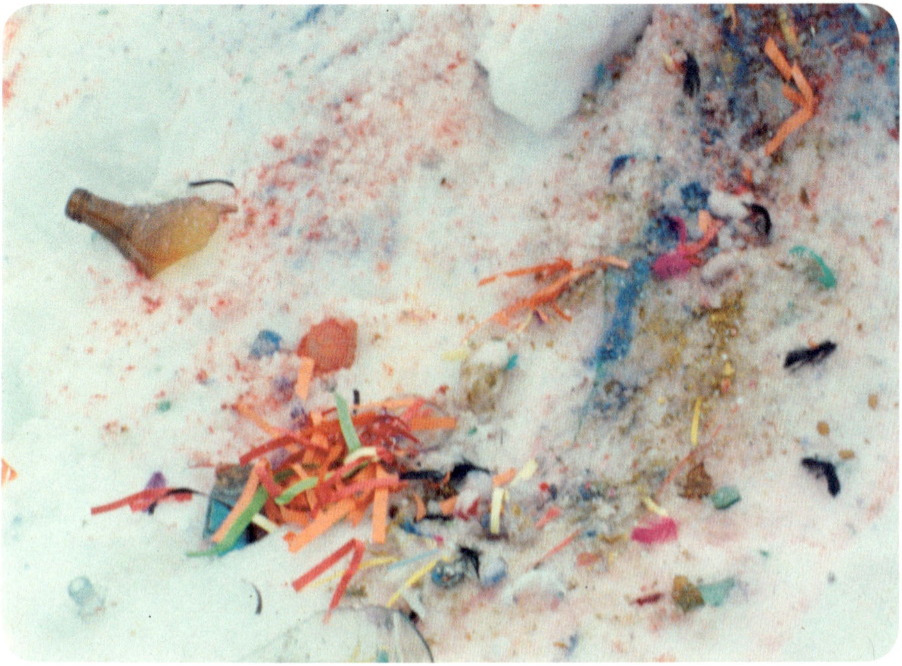

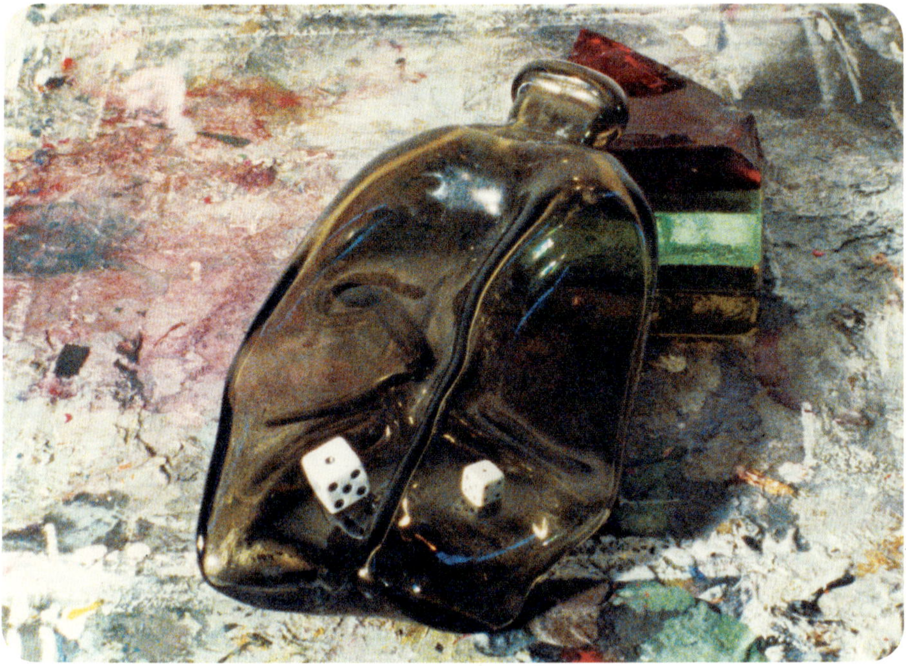

Banff

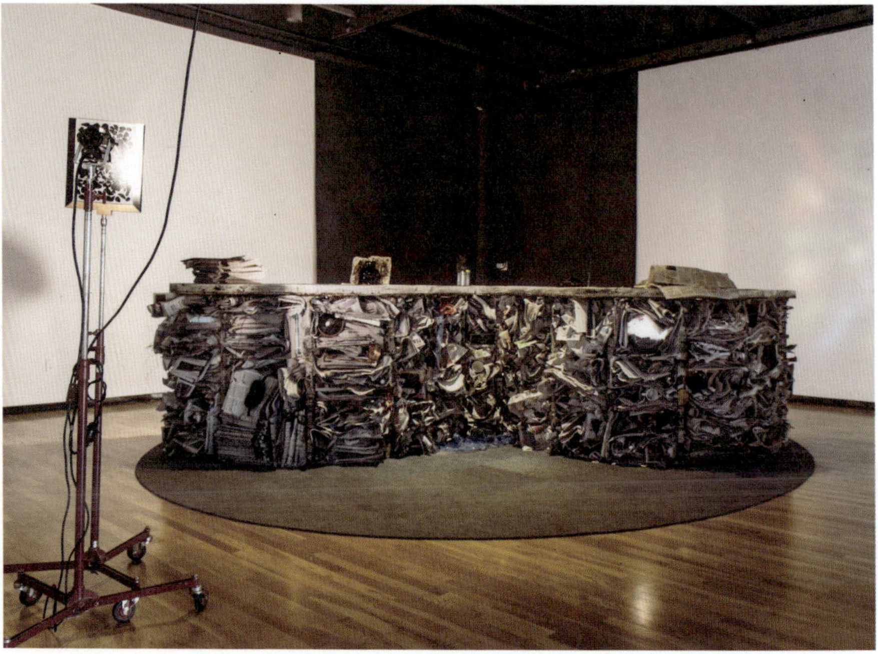

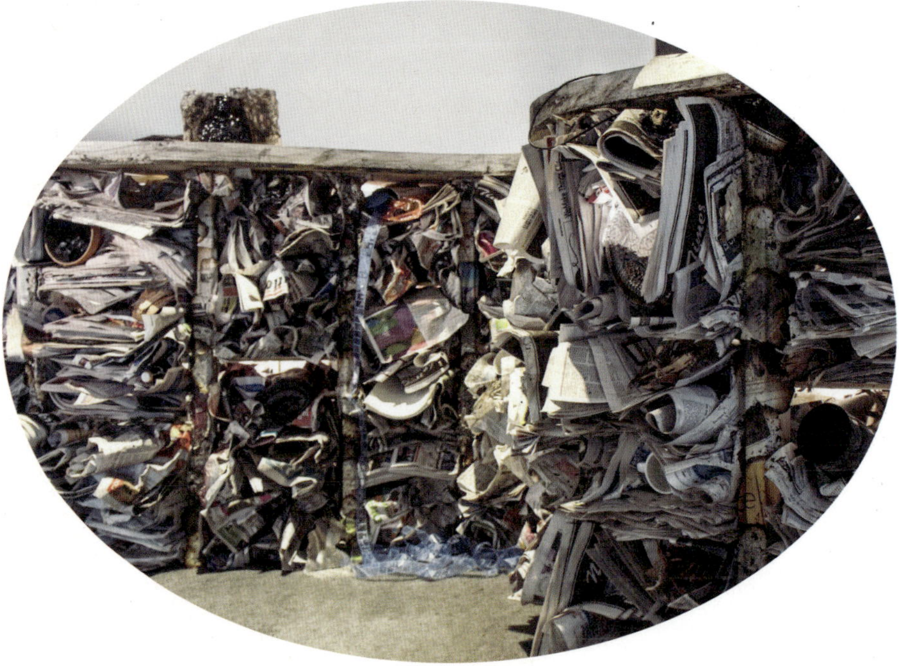

Installation views, Walter Phillips Gallery, 2013

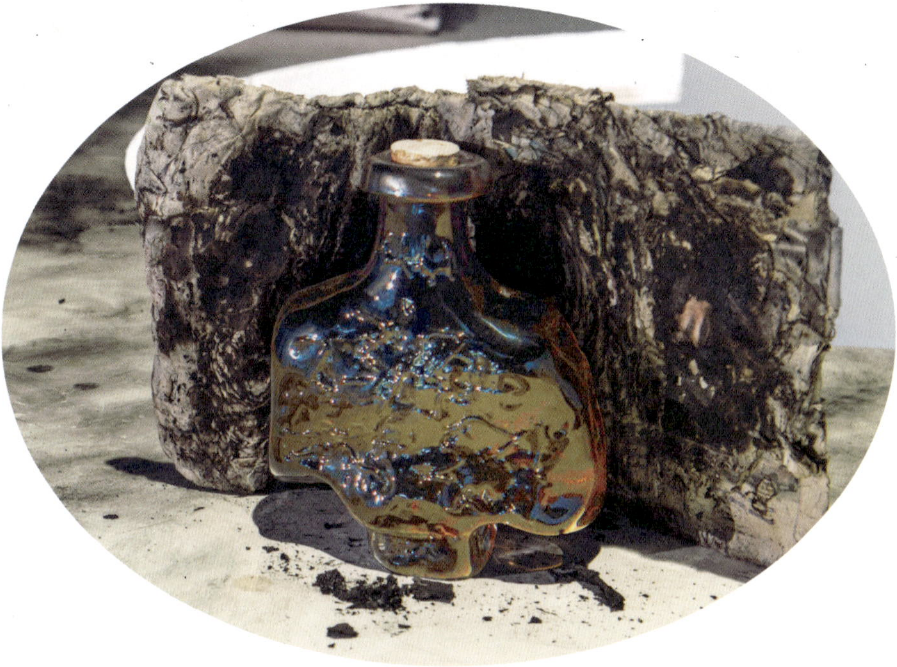

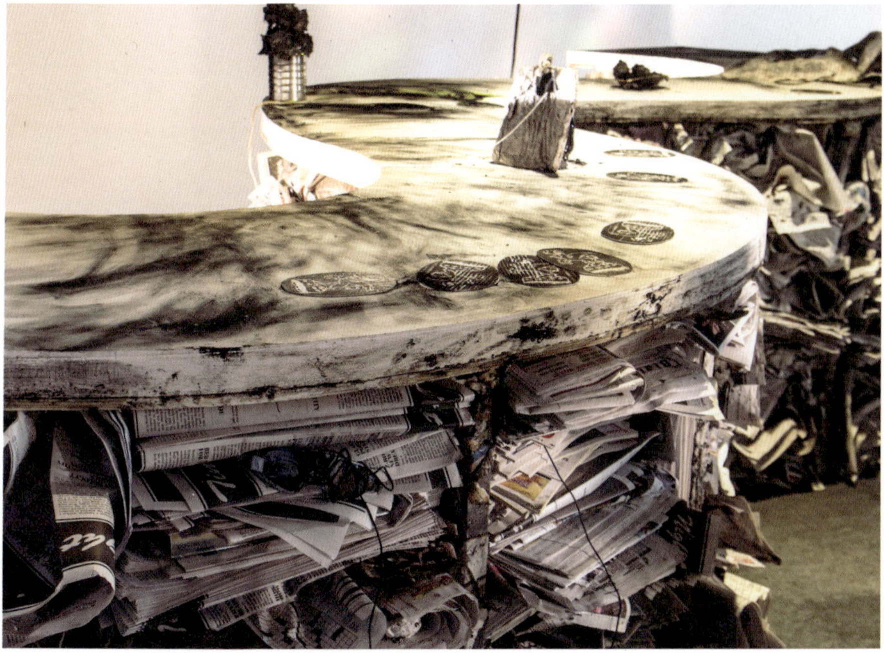

Banff

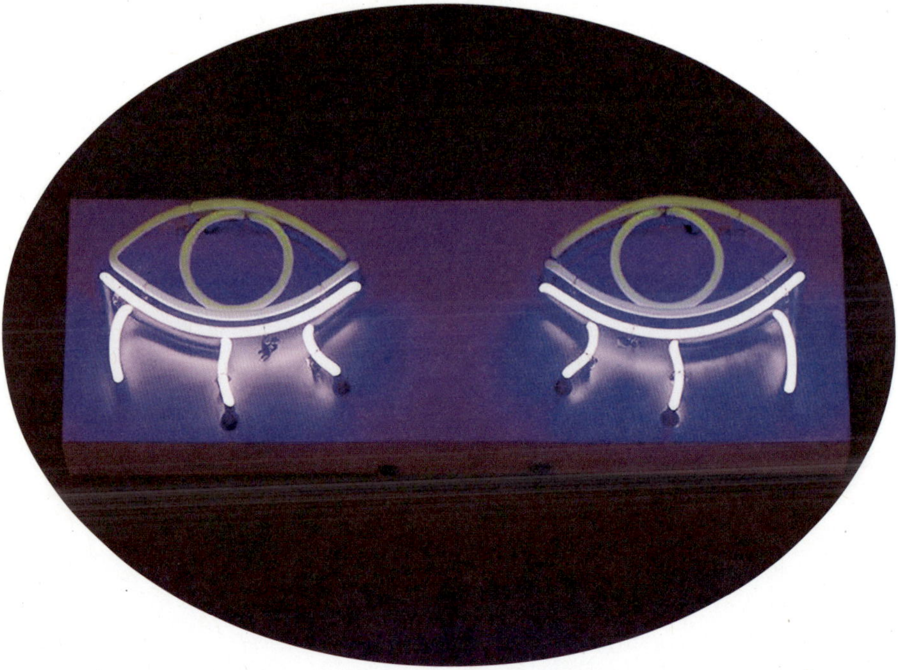

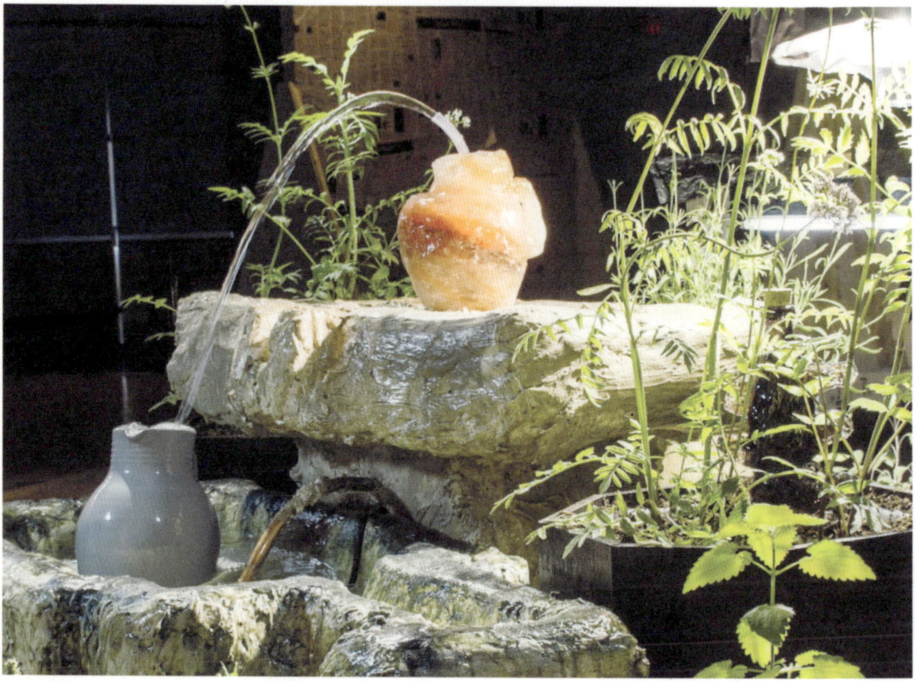

Installation views, Walter Phillips Gallery, 2013

Jesse McKee

Surreal Ghosts and Neuroplastic Ancestors

I entered the story sometime in 2012 in Banff. Julia Feyrer and Tamara Henderson had met each other some years prior at the Städelschule in Frankfurt, where they studied with artists Simon Starling and Mark Leckey. I knew Feyrer and her work from the time I'd spent in Vancouver as the exhibitions curator at the Western Front. I met Henderson for the first time while she was in residence at the Banff Centre. I visited her studio and she showed me a series of drawings of fantastical bottles, each designed to imbue characteristics beyond their form and function. There was a tall, slender, yet oblong kind of bottle. "This is *The Chance Bottle*," she said. It had been designed through a game of chance in which its proportions were assigned through a roll of the dice.

Next, we watched a few clips on her laptop of a 16 mm film that would become *Bottles Under the Influence*, Feyrer and Henderson's take on John Cassavetes's 1974 film *A Woman Under the Influence*. The film featured bottles from the collection of the Historical Museum of Wines and Spirits in Stockholm. The bottles were documented, staged, positioned, studied, projected on, tucked in bed, drunk from, baked in a kiln and shot at. They were like bodies made of glass, appearing headless, armless and footless, with lips and necks. These vessels were the characters of the film.

The Museum of Wines and Spirits documented the history of the trade of making drinks and their containers through a series of dioramas, stagings and re-enactments. After learning that the museum's nostalgic display strategies were set to be overhauled to a contemporary style, the artists were compelled to take the bottles on a night out of the museum; in the film, we see the objects come to life, animated with lighting effects and handmade trickery that recall early twentieth-century filmmaking. The film's second setting is inside the Royal Institute of Art in Stockholm, where Henderson was studying at the time. She lived in a studio that smelled of birch tar; the studio was in a former shipbuilding site and the tar was used in the walls as waterproofing. Remember this smell; it will come back to us.

Feyrer had been a resident in Banff about two years prior to my meeting with Henderson, and she made a fantastic series of daguerreotypes of still-lifes in her studio; the Morris and Helen Belkin Art Gallery later acquired this series. Some artists really thrive in the environment in Banff, with its bulk of resources, natural settings and isolation; it can be a space to check out of the pressures of daily life. I could tell that this was true for Feyrer and Henderson; Banff seemed to be productive and convivial to both of their practices.

As a curator you tend to follow your instincts. When that nagging feeling of *this ought to be* keeps coming back into your mind and heart, you make an offer, an invitation. I invited both artists back to Banff in 2013 for a month-long residency with the goal of making an exhibition together. Prior to their arrival, they spent time in Vancouver making some things. In Banff, they developed an elaborate film set. Their characters were designed from those drawings I had seen; the bottles had become real. They had carved their visions into moulds and worked with a glass studio to blow them into shape.

We met *The Pest Detective*, *The Blind Bottle*, *The Newspaper Bottle*, *The Old Hag* and *The Chance Bottle*. *The Pest Detective* was inspired by a little character you'll find on every page of the Vancouver *Yellow Pages*, a bug in a yellow detective's coat, wearing a wide-brimmed hat with holes for its antennae to stick through. He was filled with apple wine, a spirit popular in Frankfurt, where the artists first met. *The Blind Bottle* was made through a blind-folded collaboration between the artists, moulding the shape of the thing without sight, but with trust; it was filled with moonshine of a proof so strong it might make you lose your sight. *The Newspaper Bottle* was designed as an open page and is filled with a smoked whiskey, something a reporter might have sipped at a press bar after a long day. *The Old Hag* and her six mauve limbs refer to a Newfoundland legend of a spirit who visits you and sits on your chest, paralyzing your body as you come to consciousness; she was filled with a valerian tincture to encourage sleep. And finally, *The Chance Bottle* in all its glory, proud and tall, but not tasting quite right, was filled with a combination of all of these concoctions, with two free-floating dice at the bottom of the bottle.

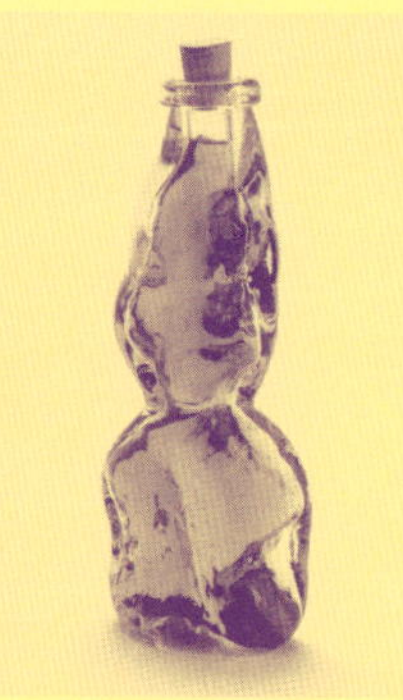

Julia Feyrer and Tamara Henderson, *Chance Bottle*, 2013

You enter the exhibition through an opaque glass-paned door that leads to *The Pest Detective*'s office, a room with a bug light hanging by its cord above a wooden desk whose surface has been inked and carved into. This surface has been used to make a woodblock print, a nod to the namesake of the gallery itself,

 Jesse McKee

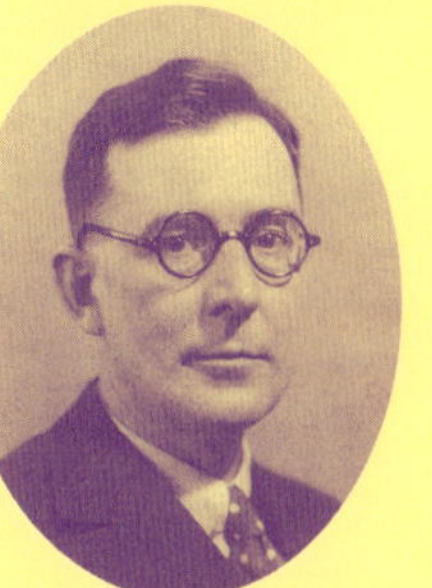

Walter J. Phillips, who was a veteran artist in this medium in the mid-twentieth century. On top of the desk you see a typewriter whose keys have been replaced with bits of seashells. Around the desk is a crushed powder, also made of seashells, that offers a protective perimeter, like diatomaceous earth scattered to repel insects. This material has been crushed between a Pacific beach stone and a piece of Rundle stone from the mountains in Banff. Over in the corner, inside a bar fridge borrowed from the halls of the residence, you find *The Pest Detective* keeping cool, while the venetian blinds hanging in the office window, a mainstay of the film noir genre, have been cut into the shape of the character.

Beyond this, a garden full of plants that encourage deep sleep and dreaming has been grown; chamomile, pineapple sage and valerian are a few of the species that have been planted here. A "communicating fountain," made from a traditional apple-wine pitcher and its replica, carved from salt crystal, spouts water between the two vessels. And there is *The Old Hag*, positioned in the earth of one of the planters. A neon sign flickers between a pair of eyes opening and shutting, phasing between pineapple yellow and violet, colouring the light coming from a series of industrial grow lights hung above the space—blasting with the power of several suns—which keep the plants nourished inside this black box of a gallery.

At the farthest point back, a massive bar has been constructed in the shape of a curved wave, stuffed with the newspaper *The Night Times*, a publication made by the artists, which, instead of reporting on crime, political upheavals and sports games, is authored by a staff of journalists who can witness dreams. As subscribers, we wake up to reportage about the most interesting dreams witnessed the night prior. The bar is the dream journalists' refuge; in the early morning light, they will tell each other tales as they sip on their smoked whiskey. The bar's seams have been sealed with that birch tar, reminiscent of the studio in Stockholm. Henderson noted that this smell would remind her of her own consciousness in a lucid dreaming state; in Stockholm, the smell would wake her every morning, grounding her in the real.

A cinema at the other far end of the gallery shows that first film, *Bottles Under the Influence*, and on your pass back, you notice the two other characters flanking the front corners of the space, *The Chance Bottle* and *The Blind Bottle*, watching over it all.

An interest in formal locations for the appreciation of craft, art and display—for example, the museum or gallery—is enmeshed with the studio and the domestic interior in

Henderson and Feyrer's films. The notion that the objects contained within these formal sites have their own histories, stories and perceptions that extend beyond what we may observe about them within everyday consciousness is intrinsic to the artists' mode of storytelling. This oneiric quality provides the staging ground for the sequel to *Bottles Under the Influence*, *Consider the Belvedere*.

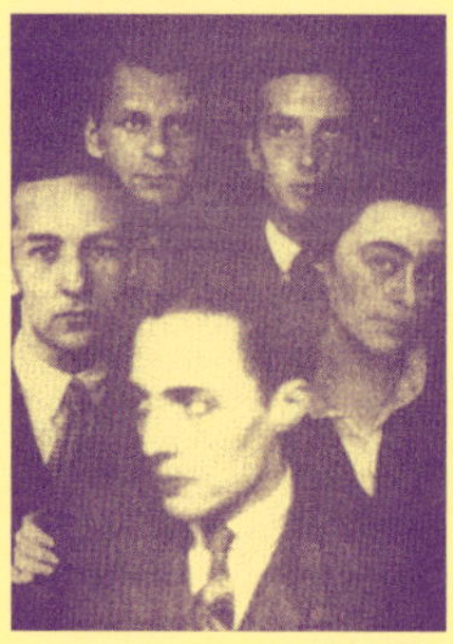

Feyrer and Henderson's sets and films remind me of the early twentieth-century surrealist group and its associated publication, *Le Grand Jeu* (*The Great Game*), led by the French writer René Daumal. This shadowy camp of authors and artists seemed to have a more ambitious cause than that of the better-known surrealists. They asked the artists of that place and time to take steps beyond just representing their hyperconscious perceptions. Once they could work in this way, what might they do in the conscious world? Where could they take each other? How would they transform themselves?

Across a series of four journals between 1928 and 1932, *Le Grand Jeu* set out a mission to offer a progressive idea around the surreal and the dream state, expanding André Breton's framing, and drawing members from his camp to theirs. With their psychic experimentations and surreal occultism, Daumal and his group set out to offer a serious study of traditional metaphysics and perception. In the foreword to the first issue of the journal, Roger Gilbert-Lecomte writes that "the Great Game is incurable, not winnable; you don't only play it once. We want to play it in every moment of our lives."[1]

This tone of *Le Grand Jeu* further resonates with the neuroplastic theories of today, which tell us that the mind can be shaped and rewired through its experiences—both conscious and unconscious ones. Both *Le Grand Jeu* and Feyrer and Henderson's collaborative practice ask you to pay more attention to the dream, not only to analyze it for its hidden messages, but also to take it seriously and value its legitimacy as a mode of being. Beyond the inquiries offered by early twentieth-century psychoanalysts, now, nearly a century later, studies have taken psychoanalysis into the realm of observed science through the discovery of the neuroplastic capabilities of the brain. These are the observed changes that the brain can make to its own structure and function in response to experience, both real and perceived. Writing on these observations, Norman Doidge remarks:

Psychoanalysis is often about turning our ghosts into ancestors ... We are often haunted by important relationships from the

Jesse McKee

past that influence us unconsciously in the present. As we work them through, they go from haunting us to becoming simply part of our history. We can turn our ghosts into ancestors because we can transform implicit memories—which we are often not aware exist until they are evoked and thus seem to come at us "out of the blue"—into declarative memories that now have clear context, which makes them easier to recollect and experience as part of the past.[2]

Feyrer and Henderson's collaborative films echo these qualities. They devote their practice to muddling through the realms of an ongoing narrative of the alter-conscious, straddling the gap between dream and the waking world. Focusing on the dream space through sustained practice has rewired their collective perception as a pair, and a sort of third collaborator has emerged, an energy that moves between them amid conscious and unconscious realms. They've developed the ability to open this door of perception and possibility whenever they choose.

This aspect of their collaboration can be seen in their characters, which evolved from singular objects in the first exhibition at Walter Phillips Gallery—a collection of bottles—to a series of interdependent unions. The characters were remade with the support of the Department of Chemistry's glassblowing workshop at the University of British Columbia and exhibited as part of the exhibition *The Last Waves* at the Belkin in 2016. There, the *Communicating Vessels* were paired, connected through glass shafts and tubes. The characters and their contents had mixed, and become a new thing.

Thinking through the surreal histories of *Le Grand Jeu* in relation to Feyrer and Henderson's practice with the philosophical implications of contemporary brain science brings me to some deduction through the work of French philosopher Catherine Malabou, who is best known for her work on plasticity. Malabou has forged new connections across such fields as philosophy, neuroscience and psychoanalysis and their fundamental entanglements with cultural, political and social life. Working with post-structuralist and post-critical methodologies, she addresses the work of philosophers Kant, Hegel, Freud, Heidegger and Derrida. Her writing engenders a reconsideration of keywords and foundational concepts such as subjectivity, affect, gender, sex, feminism, neoliberalism, sovereignty, justice and trauma, to name a few.

The concept of plasticity has an aesthetic dimension (sculpture, malleability), just as much as an ethical one (solicitude, treatment, help, repair, rescue) and a political one (responsibility in the double movement of the receiving and the giving of form). It is therefore inevitable that at the horizon of the objective descriptions of brain plasticity stand questions concerning social life and being together. To expedite matters, let us reduce these to one option: Does brain plasticity, taken as a model, allow us to think a multiplicity of interactions in which the participants exercise transformative effects on one another through the demands of recognition, of non-domination, and of liberty? Or must we claim, on the contrary, that, between determinism and polyvalence, brain plasticity constitutes the biological justification of a type of economic, political, and social organization in which all that matters is the result of action as such: efficacy, adaptability—unfailing flexibility?[3]

Consider the context of Vancouver now, a place that is eight years on from the mega-event of the Olympics and rapidly veering toward an elusive mono-culture triggered by the gentrification of most of its neighbourhoods. Parcelled with the economic entrapment of neoliberal redevelopment are psychic wounds and a diminution of time, self-determination and pleasure. Alternate perceptions offered through dream and escape are not only a proposition against this unceasing momentum, but also a necessity for survival and resilience amid conditions that close possibility. Feyrer and Henderson don't offer a purely escapist position, but rather one that reminds us that the way things appear around us are not always as clear and fixed as they seem. It returns to us some agency and asks us to exploit those openings as much as possible—to make our brains and the world out of our plural perceptions of it.

Feyrer and Henderson's perceptions are first encountered as a visitor to these exhibitions, which offer the residual presence of objects and architecture haunting spaces cast as abandoned film sets. These spaces become places to contemplate the dormant but dreamy periods between the shooting, editing and viewing of a film. A slowed transition from environment to moving image is informed by the ghostly realm of a psychoanalytic haunting, which is produced, finally, in the film, its inherited ancestor. This process speaks of the neuroplastic effects of the dream worlds brought into waking life, offering a criss-crossed narrative drawn from the artists' visions, seen through varied states of perception, in the studio, the gallery, the home and the city.

1
H.J. Maxwell and Claudio Rugafiori, eds., *Le Grand Jeu: Collection Complète* (Paris: Editions Jean-Michel Place, 1977), issue 1 (Summer 1928), p. 1.

2
Norman Doidge, *The Brain That Changes Itself: Stories of Personal Triumph from the Frontiers of Brain Science* (New York: Viking, 2007), 243.

3
Catherine Malabou, "Plasticity's Fields of Action," in *What Should We Do with Our Brain?* (New York: Fordham University, 2008), 30-31.

 Jesse McKee

Alex Klein

Somniloquy

I begin writing while under hypnosis, having decided on this method as a way to reach deep down, to relinquish to the associative and to connect my innermost thoughts with the computer keyboard. As I submit to the process of hypnotization I attempt to dismantle the restraints imposed by consciousness, to unburden myself from the armour of the body and to eliminate the contaminants of the outside world. My muscles relax, my mind goes elsewhere and the present disappears. A pulsing hum is interwoven with a robotic voice: "Start writing, start writing, start writing. Writing is joy when you are in a peaceful state. I describe what I have seen or done from different perspectives. Writing is my life. Writing is my passion. Writing is joyful. There is no such thing as writer's block ..."[1] I disappear into the jumble of these words. I have no concrete sense of time.

Hours pass and as I emerge from my trance, I cannot be sure if I am fully awake. My mind drifts and I begin to ruminate on one of my favourite films, Vincente Minnelli's 1970 Technicolor musical, *On a Clear Day You Can See Forever*. The film stars Barbra Streisand as Daisy Gamble—a self-described ordinary girl from Mahwah, New Jersey and a serious smoker who can make flowers grow, anticipate when the telephone will ring and locate lost items—and Yves Montand as Marc Chabot—a sophisticated skeptic, professor and psychiatrist with an expertise in hypnosis. In an attempt to kick her habit Daisy consults Dr. Chabot for a hypnotherapy session. In a thick French accent he lulls her:

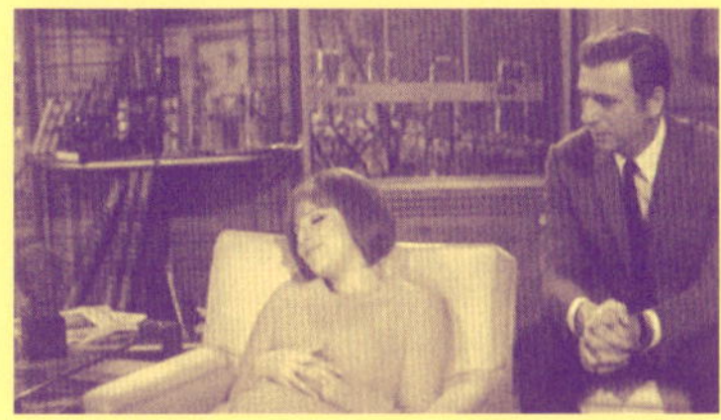

On a Clear Day You Can See Forever, dir. Vincente Minnelli, 1970

"Your eyelids are now heavy, your arms are numb and heavy, your legs are dull and heavy and you give yourself to sleep. A deeeeeep sleep."[2] In no time Daisy is under his spell. When he asks her to tell him "everything you can about yourself, beginning with your name," she rouses, momentarily struggles to locate her identity and firmly declares with a newly pronounced British accent: "My name is Melinda. Melinda Winifred Waine Tentrees!" Startled, he eventually comes to realize that in

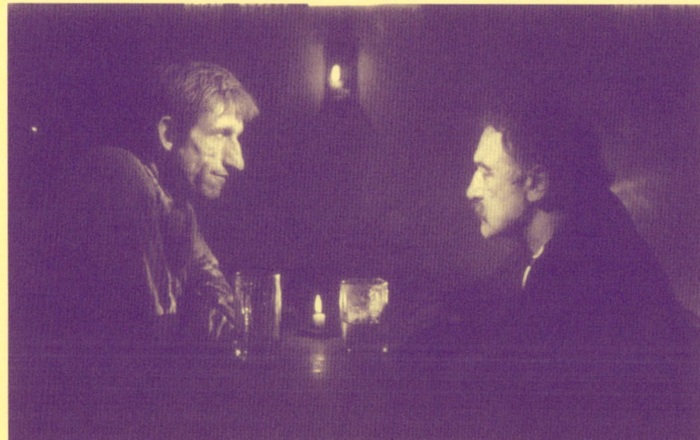

his effort to cure Daisy of her nicotine addiction he has unwittingly conjured a past life, thus setting the stage for an unusual ménage à trois.

If hypnosis in this instance is a narrative device that complicates fixed notions of personhood, for director Werner Herzog, it is a serious tool for filmmaking. While Herzog has employed hypnosis at various times in his career (and famously on occasion with chickens) his 1976 film *Heart of Glass* is the most notable of these experiments. The film tells the story of a small Bavarian village that falls prey to a collective form of madness following the death of a master craftsman who held the secret to making a special rose-coloured glass. In order to produce the effect of a "kind of stylized somnambulism," Herzog had the majority of the cast perform their lines while in a mesmerized state.[3] Although he originally intended to work with a bona fide hypnotherapist, Herzog ended up beginning each filming session by inducing the actors himself, ultimately merging the professions of filmmaker and hypnotist.

For critic Roger Ebert, this resulted in the actors performing their lines like zombies with a strange delivery of both "dread and certainty." With their individual mannerisms erased it is possible that what we are actually hearing is Herzog's own inflection. In effect, "he is acting through them."[4]

Herzog's wish to speak through his cast also pertained to his audience. He remembers wanting to extend this idea further by literally hypnotizing theatregoers through the screen while they watched the movie, summoning them out of their daze at the end. He only abandoned the idea after considering the potential liabilities.[5] If hypnosis allowed Herzog to portray an "inner state" on celluloid, it also acted as a kind of metaphor for the very process of making and potentially viewing films. He explains:

> Cinema per se has a hypnotic quality to it. I often find myself in an almost unconscious state on the film set, having to ask the person doing the continuity what scenes have already been done and what work remains... It's as

Alex Klein

if I were at a drunken party and somehow arrived home without being aware of it. The next morning three policemen are standing by my bedside, accusing me of having killed someone the night before.[6]

Here the film is likened to a crime scene while its production is dependent on a momentary loss of self and memory. Like the village confronted with the glassblower who shepherded his ruby secret to his grave, a lapse in the mnemonic can produce unexpected, if sometimes dangerously chaotic results for art and history alike. If for Herzog the film set provokes a state of unconscious being, perhaps the camera is there to both guard against amnesia and to provide a kind of symbolic correlate between the ruby glass and the ground glass, with the lens acting as a filter between the internal and the external world.

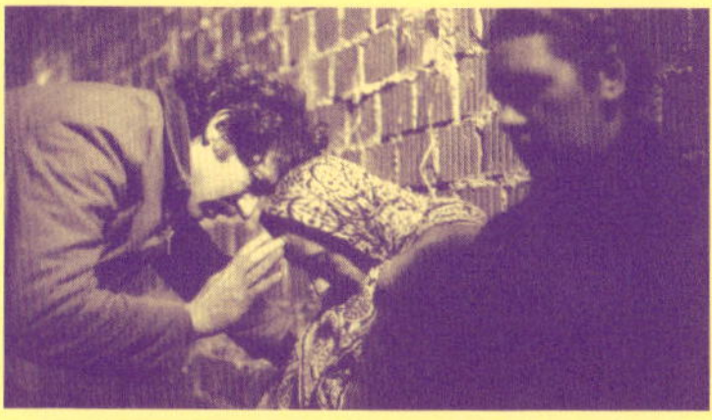

Werner Herzog on the set of *Heart of Glass*, 1976

Of course, the surrealists famously attempted to access and record the subconscious by reconciling chance operations and automatic writing with the immediacy and supposed veracity of the fixed photographic eye.[7] Through this conjunction they rejected the mastery of straight image production and linear representational narrative in favour of alternate conduits and articulations of perception.

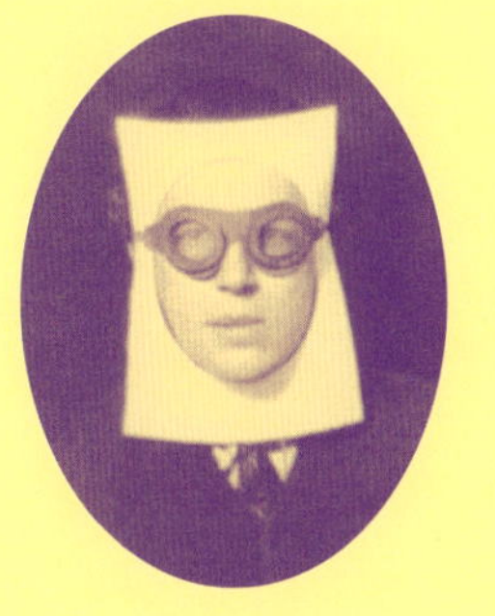

André Breton (1896–1966)

Writer André Breton reflected on the underlying nature of surrealism and its connection to the everyday in his 1932 book *Les Vases communicants* or the *Communicating Vessels*.[8] For Breton dreams act as a passageway between the experience of the world and interiority. It is precisely this space between sleep and wakefulness that contains transformative potential and the twilight zone in which artists Julia Feyrer and Tamara Henderson work.

Feyrer and Henderson's collaborations, which move fluidly between film, sculpture, painting, installation, text, performance and book-object, are driven by lived experience and arrived at by means of automatism, altered states, alchemical processes and psychic inquiries. While layered references to cinema and literature abound, the artists are equally interested in the symbolic significance of the materials they use. In their three interconnected exhibitions, *The Last Waves* (2016), *Consider the Belvedere* (2015) and *Bottles Under the Influence* (2013), the gallery performs a doubled function. It is both a space to display and provide context for the artists' sculptural ensembles and 16 mm films as well as a movie set and site of future artistic production. Occupying several temporalities at once the exhibition forms a recursive loop in which viewers are simultaneously looking backwards and forwards as if they were a Klein bottle or an ouroboros.

The destabilization of time and artistic agency is also key to surrealism and one way in which critics have attempted to dismantle its misogynistic overtones. While on the one hand it is difficult to deny surrealism's aggressive fetishization of the female body, for art historian Rosalind Krauss one might also locate within these works a radical gesture that insists on the imaging of gender as a construction rather than a biological given. She argues that this slippage between masculine and feminine is not solely relegated to the surrealist text or image, but is embedded in its very production. As such, "it breaks down the difference between those formerly positioned opposites—author and reader—and thus between the inside and the outside of the text."[9] Through diaristic, automatic, hallucinatory and responsive techniques neither the individual viewer or artist, nor reader or author, is privy in advance to the final outcome. It is this displacement of traditional hierarchical relationships that produces what Krauss sees as a feminization of "the viewing subject in a move that is deeply antipatriarchal."[10] This subversion is how I understand Feyrer and Henderson's contemporary deployment of surrealist strategies. Similar to the uncertain footing that Krauss describes in her writing on this historical avant-garde, the artists slip and slide between the identities of their individual authorship, between objecthood and the role of their audience. To walk into one of Feyrer and Henderson's installations is to become simultaneously a passive viewer, an active collaborator and a character in one of their scenarios. It also sometimes results in becoming inebriated.

Certainly intoxication has taken place in their exhibitions through the copious consumption of alcohol, but it is also a visual effect and a subject of fascination for the two artists. In their film *Bottles Under the Influence* (2012)—a loose reference to John Cassavetes's filmic inquiry into psychosis and sexuality, *A Woman Under the Influence*—the artists worked with glass bottles from the collection of the Historical Museum of Wines and Spirits in Stockholm, which are embodied as actors to be staged, observed, projected on, used and destroyed. Alongside the film, the artists penned a drinking song for women, which is a provisional script for future films as well as a song that was performed at ICA by opera singer Lauren Pearl Eberwein, scored by composer Tony Solitro and accompanied by a special cocktail.[11]

The second film, *Consider the Belvedere* (2015)—a nod to David Foster Wallace's meditation on the perverse pleasure taken by gourmands in the preparation of lobsters—premiered at ICA and takes on a more narrative structure as it follows new bottle characters, fabricated by the artists in collaboration with professional glassblowers,

Alex Klein

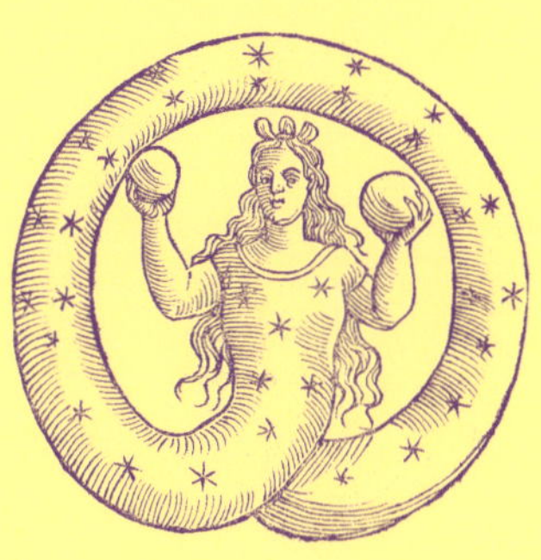

Cesare Ripa, Ouroboros
from *Iconologia*, 1669

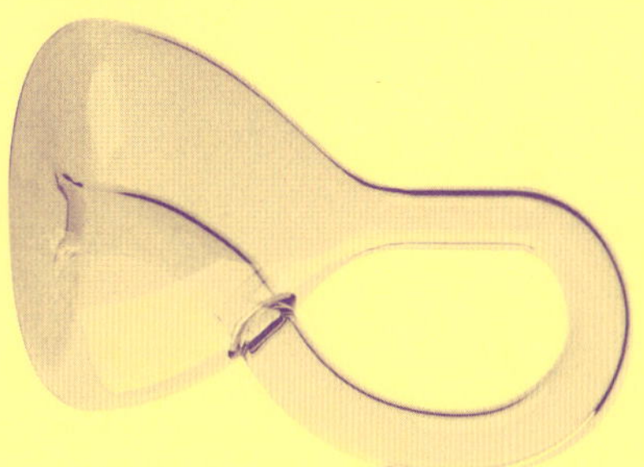

Klein bottle

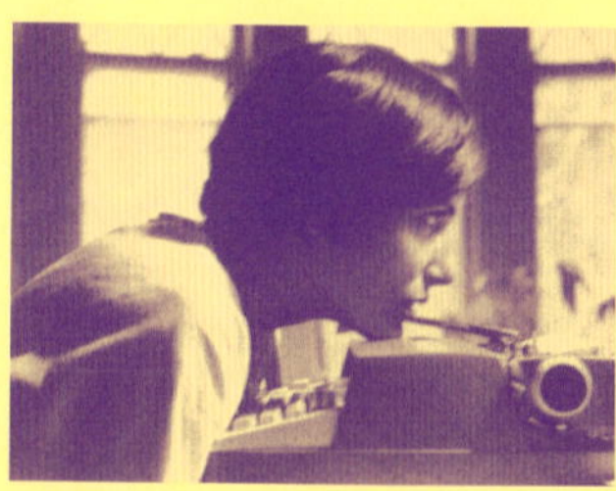

Rosalind Krauss, from the cover
of *Perpetual Inventory*, 2010

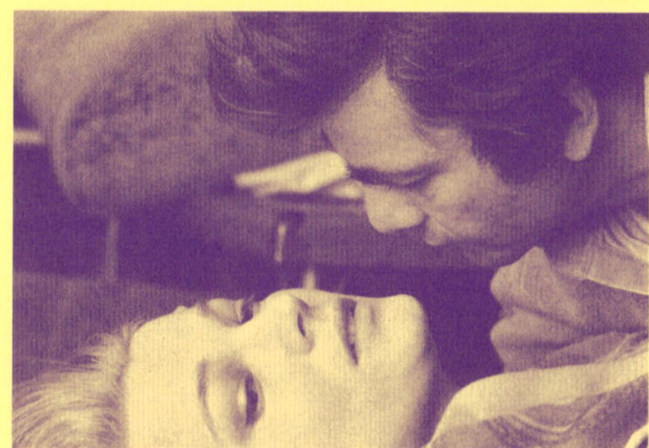

Gena Rowlands and Peter Falk, *A Woman Under the
Influence*, dir. John Cassavetes, 1974. Photo: Sam Shaw

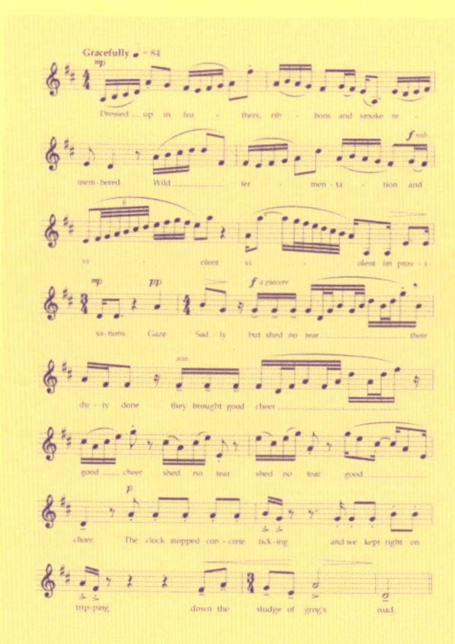

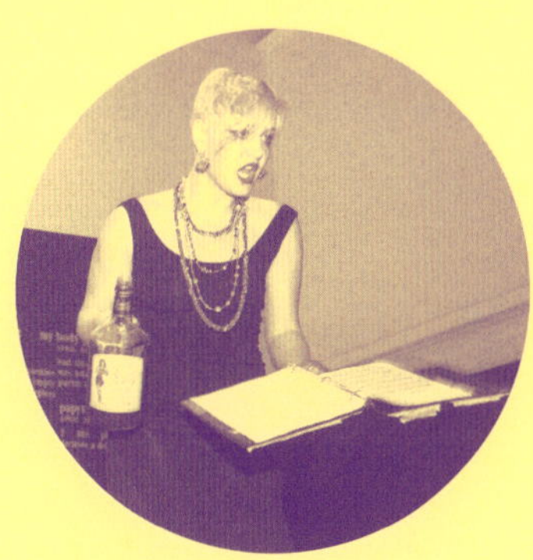

Drinking song score, *Les Bouteilles
de la Table Ronde* composed by Tony
Solitro and performed by soprano
Lauren Pearl Eberwein at ICA

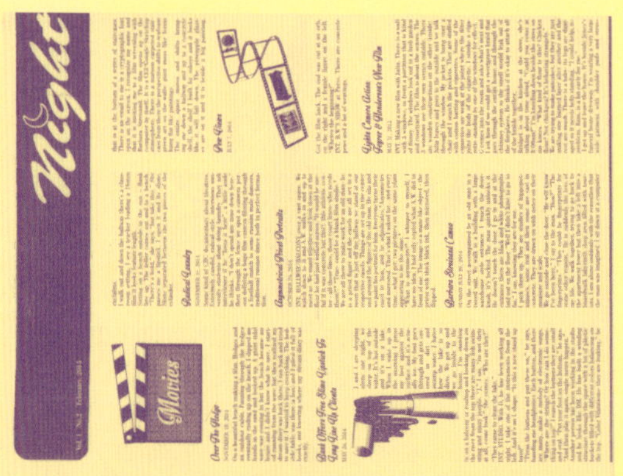

Julia Feyrer and Tamara Henderson,
Night Times News Vol. 1, no. 2, February 2015

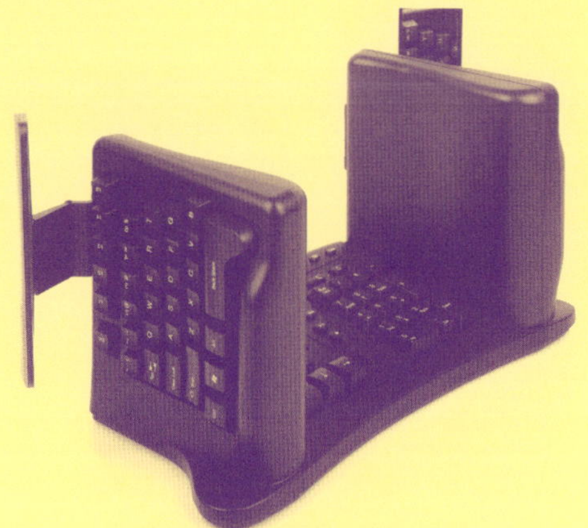

SafeType™ keyboard

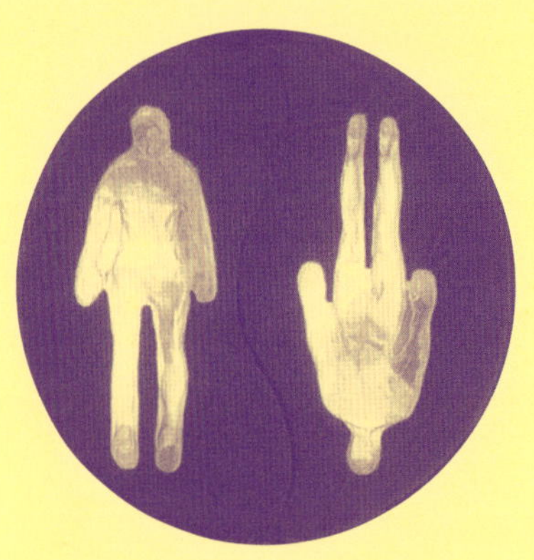

Julia Feyrer and Tamara Henderson,
The Aura Readers, 2015

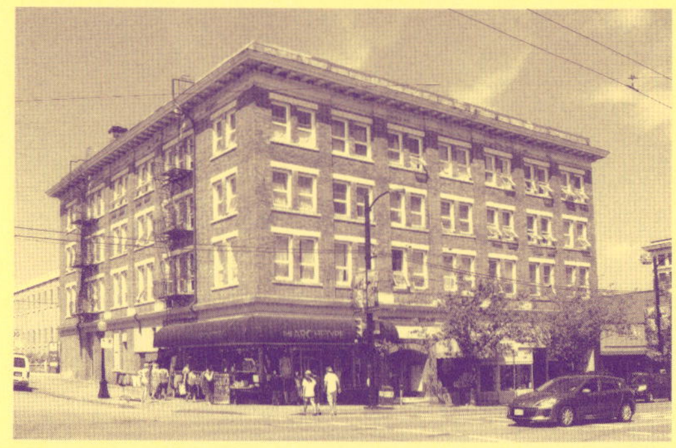

Belvedere Court, 2545 Main Street, Vancouver, built 1912

         Alex Klein

through a kind of film noir detective story that would seem to channel Herzog's association of film with a crime scene. These "vessels," with names such as *The Pest Detective*, *The Blind Bottle* and *The Old Hag*, were filmed in the set of their previous exhibition at Banff and on location in Vancouver at the Belvedere apartment building, where both artists had been living at the time.

While on film these bottle characters are awakened through techniques that recall the kind of special effects found in early cinema, within the installation at ICA they lay dormant as sculptural props in a *mise en scène*. Upon entering the gallery-cum-film set one was invited to hang out at *The Night Times Press Bar*, where visitors could peruse *The Night Times News* (a newspaper recounting the artists' reveries) and were encouraged to record their own private dreams for public display on a large projection and for possible inclusion in future issues of the newsprint journal. At times this work was aided by a dream stenographer who sported custom-fitted silver shoes and whose paper trails of transcribed dreams were strewn around the room. The bar itself was a miniaturized replica of the Belvedere building that included windows with mystical dioramas and a new cast-iron container/character, *The Boiler Room Bottle*. The bar's structure was constructed from handmade bricks made out of newspaper and mortared together using a specially scented Scandinavian pine sap that hung thick and sweet in the air. And when the drinking song was performed a team of dream bartenders arrived to serve libations.

After all of this drinking and dreaming it was natural to move on to *The Hotel Room*, where the bottles from the film were showcased in their hotel minibar "offices" alongside hotel paintings and a screening of *Bottles Under the Influence*. On a carpeted raised platform were situated two beds and a nightstand that was also a fountain. Each bed held the impression of the figure of one of the artists, re-emphasizing that to be awake and asleep are in this case deeply imbricated. Upon closer inspection the impressions were actually glowing pools decorated by an array of colours that had been determined by individual aura readings that took place at the museum. The frames of the beds each in the shape of a half-moon so that they could be pushed together to create a single form were undoubtedly a metaphor for Feyrer and Henderson's relationship as artists and collaborators. Journeying out of the room you arrived at *The Beach*, where naturally occurring fluorescent rocks glowed, awaiting their documentation and activation in the forthcoming film, *The Last Waves*, which they began in the exhibition at ICA. This was also where a new version of *The Blind Bottle*, which is made out of melted 3D glasses, lived and where one could watch the Belvedere film while sitting on a stuffed snake made from beach towels.

The refuse from the beach washed ashore and was enmeshed in the sculptural screens that also functioned as cucolorises that would be used to create shadows and optical effects in the artists' next film. On the cucolorises, among the beach debris, one detected items such as a telephone, ads from the *Yellow Pages* and copies made from a trade magazine for the professional administrative assistant, *Canadian Secretary*. There was also a new bottle, *The Secretary*. She is in the shape of two fingers "walking," and was coincidentally filled with a ruby-coloured substance. Suddenly one was aware of the installation as a site not just of transcription, but of transmission, one whose many modes of textuality take on a gendered inflection that gently oscillates between a meditation on the labour of female writing and an enactment of an *écriture féminine*.

Yet again the artists have placed us on unsure footing and it is at this point that I hazily remember my hypnotic experiment that occasioned this essay. Trying to remember being in a trance is similar to the fuzzy sensation of recounting a dream or describing the work of Julia Feyrer and Tamara Henderson. Eventually these installations, like any film set, are dismantled, the bottle protagonists go home and all that is left behind are a collection of props and raw materials. But the films, while not the same as the disorienting experience of their installations, are at least proof of the crimes committed the night before. Ultimately, for Feyrer and Henderson, our perception of the world and understanding of time are both mediated and made possible by the camera. It serves as a kind of conduit to explore the connection between the subconscious and the everyday, becoming itself a "communicating vessel."

 Alex Klein

1

"Overcome Writer's Block Hypnosis," https://www.youtube.com/watch?v=3HVsrTRUwcM.

2

Yves Montand, *On a Clear Day You Can See Forever*, directed by Vincente Minnelli (Hollywood: Paramount Pictures, 1970).

3

Herzog observes: "The potential for visionary and poetic language is revealed through hypnosis. I wanted to provoke poetic language from people who had never before been in touch with such things." He goes on to say that some of his other films "were attempts to render on screen, for everyone to see and experience, certain inner states." As cited in Paul Cronin, *Werner Herzog: A Guide for the Perplexed. Conversations with Paul Cronin* (New York: Farrar, Straus and Giroux, 2014), 135.

4

Roger Ebert, "Heart of Glass," http://www.rogerebert.com/reviews/great-movie-heart-of-glass-1976.

5

Cronin, 138–39.

6

Cronin, 132.

7

See Rosalind Krauss, "The Photographic Conditions of Surrealism," in *The Originality of the Avant-Garde and Other Modernist Myths* (Cambridge, MA: MIT Press, 1986).

8

In scientific terms, a "communicating vessel" describes two or more containers that are linked together and, as a result of gravity and pressure, will hold the same amount of liquid no matter how much is added to either container.

9

Rosalind Krauss, "Claude Cahun and Dora Maar: By Way of Introduction," in *Bachelors* (Cambridge, MA: MIT Press, 1999), 15.

10

Krauss, *Bachelors*, 17.

11

At the Belkin Art Gallery, the drinking song was performed by Kallie Clayton and Scott Rumble, with Vivienne Bessette's NRG drink and the Magnussonian Twist cocktail, named after the Belvedere's Peter Magnusson, served alongside.

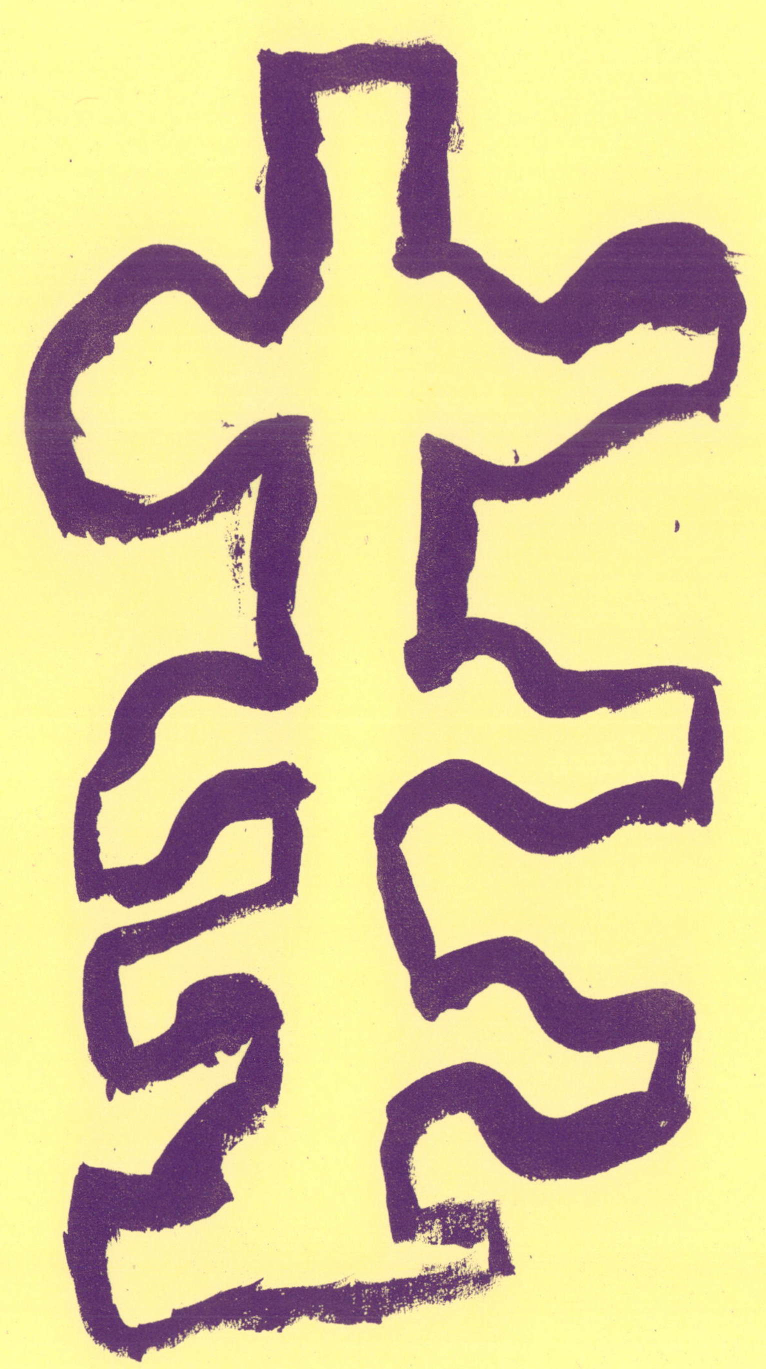

Consider the Belvedere

ICA Philadelphia

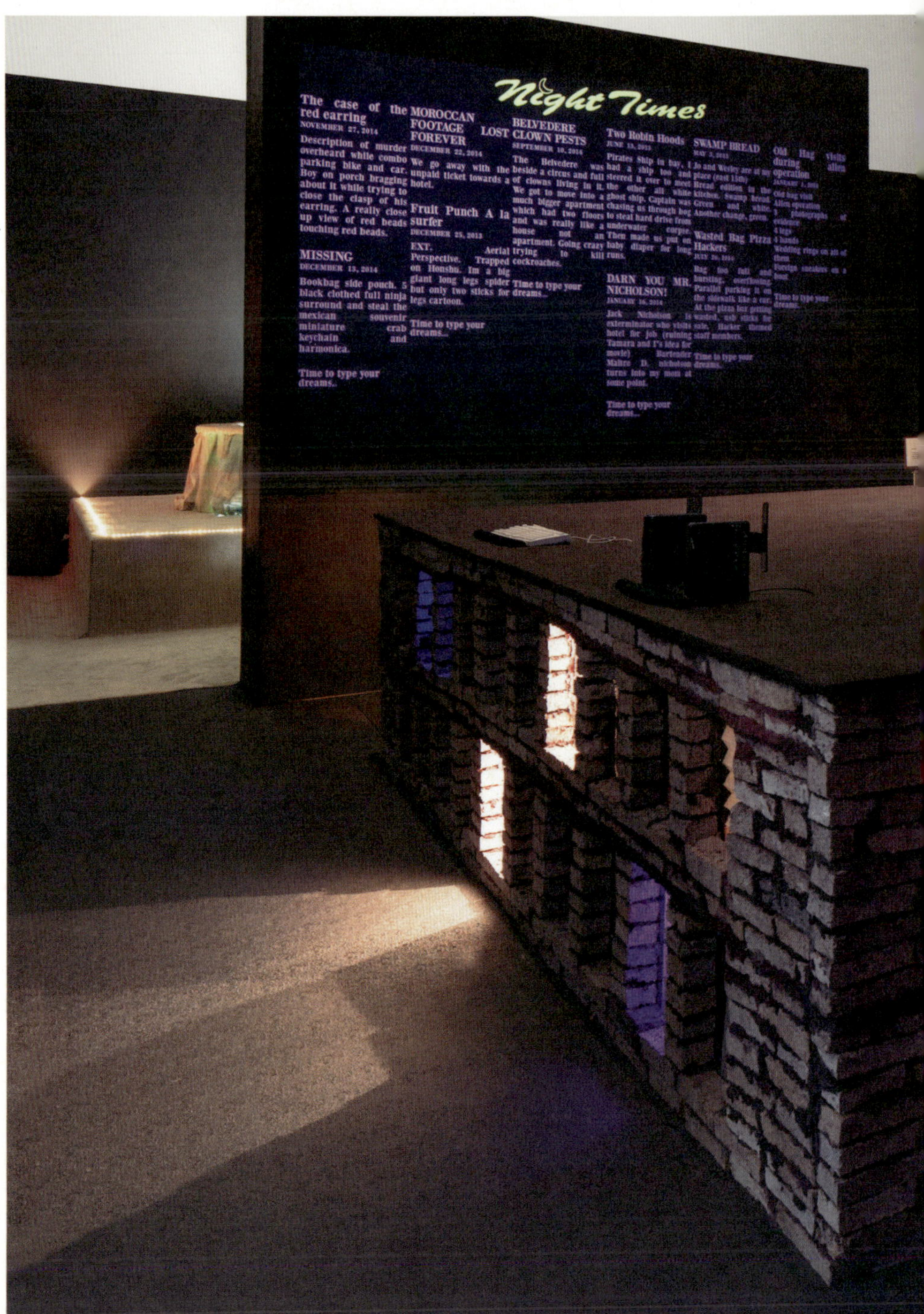

The Night Times Press Bar, 2015

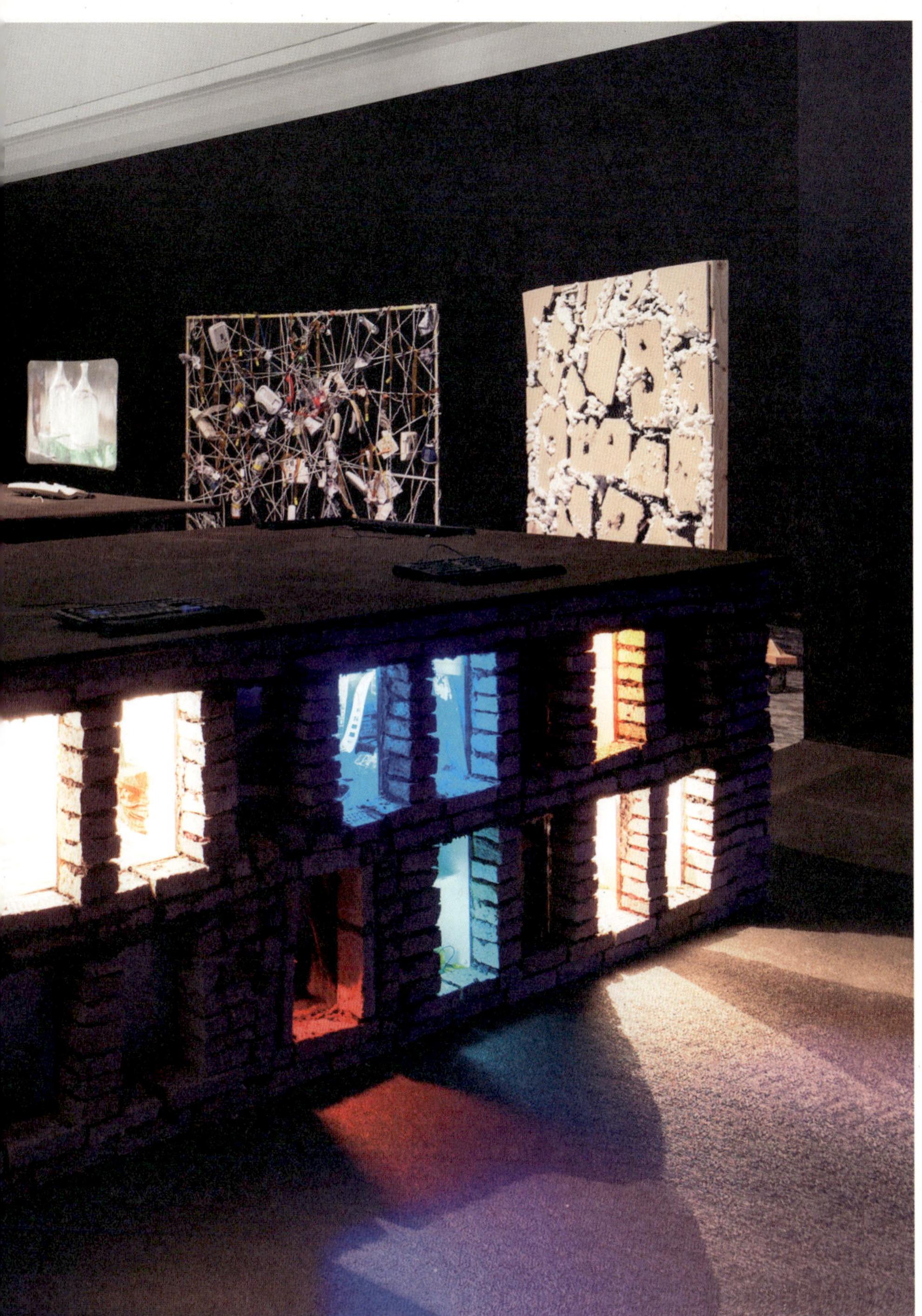

Installation view, ICA Philadelphia, 2015

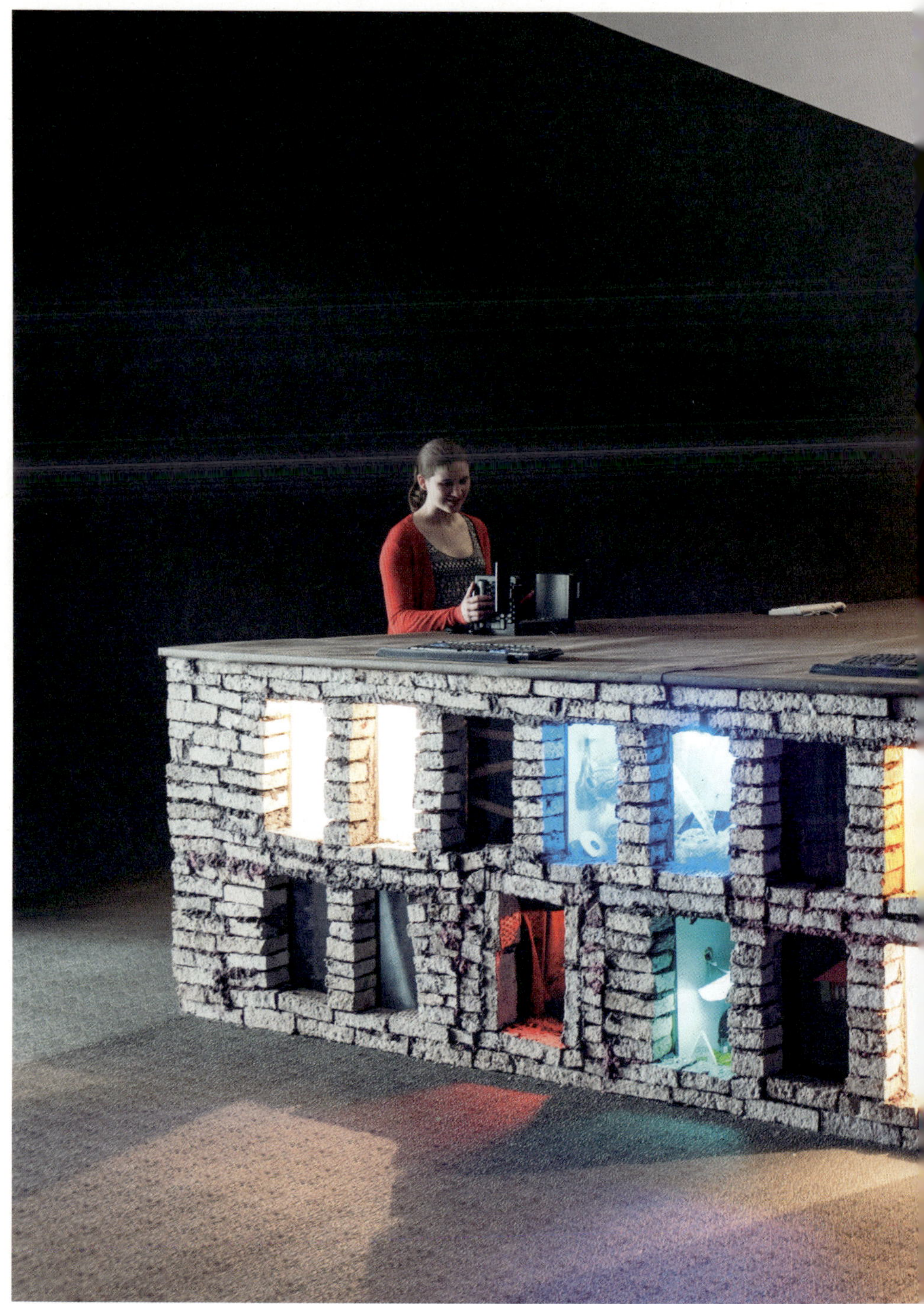

The Night Times Press Bar, 2015

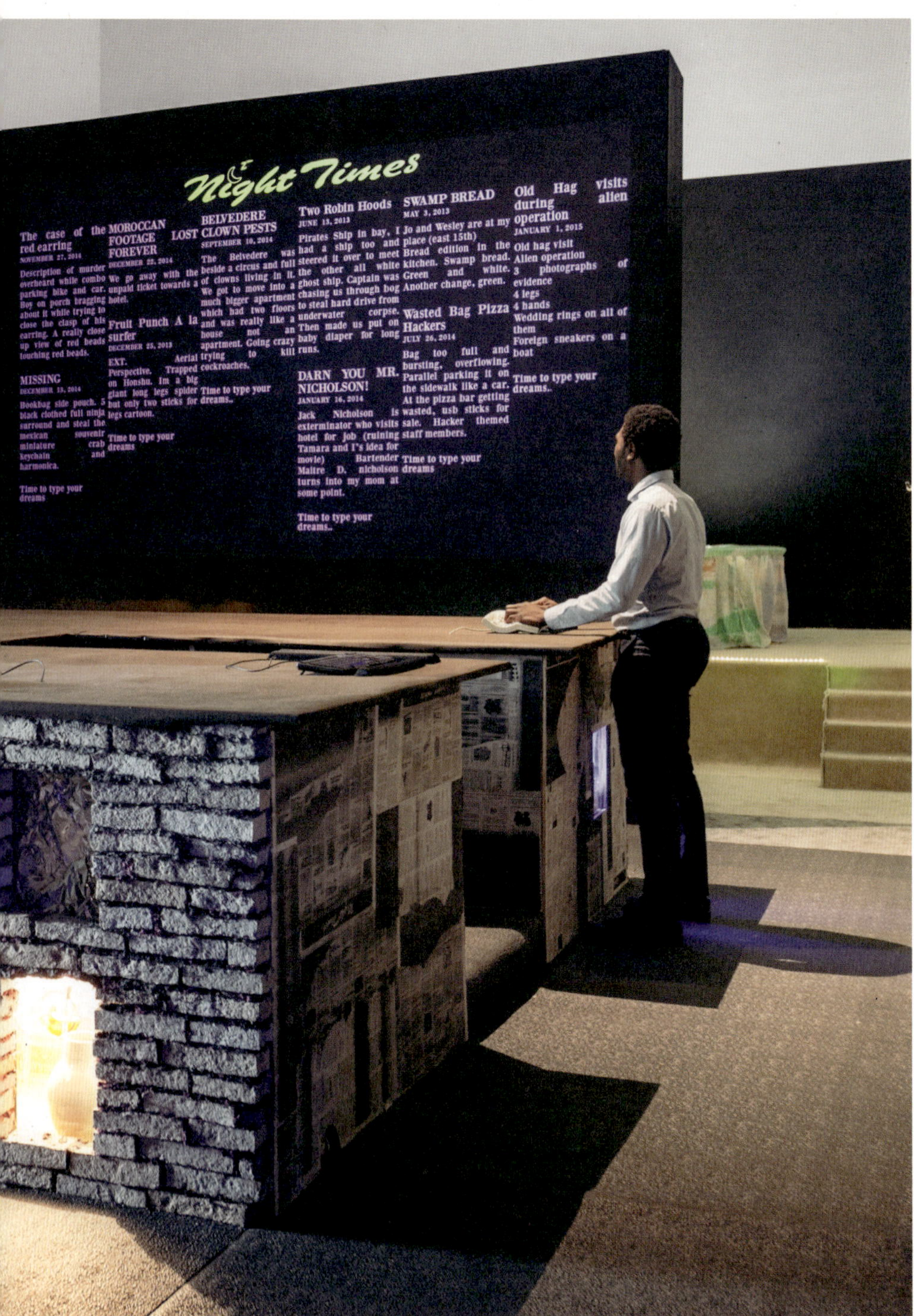

ICA

Installation view, ICA Philadelphia, 2015

69

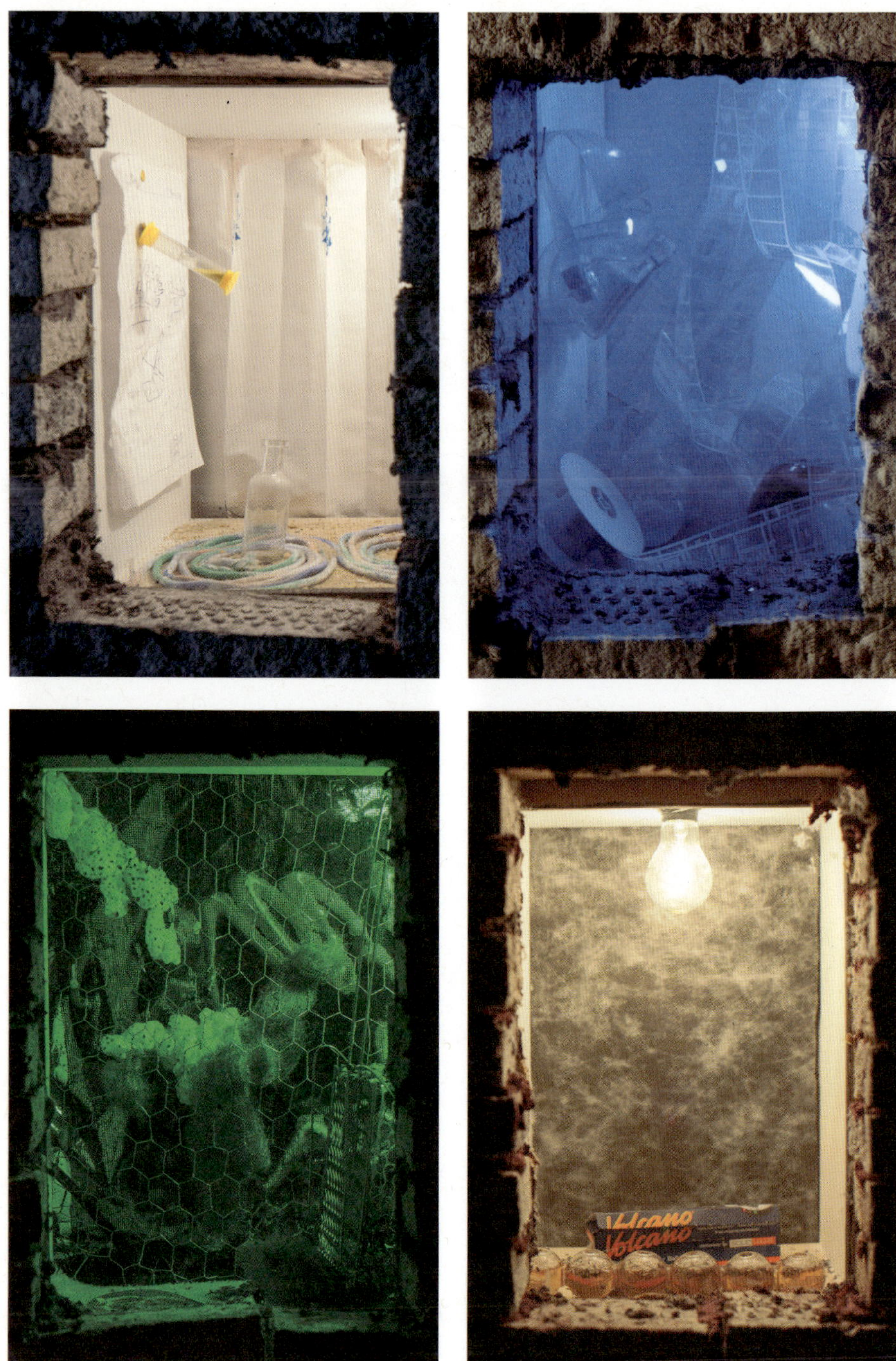

The Night Times Press Bar (details), 2015; installation view, ICA Philadelphia, 2015

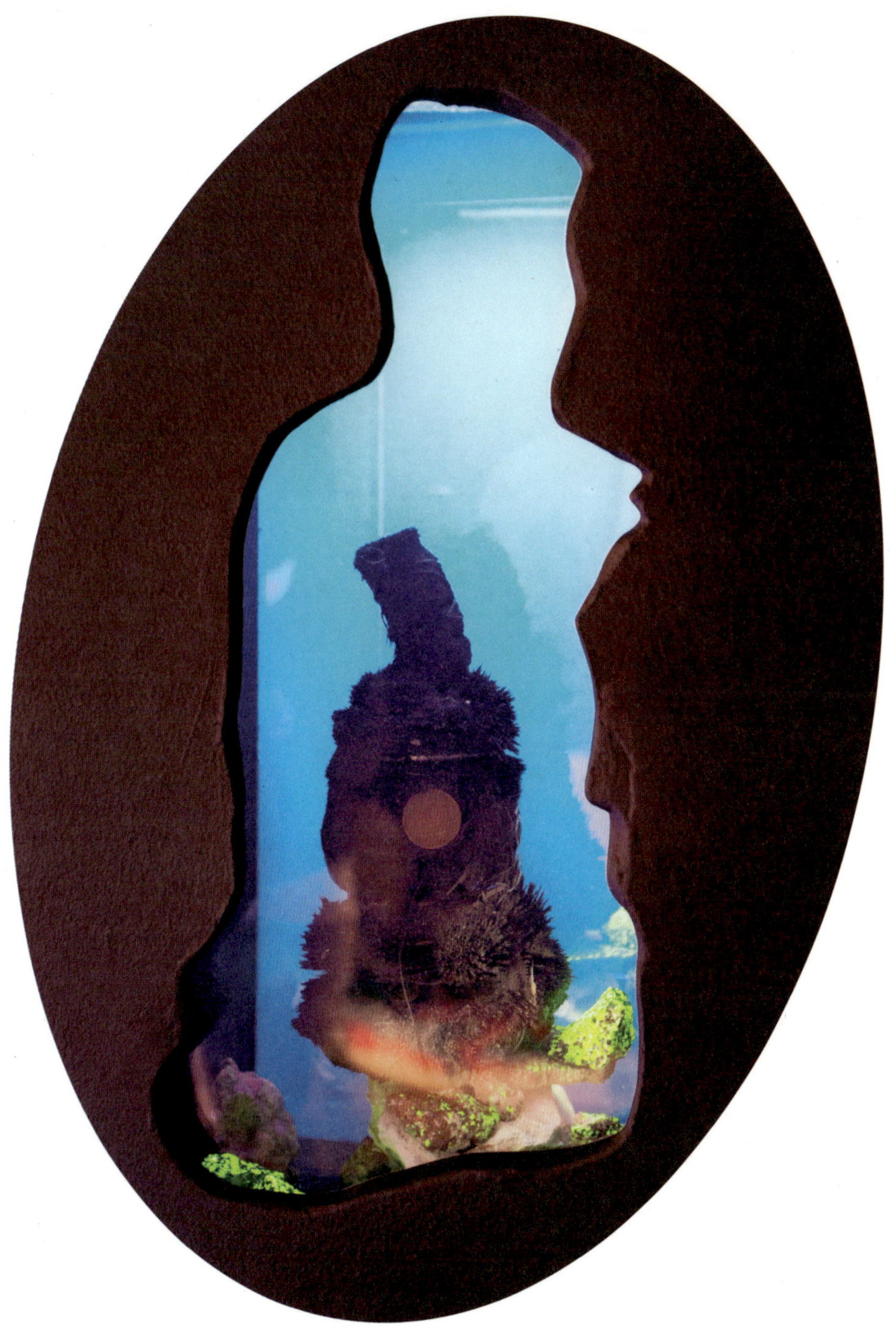

Chance Bottle, 2015; installation view, ICA Philadelphia, 2015

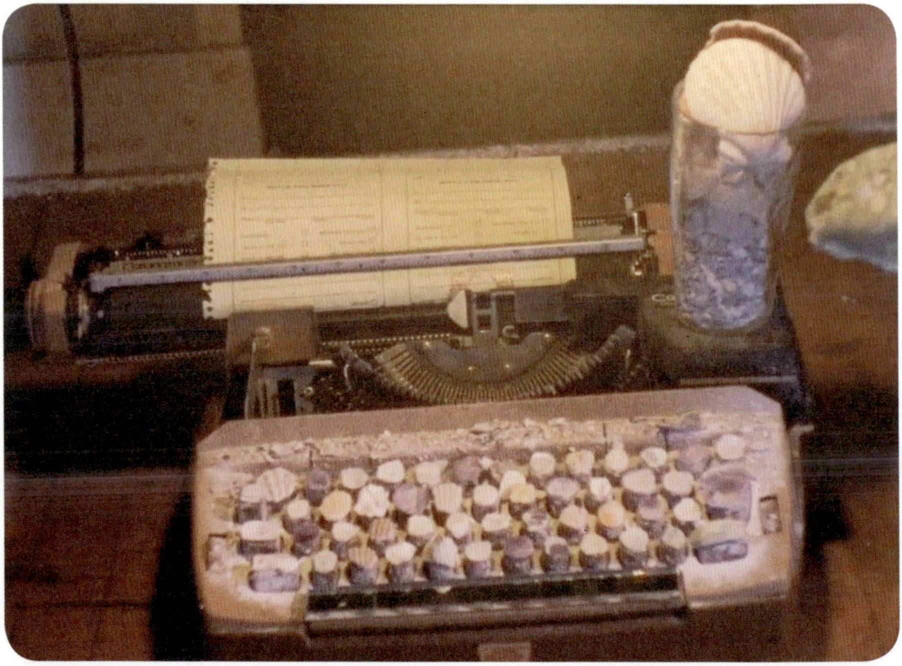

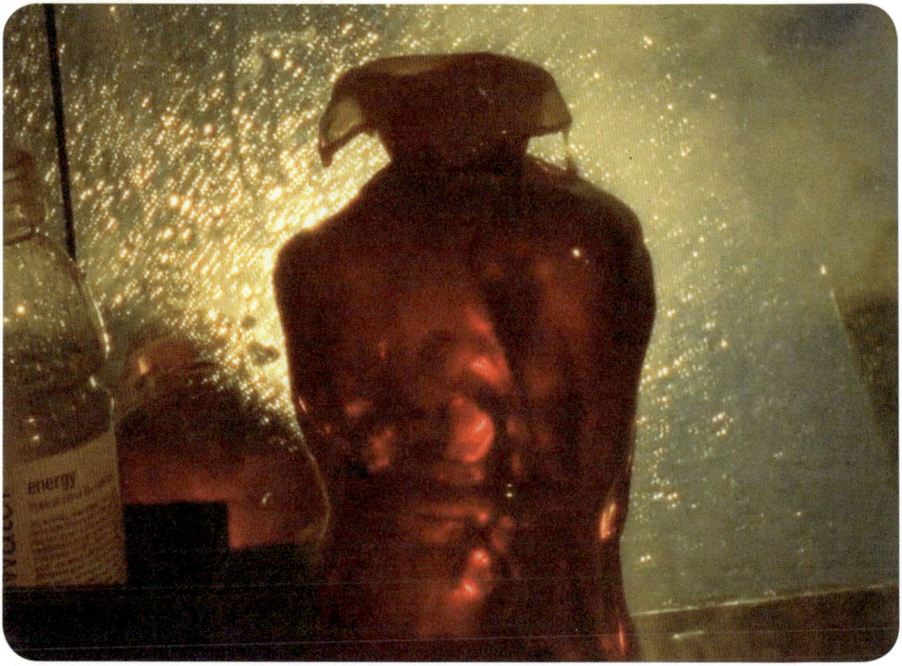

Consider the Belvedere (film stills), 2015

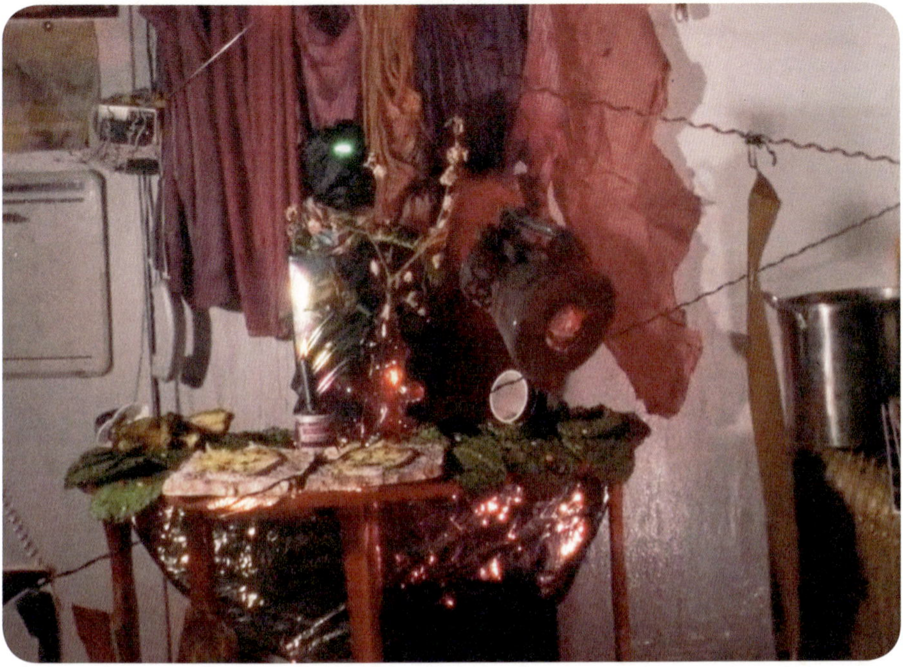

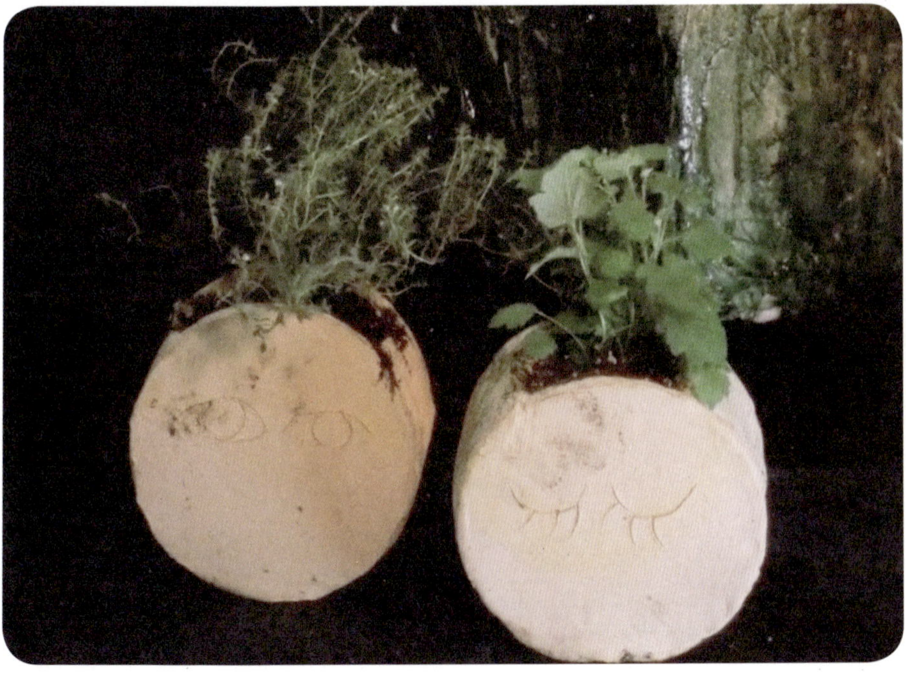

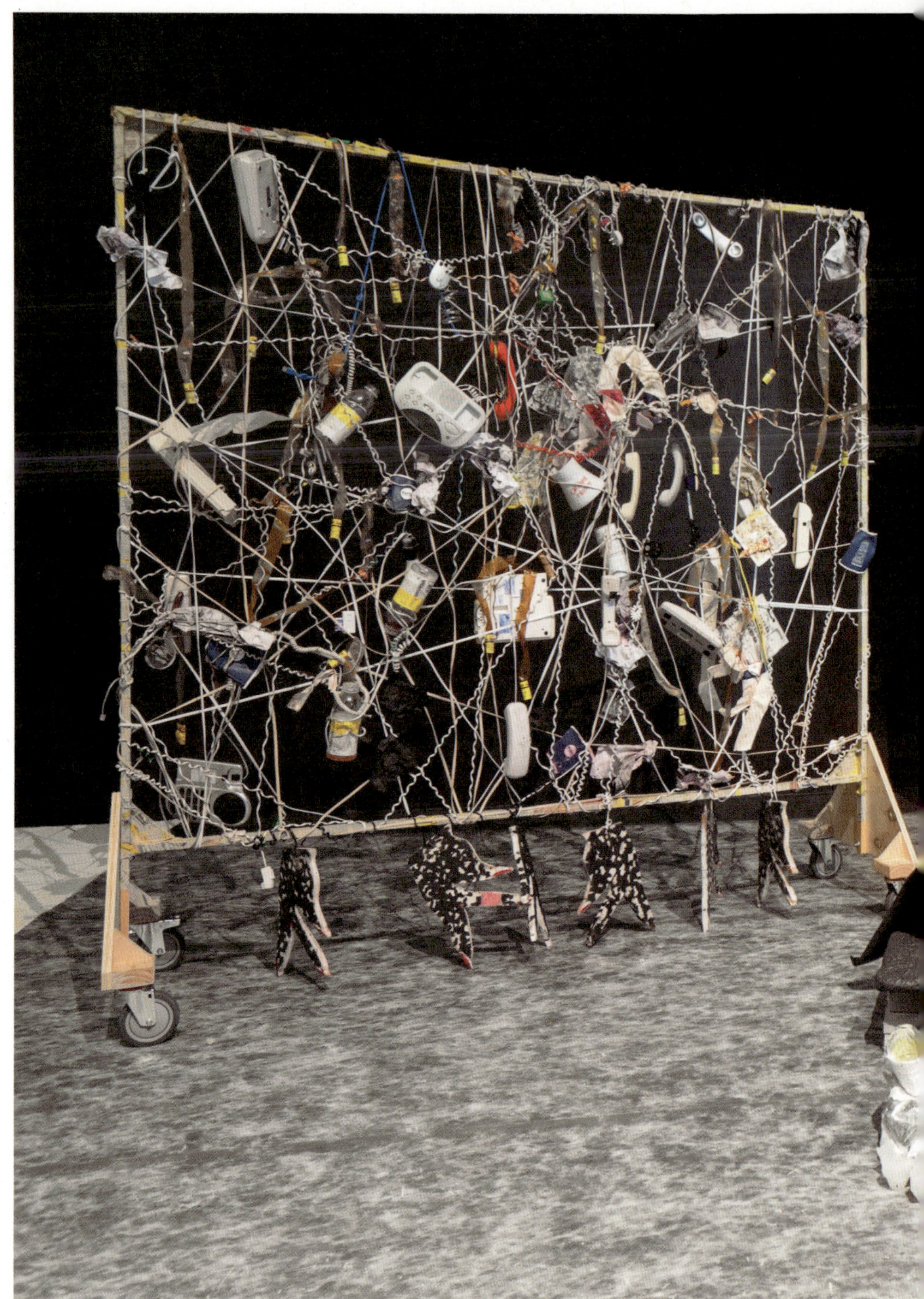

From left: *Secretary Cucoloris; Stenographer Ensemble; Exclusion Cucoloris*, 2015

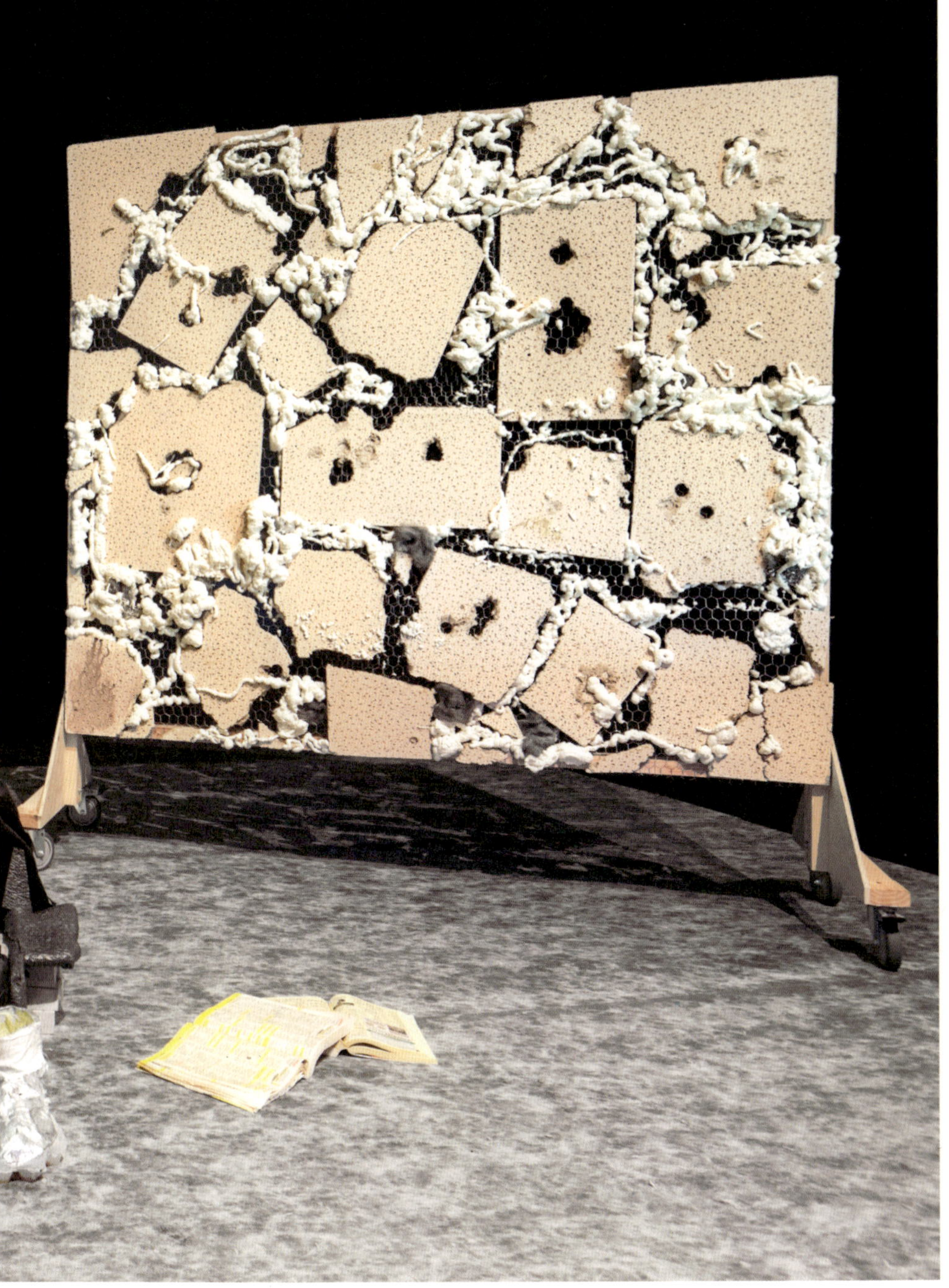

Installation view, ICA Philadelphia, 2015

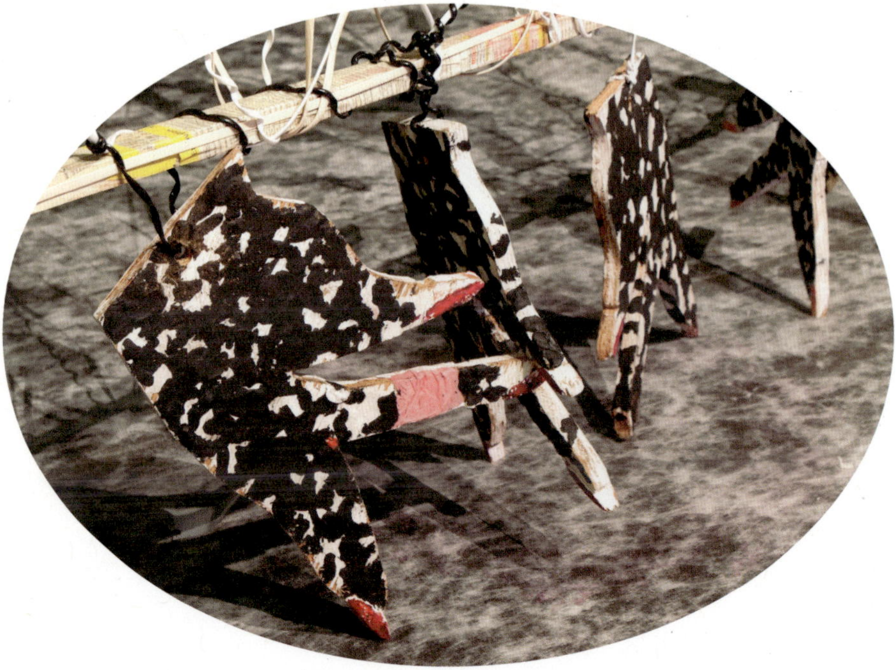

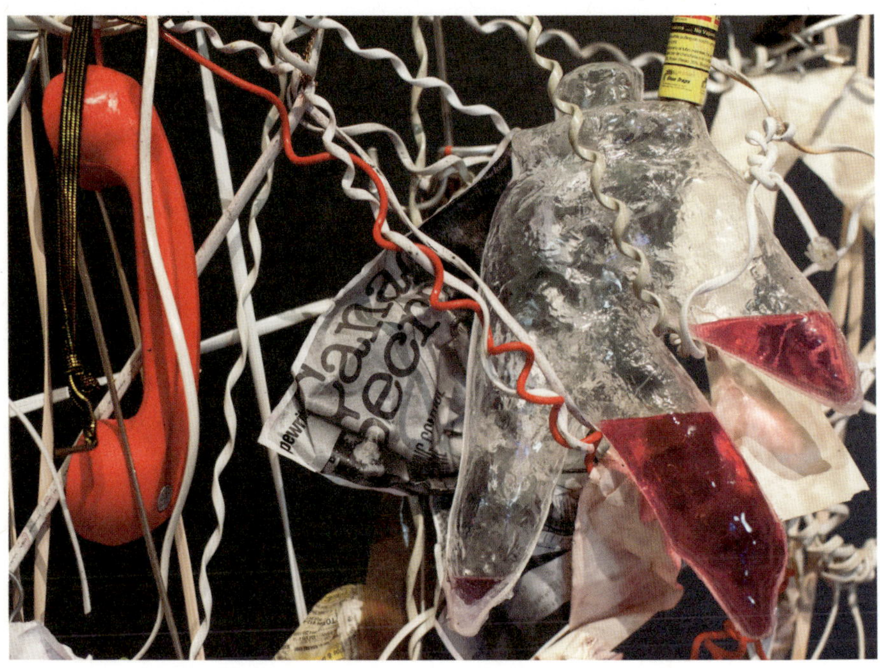

Secretary Cucoloris (details), 2015;
installation view, ICA Philadelphia, 2015

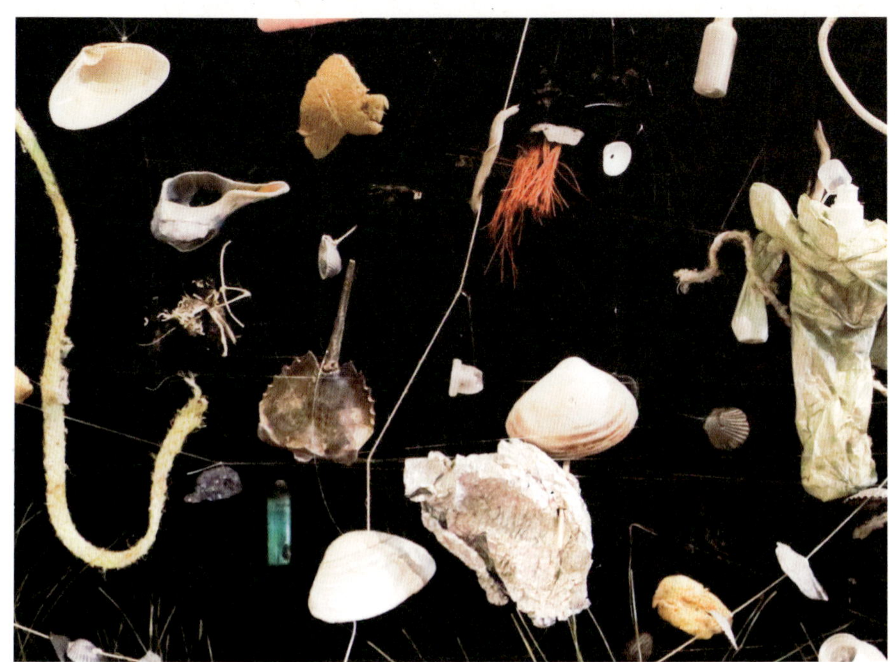

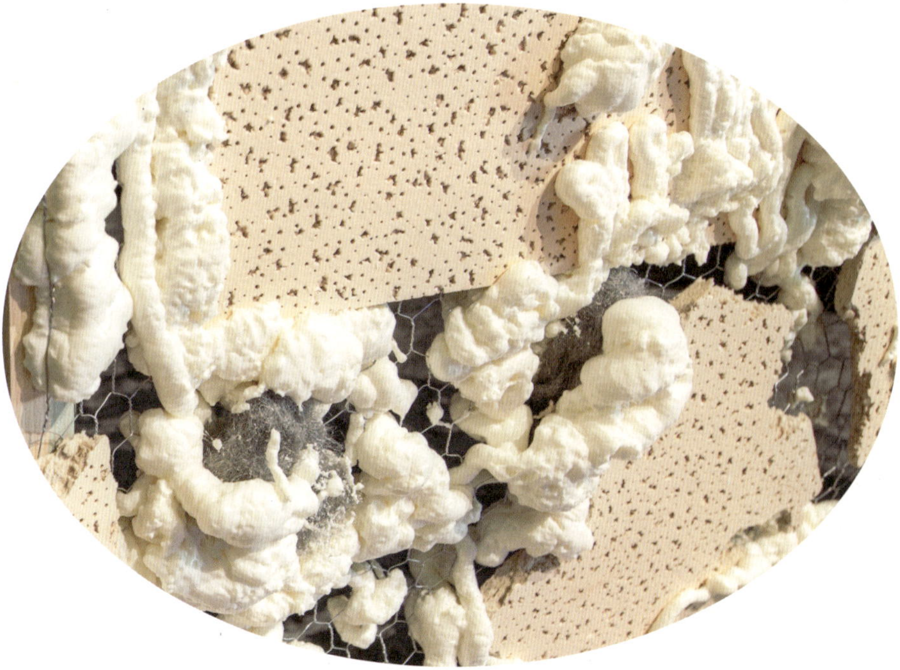

Beachcomber's Cucoloris (detail); *Exclusion Cucoloris* (detail), 2015;
installation view, ICA Philadelphia, 2015

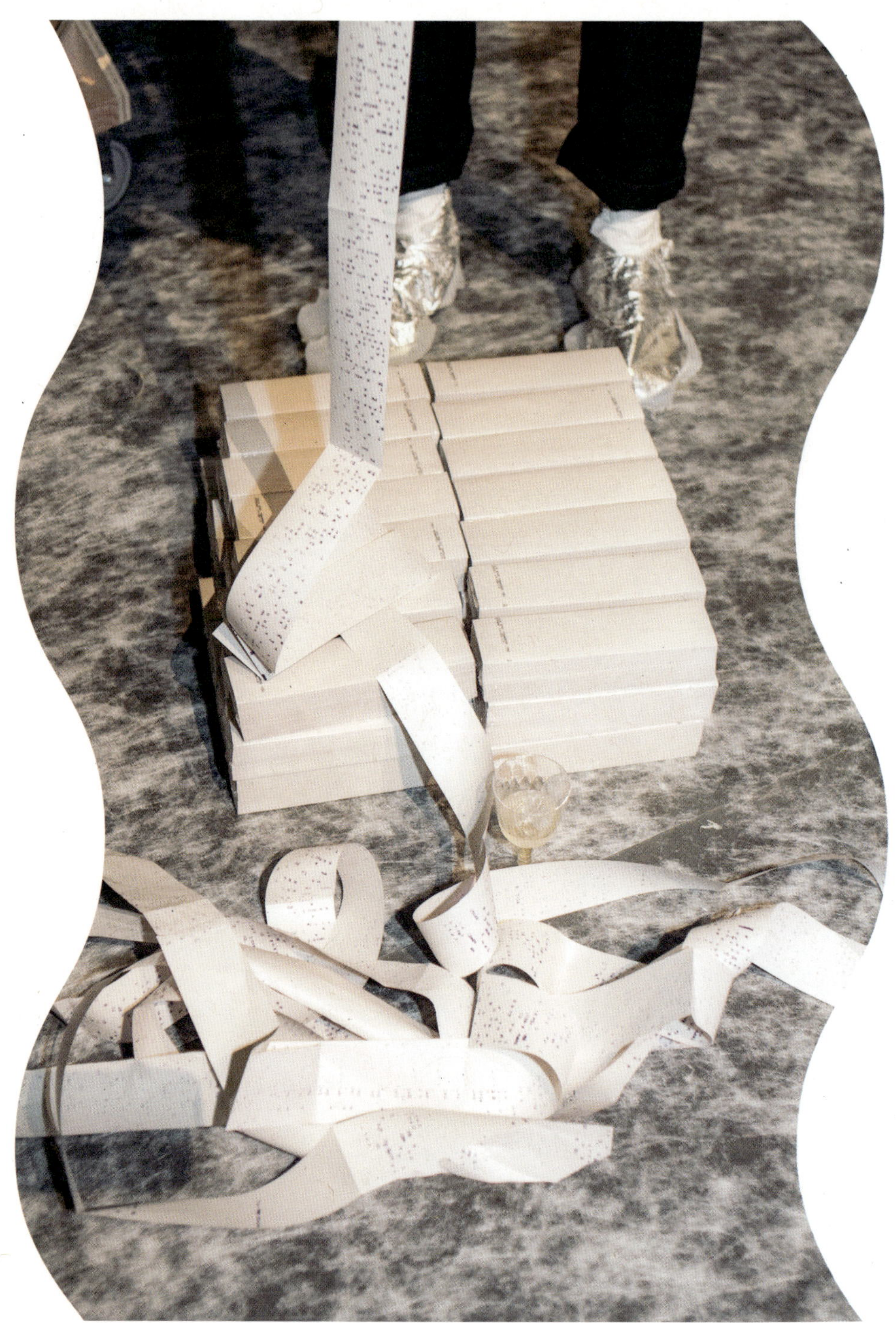

Installation view, ICA Philadelphia, 2015

Night

Movies

Over The Hedge
NOVEMBER 18, 2014

On a beautiful beach making a film. Hedges and an outdoor cabin. Panning through the hedges eventually ending up on the beach. I dipped my hands in the sand and looked up. A giant tidal wave was coming in but the beach became my house and I didn't know what to save. I started running from the wave but then realized my dream diary was back there. I ran back and tried to save it. I wanted to keep everything. The bedside table was there (a box) and I piled it full of books, not knowing where my dream diary was exactly.

Bank Offers Free Slime Lipstick To Long Line Up Clients
MAY 26, 2014

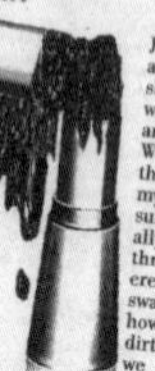

J and I are sleeping alone one night, we sleep on top of the water. It's hot outside and it's on a lake. When I wake up in the morning I press my foot against the surface and it's actually ice. My foot goes through and gets covered in dirt and swamp water. J hates how the lake is so dirty. We get up and we go inside to the house. I'm standing in on a balcony or rooftop and looking down on the river from the top there are many fish swimming and many people. "J," I say, "its not dirty at all, come look." She comes. "Who are they?" "They came to clean the lake."

INT. STUDIO. With D, he has been working all night. I take one of the instruments from the left. And it's an L shape. "Is this a new stand up bass?"

"Press the buttons and put these on," he says, handing me headphones. Each button, and there are many, make a melody of electronic songs. "Where are the strings? Or how can I do something on top?" I search the buttons they are small and oval. "Put your foot on the bottom," he says. "And then play it again, single notes happen." Another person has been working in the studio and he looks like DM. He has built a winding structure through the space with a lot of plastic buckets filled with different colors balancing on the top. "Color Vibrations- they are leaking," he exclaims.

I walk out and down the hallway there's a classroom setting, I see a teacher loading a 16mm film it looks feature length.

Sitting on a bench outside in the sun – Bank line up. The teller comes out and to a bench. "There's a hold," she says, "but take this." She passes me a lipstick. I open it and its slime, Slime separated between the two pieces of the cylinder.

Radical Laundry
NOVEMBER 10, 2013

Some kind of CBC documentary about theatres. Extremely candid, radical style, interviews university students about doing laundry. They ask interviewer if he "loves it here", a little aside he thinks. "I don't spend any time down here." then through the fence we spot a camera person dollying a huge film camera filming through a football match to some russian male dancers, traditional russian dance both in perfect formation.

Asymmetrical Priest Portraits
OCTOBER 26, 2014

INT. HALLWAY/BALCONY over a vast space. We watch down to it and A.W. walks in and up to meet us. We stand together and look down at the floor he had just walked across. "It would be useful if it was concrete but this?- this athletic center - all those lines, those court lines- who needs them?!" "True- could be a blank film studio." We are all there to make work for an old man- he is a priest figure and the easels are all set in a room that is just off the hallway we stand at our respective easels. Things are set up in the center and around the figure of the old man. He sits and we paint his portrait for him. Everyone turns their easel to him, and he adjudicates, "Asymmetry and mirrored. That's what I asked for...and every time...what I get: two pictures on the same plain appearing to be the same."

"What is asymmetry?" I whisper to myself, I have no idea. I had only copied what A.W. did in front of me. The image is a maze like object - the priest with thick black ink, then mirrored, then flipped.

Barbara Streisand Cameo
SUNDAY JULY 20, 2014

On the street accompanied by an old man in a tweed suit. We walk to a building with a large warehouse style entrance. I touch the doorknob, it's locked. The man quickly unlocks it. He doesn't touch the door. I go in and at the entrance there are black and white photographs laid out on the floor. "Well I didn't have to go so far," I say, knowing they are for me. I pick them up. They are studies of hippopotamuses, some real and then some are cast in concrete. They are drawn on with notes on their measure and scale.

We go outside and close the door. "He will know I've been here," I say to the man. "How?" "The fingerprints." "They could be fingerprints for some other reason." He is suddenly the love of my life. We walk together, trying to go back to the apartment tower but then take a left into a boardwalk labyrinth shop area filled with tourists. I am alone suddenly with the sensation that the man was imagined. I sit down at a computer that is at the bottom of a series of staircases. There is an email to me in a cryptographic font open on the screen, I recognize my name and that it is inviting me to a film screening with Barbara Streisand. The film opens up on the computer by itself. It is a CGI/Google Sketchup atmosphere. There is a maroon carpeted staircase from there the perspective shifts to seafoam green art on the walls: giant moss like forms hung flat like paintings.

The entire space moves and shifts bringing me down a hallway and up to a concrete shelf, the shelf I built for sobeys and it looks like it will fall down. The pineapple glasses are on it and it is beside a big painting.

Pew Views
JULY 7, 2014

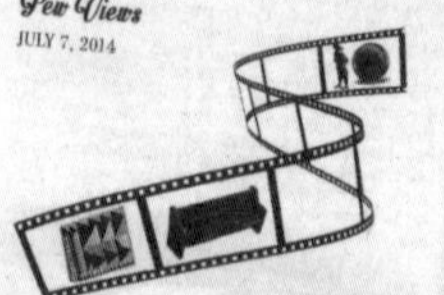

Got the film back. The end was cut at an orb, on the right and a female figure on the left. "Wheres the beginning?" INT. B.W'S SHOW at Peres. There are concrete pews and a lot of weavings.

Lights Camera Action: Feyrer & Henderson's New Film
MAY 11, 2013

INT. Making a new film with Julia. There is a wall with 3 windows, in front a partition that is kind of flimsy. The windows look out to a lush garden and courtyard. The film is about the senses. The 3 windows see their own scenes outside. There are wooden constructions on the other (inside). Julia leaves and goes to the outside and we talk through the window. My jacket is hung over a chair and I search the pockets. They are stuffed with cotton batting and cigarettes. Some of the cigarettes are weak at the point where the filter joins the body of the cigarette. I smoke a cigarette standing by one of the windows for effect. G comes into the room and asks what's next and I ask him if we could get a sweetgrass braid that goes through the entire house and through the chimney system so the smell would leak out of the fireplaces. He thinks if it's okay to attach all of the braids together.

Bridget is -in the kitchen at the stove, she's talking about time aloud, "Could you come at 8:00am?" I'm kneeling down beside the stove on my knees. "What kind of flour is this? Chicken flour? Not chickpea? It's behaving strangely." We are trying to make pancakes, but they are just making one burned layer after another and the rest are mush. There is a baby- its legs are damaged so it needs help standing. "I could help, no problem, 8am, is a bit early for me." I get up and leave the house. It's beside Jones's funeral home driveway. I'm wearing a very large wide garment with shoulder pads and struc-

RAT HOLE LEADS TO SECRET PENTHOUSE CHEF MOM
OCTOBER 17, 2013

Which rat under the floor broke in popped the plug as I was frantically pouring more rat poison down, stuffing steel wool and building a cardboard contraption. Lost in Kerrisdale driving some giant cadillac convertible, discovered the pineapple. 70's themed mansions unbelievable and sphinx shaped. Definite middle eastern vibe. Another scene, apartment on 10th all wood panelling, excellent original condition. Snuck in the front door and down the boiler room. Old hunchback landlord was down there looking for something. Secret room with crazy vintage rat traps.

Back to the white rat, the hole gets bigger and bigger. I climb in and realize I've discovered a secret penthouse apartment, it's beautiful and giant plastic in a crystal clear material unload it from the tow truck and the kittens crawl it with feather dusters. The kittens crawl cutely towards the big boiler as though it is their mom, leaving big fat cat on the headboard while they take their places in its coal holes.

CORKING THE INFESTATION OF RED FET
MARCH 9, 2013

A series of rooms connected to a hill. I work there. I pull a boombox into the center and turn on Bruce Springsteen. All along the baseboards wasps and various other insects have borrowed into the wood. There are a couple of corks plugging up most of the them and one is open revealing a very vicious red fly that has the reputation of a terrible sting. I wait for it. There is a small fly swatter hanging as well as a newspaper to swat at the bugs when they try to leave the hole. I give up after a while and go to the other room. We are inside and we see Main Street (Mel's). Although we didn't want to be bothered there is someone scraping and drilling at the wood; someone is carving new handles to get in with. I ask from one side to the other. I'm building a new chair its so big I

INSECT GODDESS SUMMONS RARE SPECIES
MAY 7, 2013

We had to bring a supply to our backyard garden house. I climbed over the hedges instead of walking around. It's too early for that. "They are too dry." The women with me said. The whole hedge flipped forward and inside there were gigantic bugs. I picked up the hedge and tried to make it back in place again. They came to the door pretty fast and noticed me. They let us in anyway. Massive interior. She was waiting for me in a large open room with slanted glass ceilings and tiled floors. Her figure was ob-

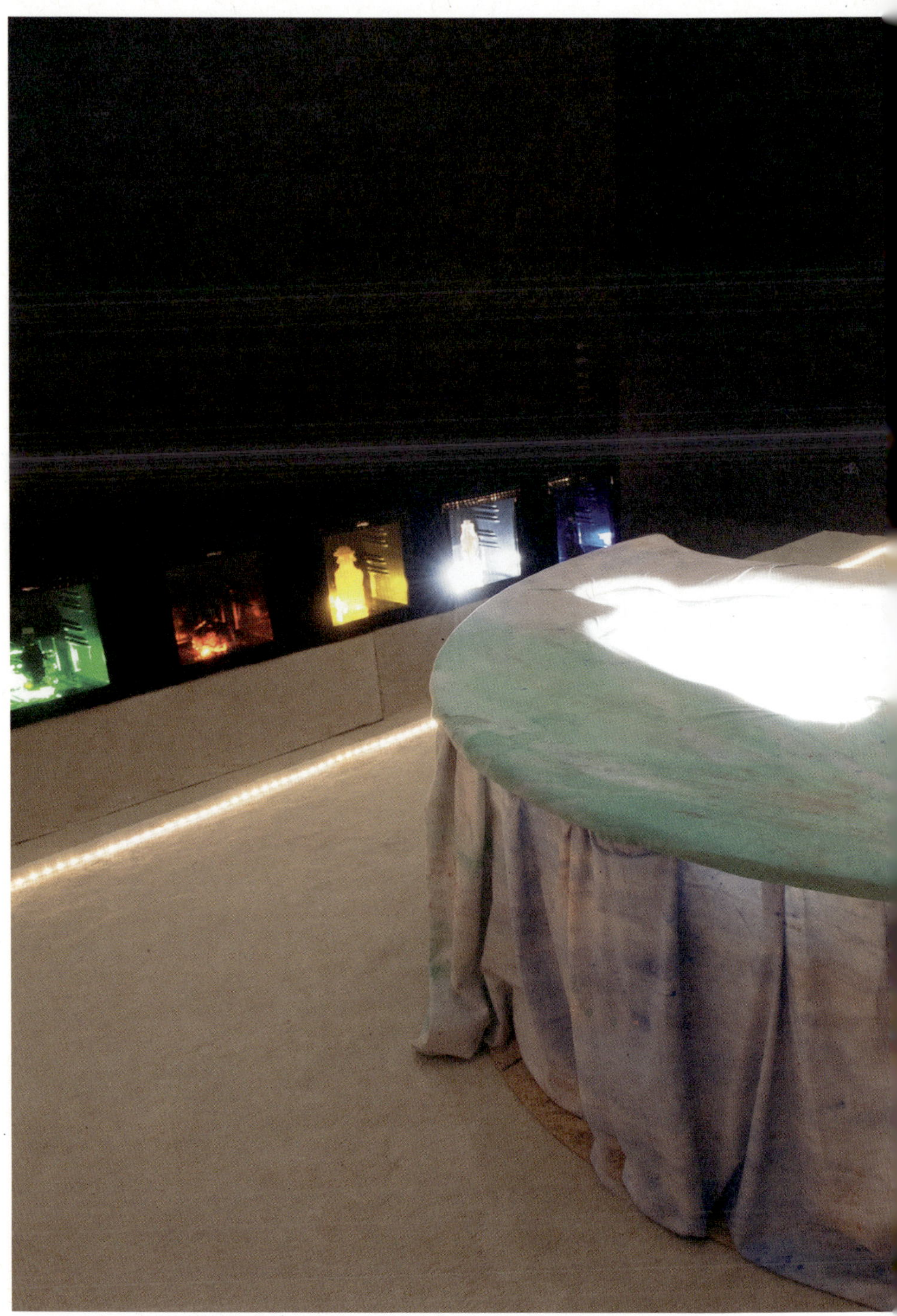

Installation view, ICA Philadelphia, 2015

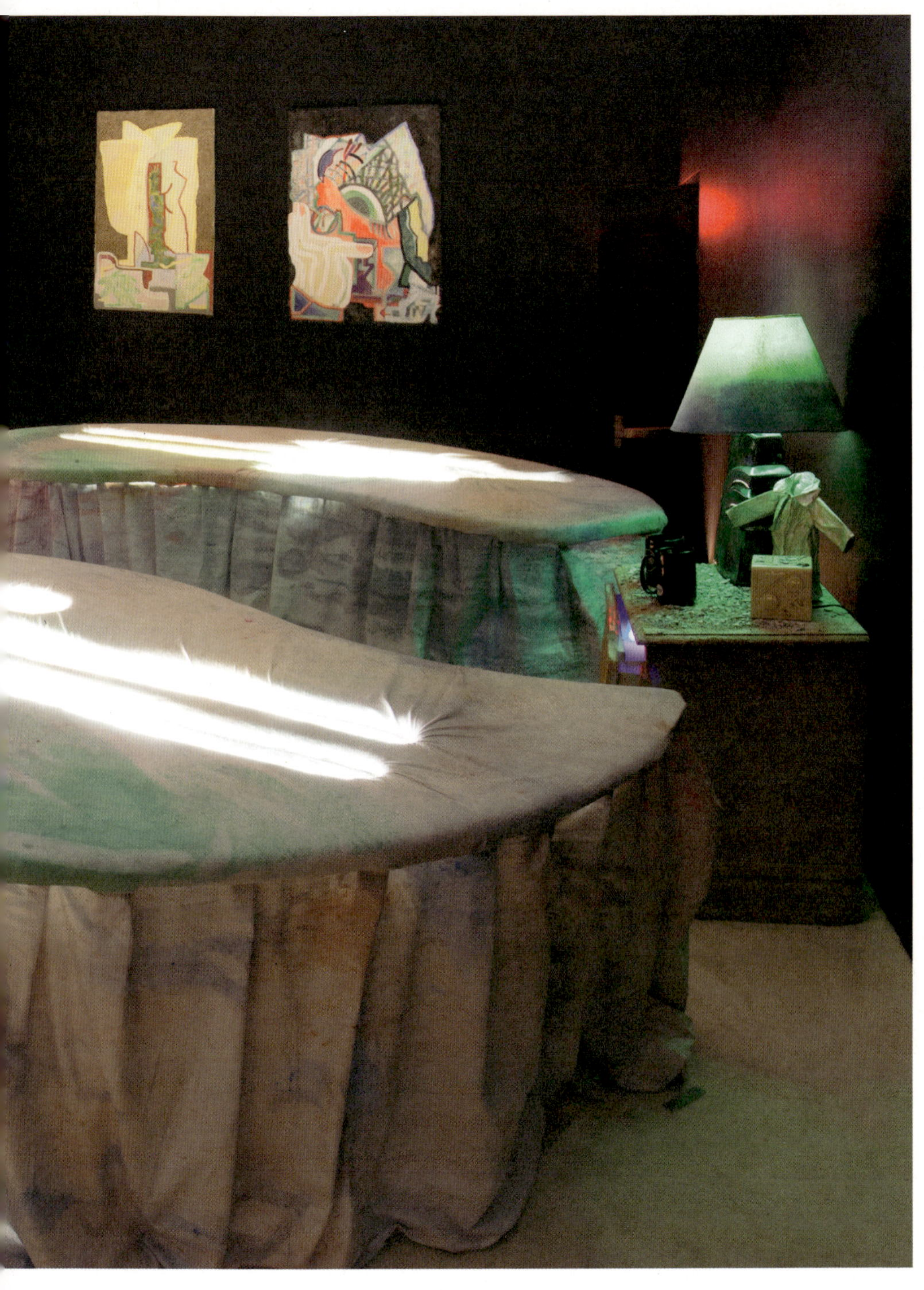

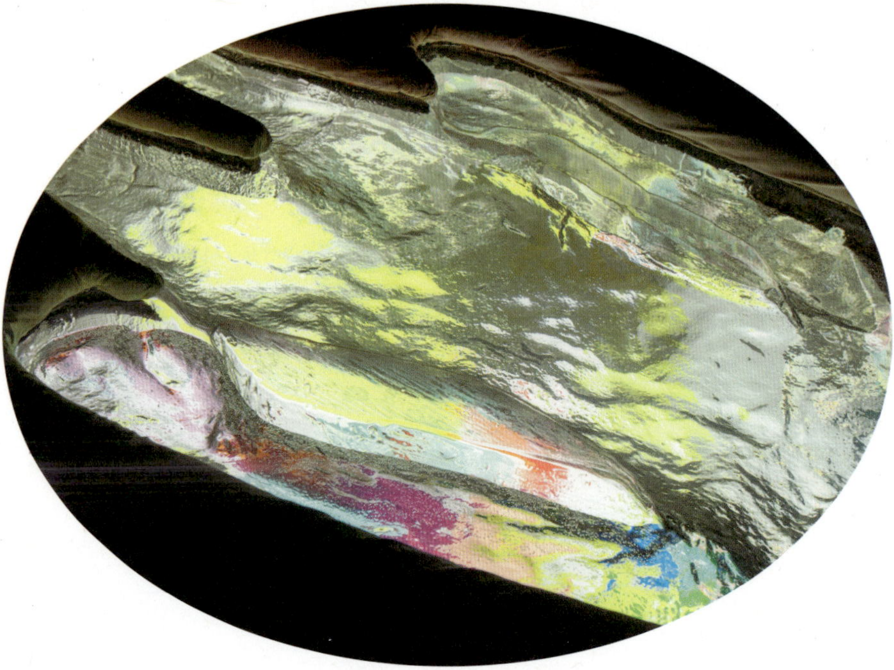

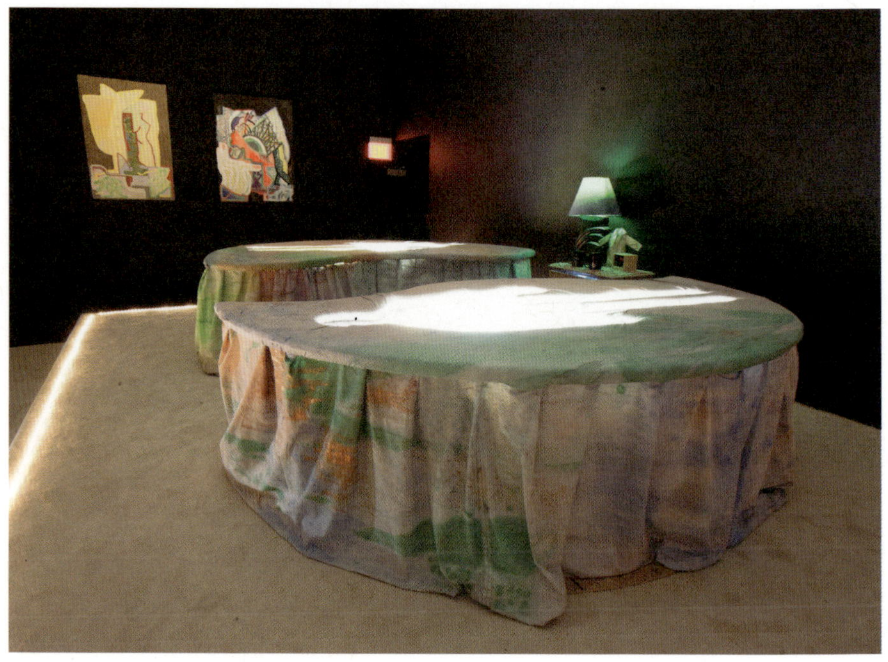

The Aura Readers (details), 2015

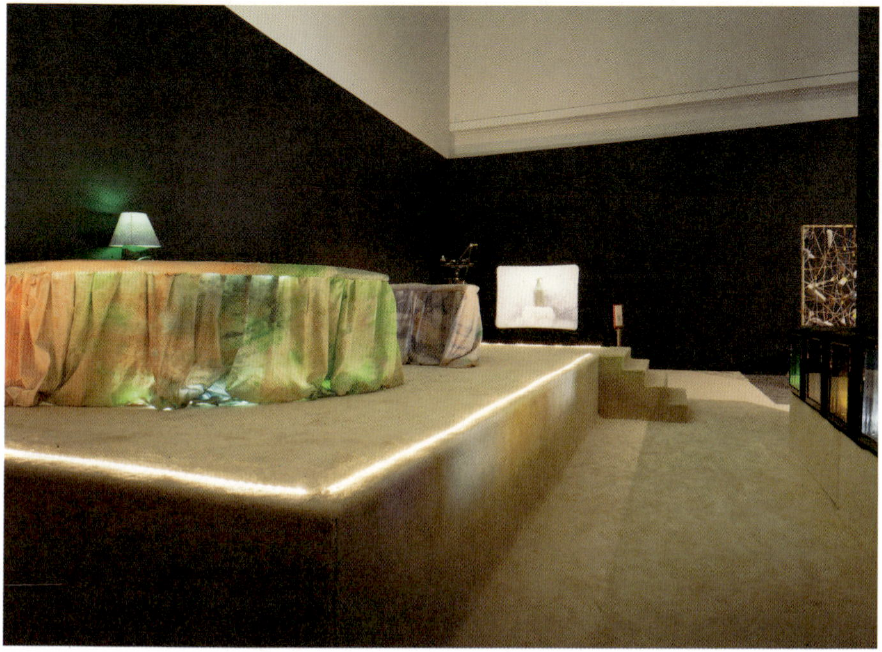

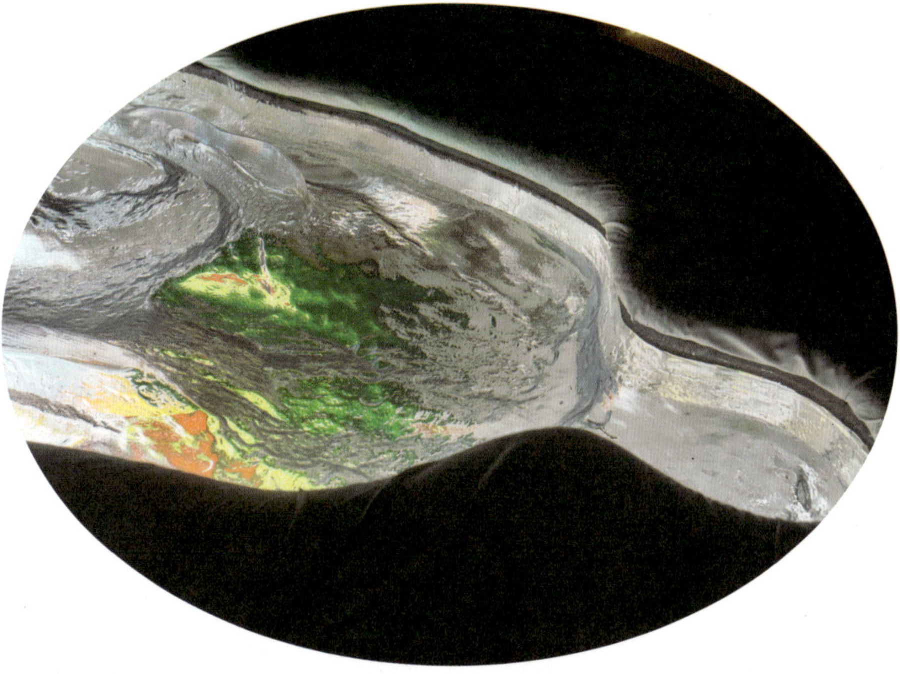

Installation views, ICA Philadelphia, 2015

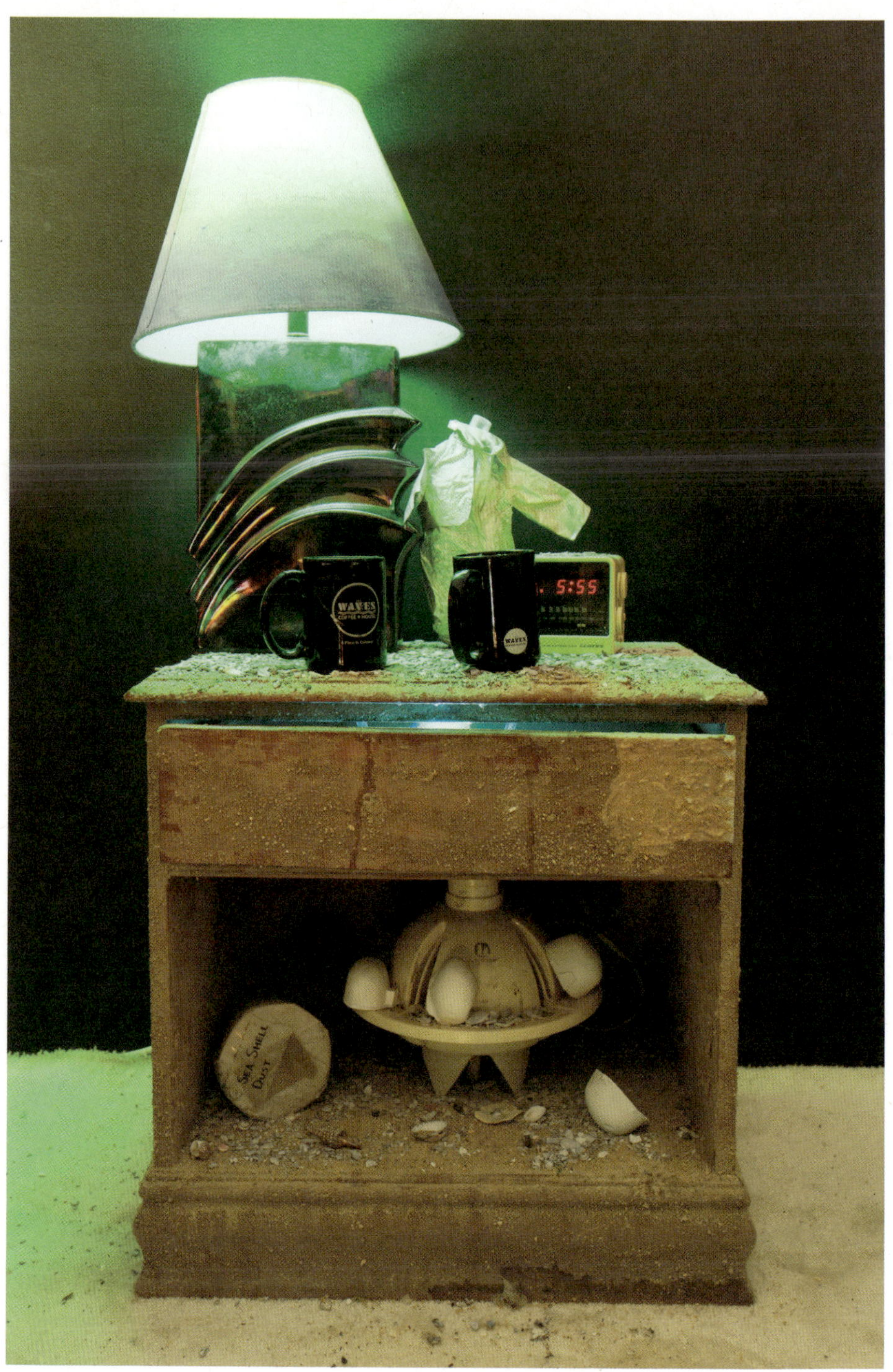

A Place to Connect, 2015; installation view, ICA Philadelphia, 2015

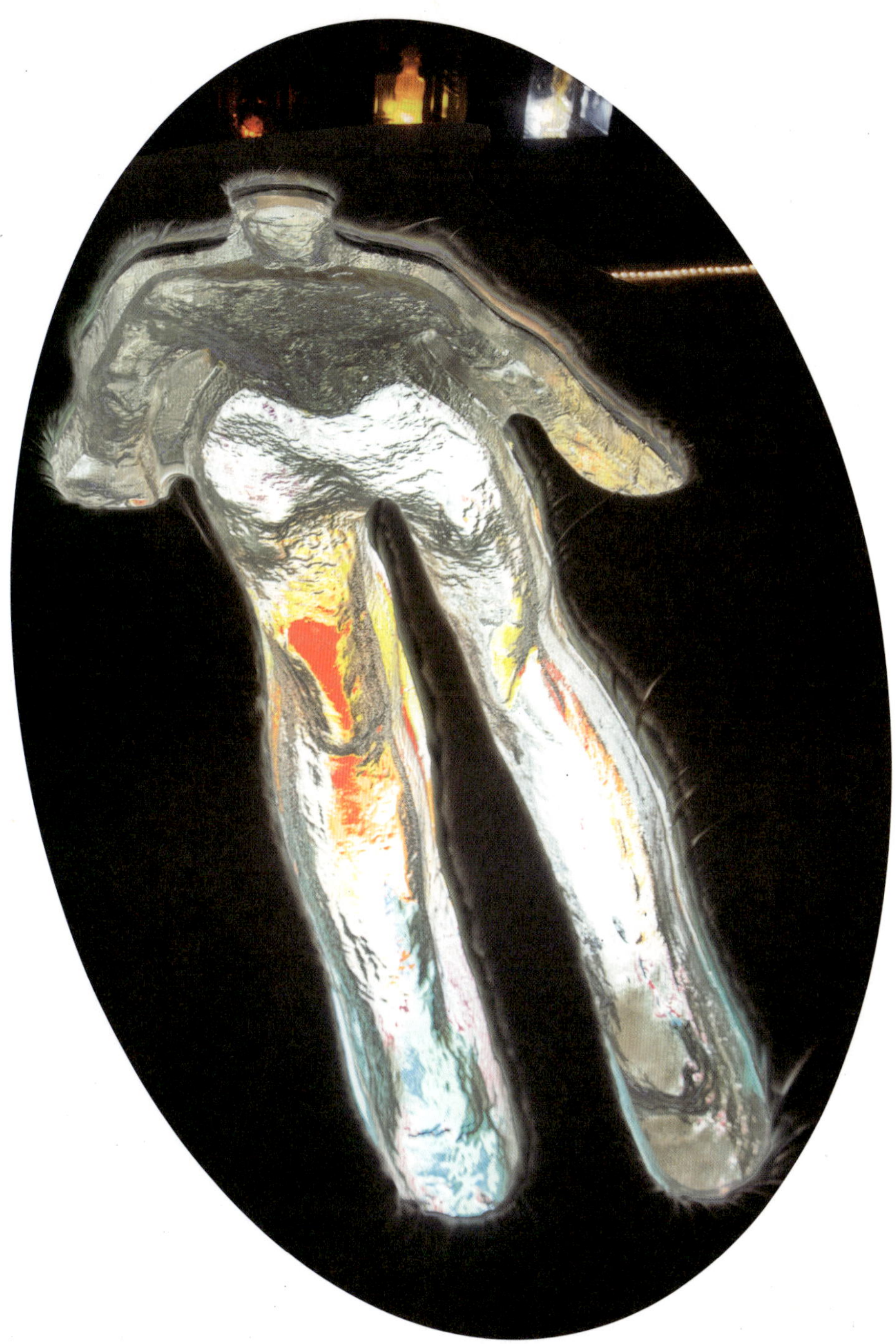

The Aura Readers (detail), 2015; installation view, ICA Philadelphia, 2015

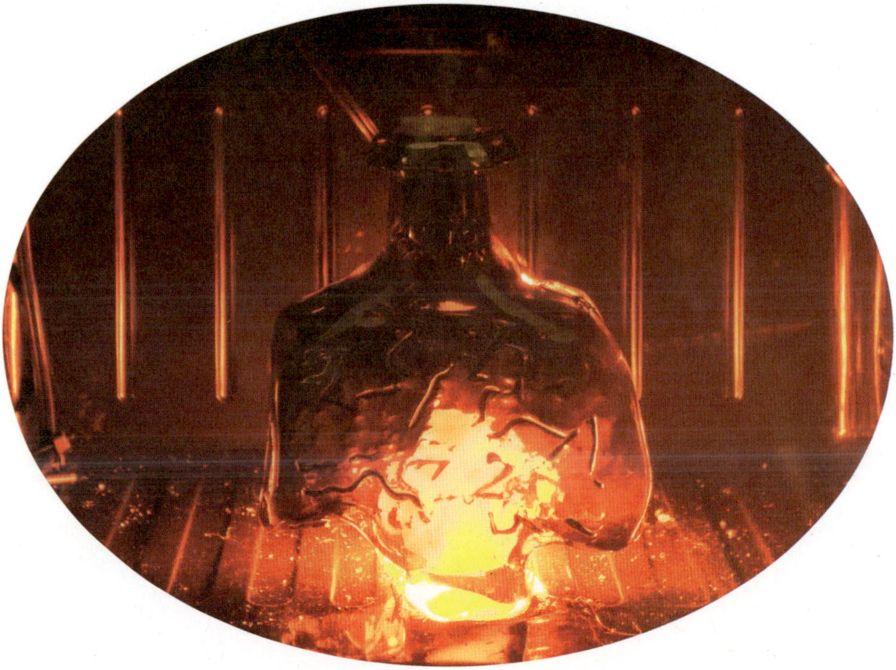

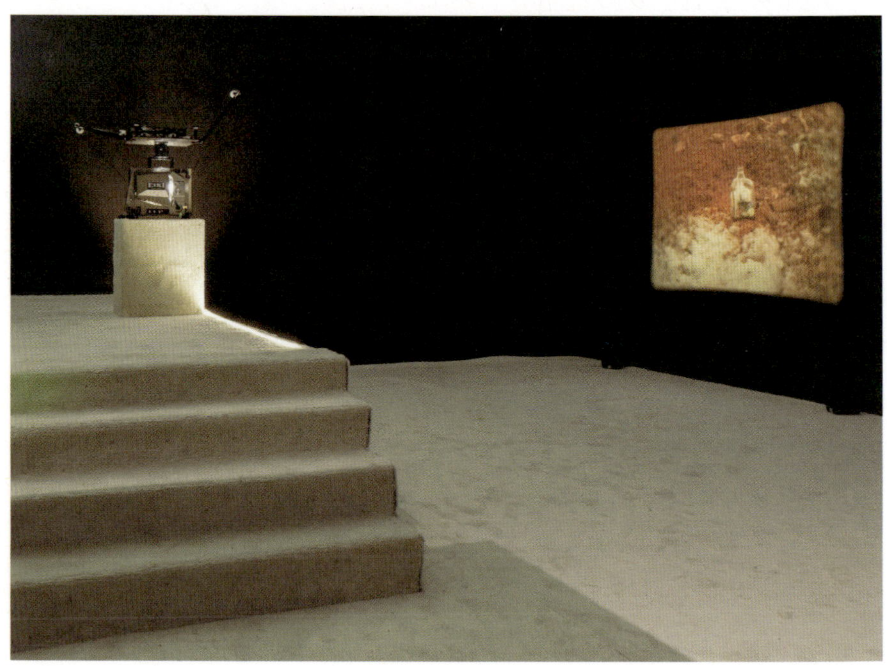

Installation views, ICA Philadelphia, 2015

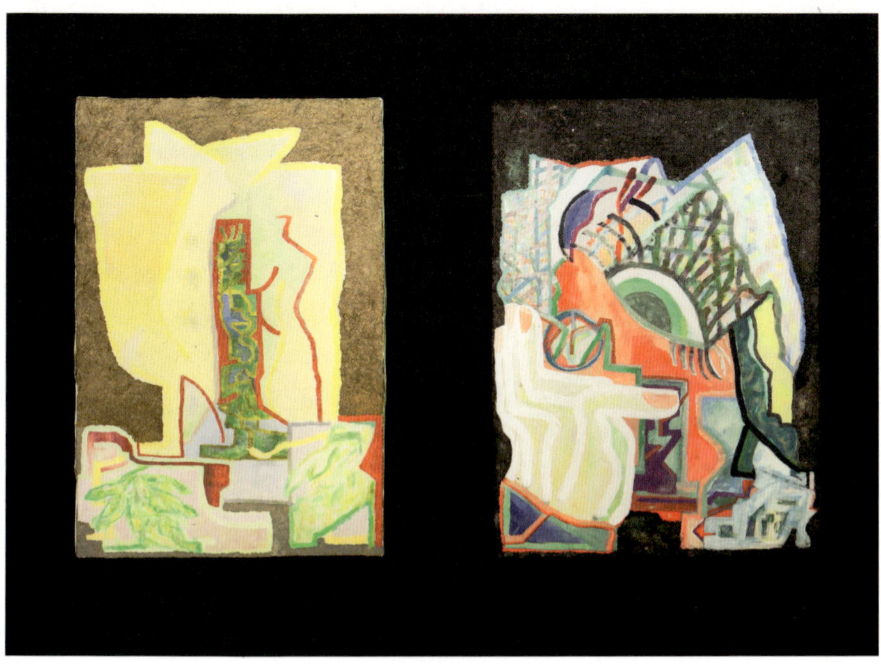

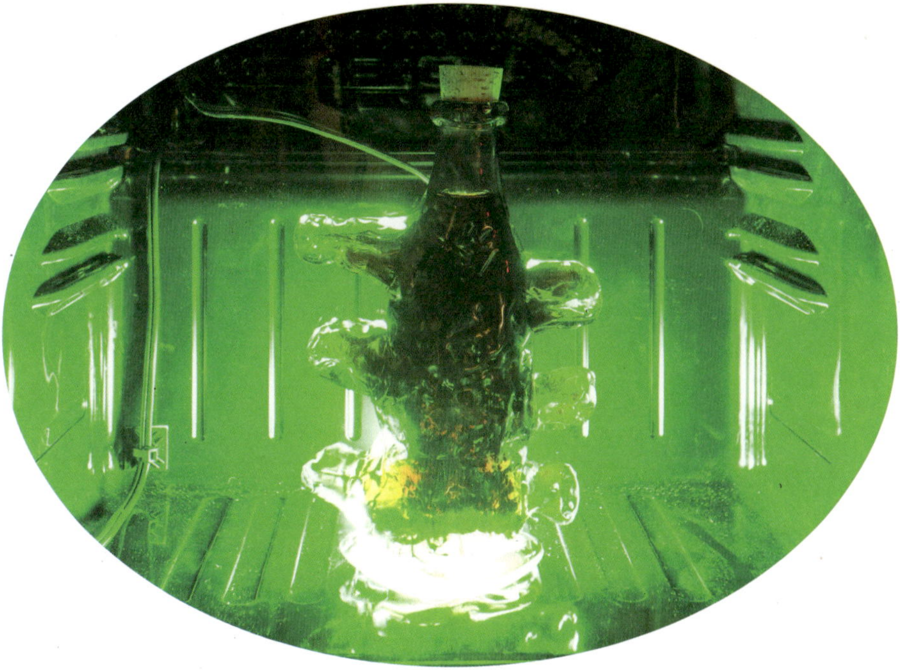

Installation views, ICA Philadelphia, 2015

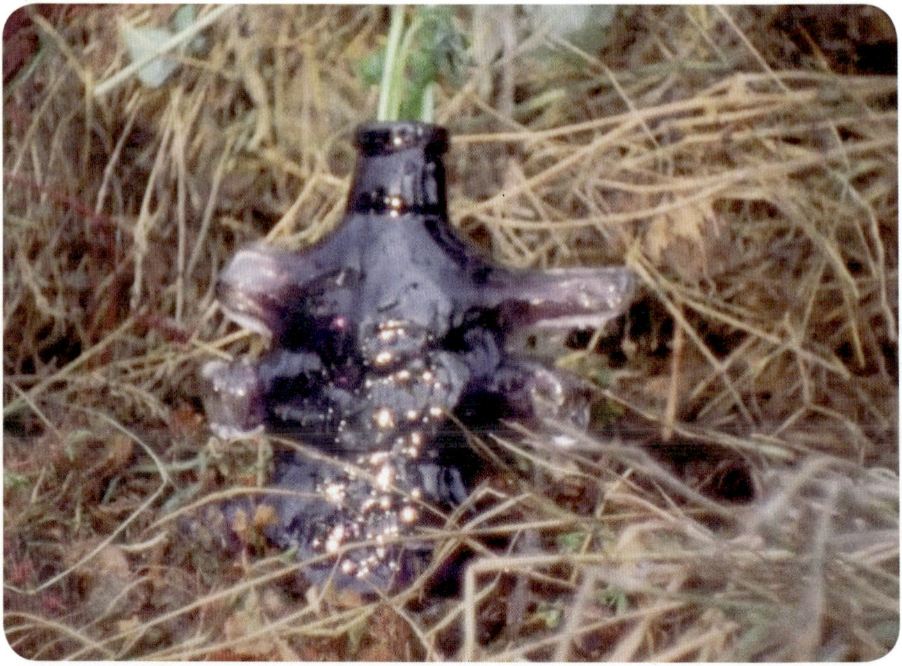

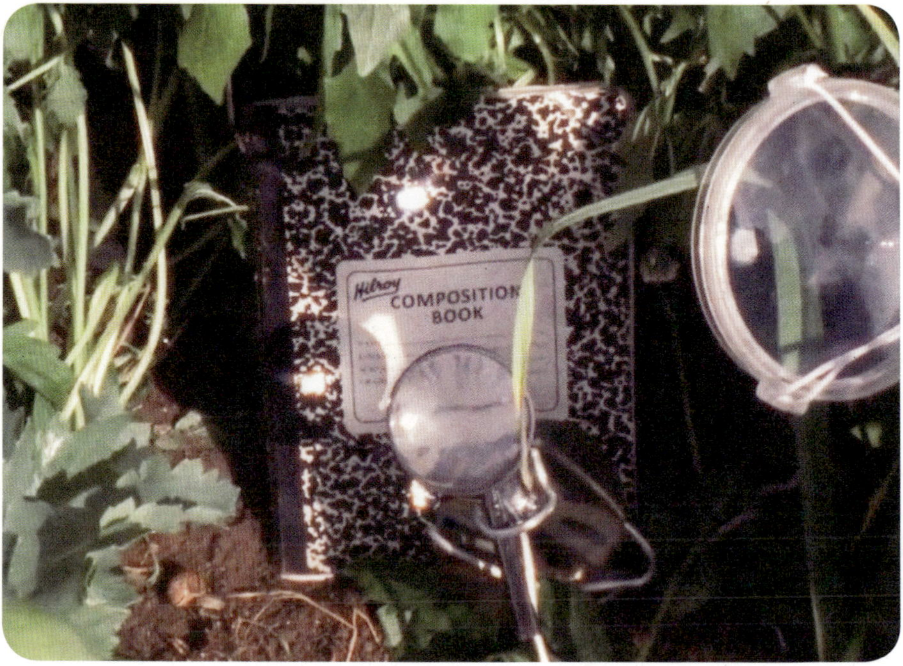

Consider the Belvedere (film stills), 2015

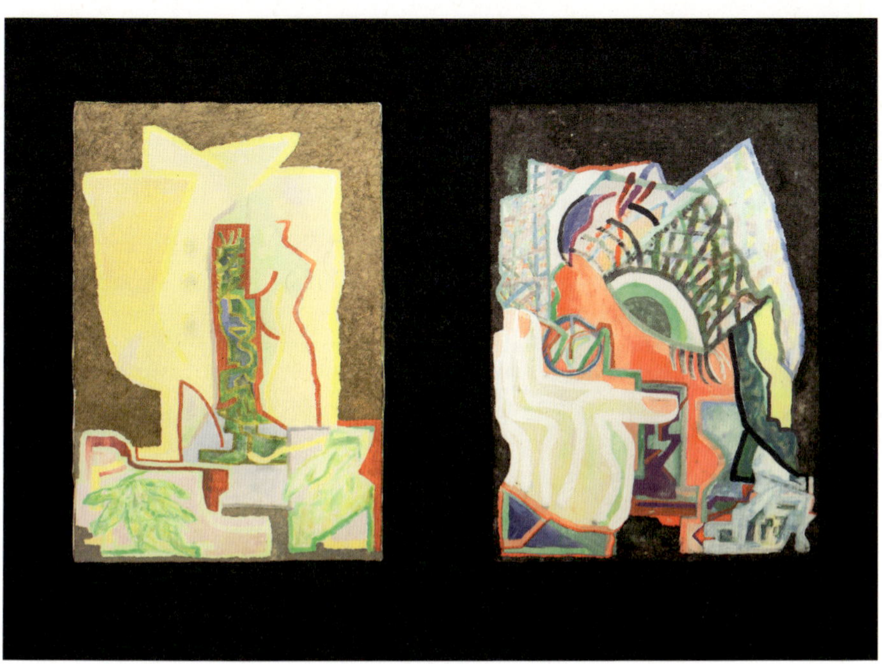

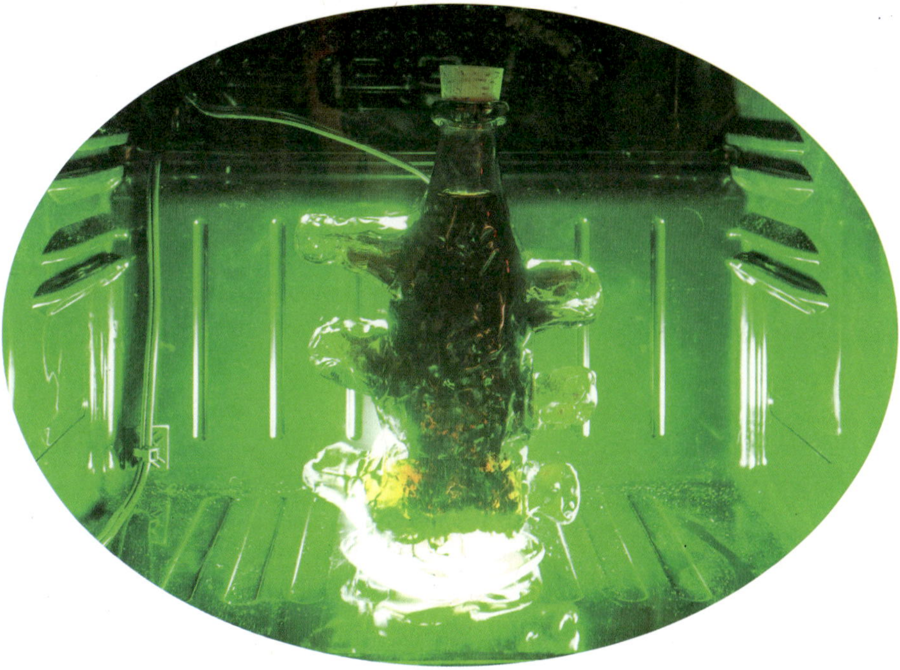

Installation views, ICA Philadelphia, 2015

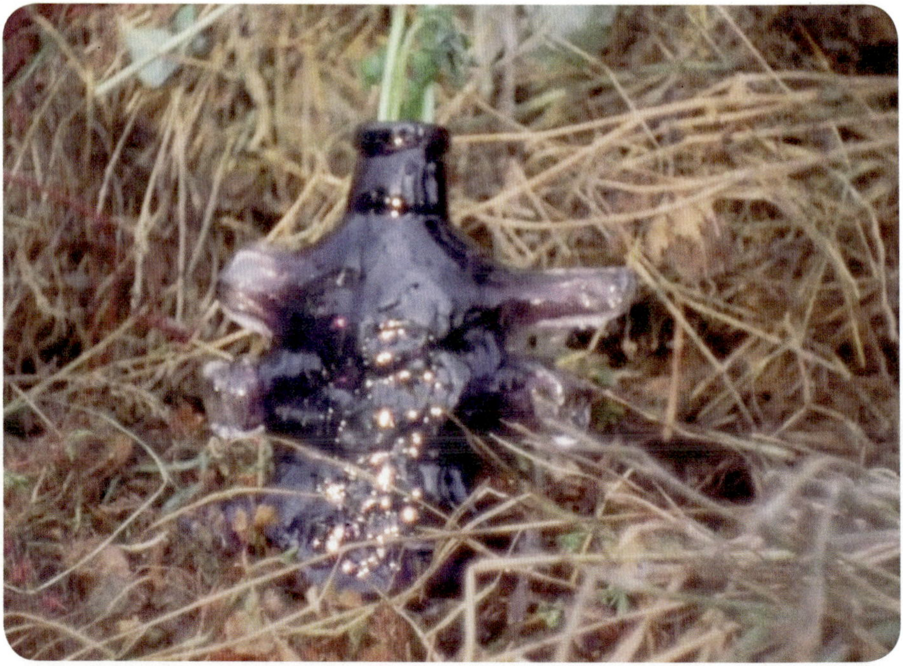

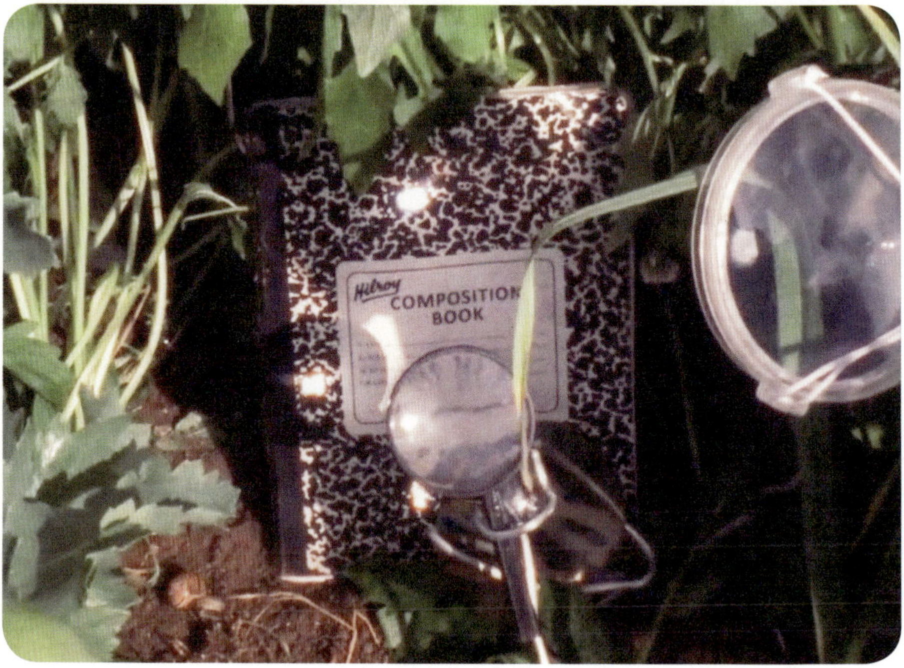

Consider the Belvedere (film stills), 2015

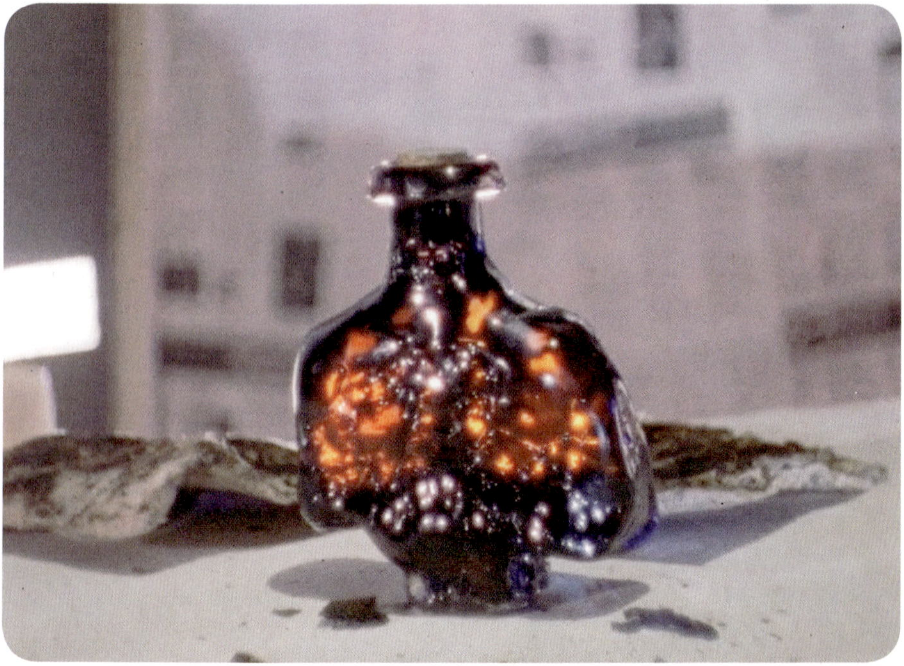

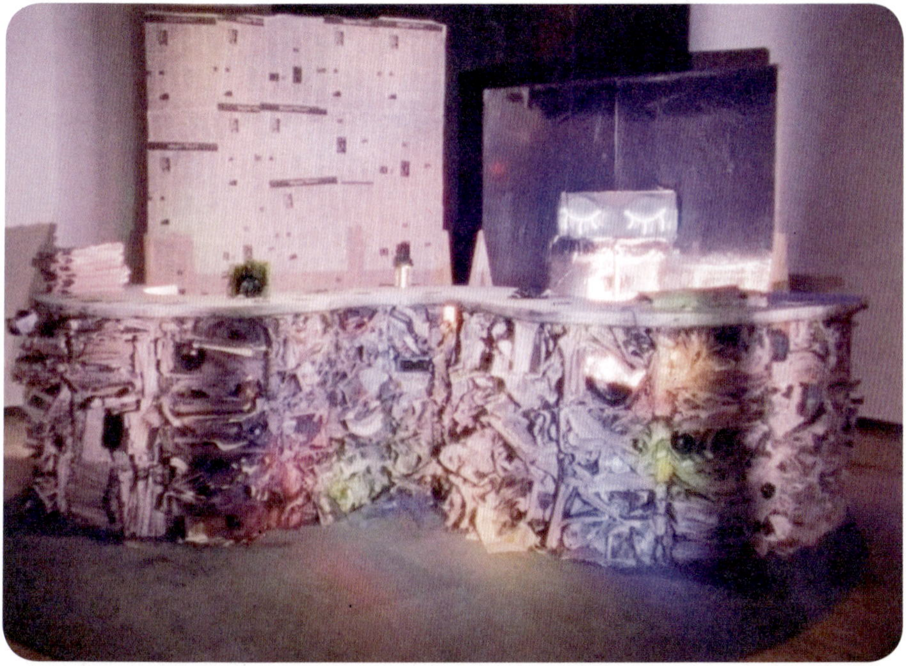

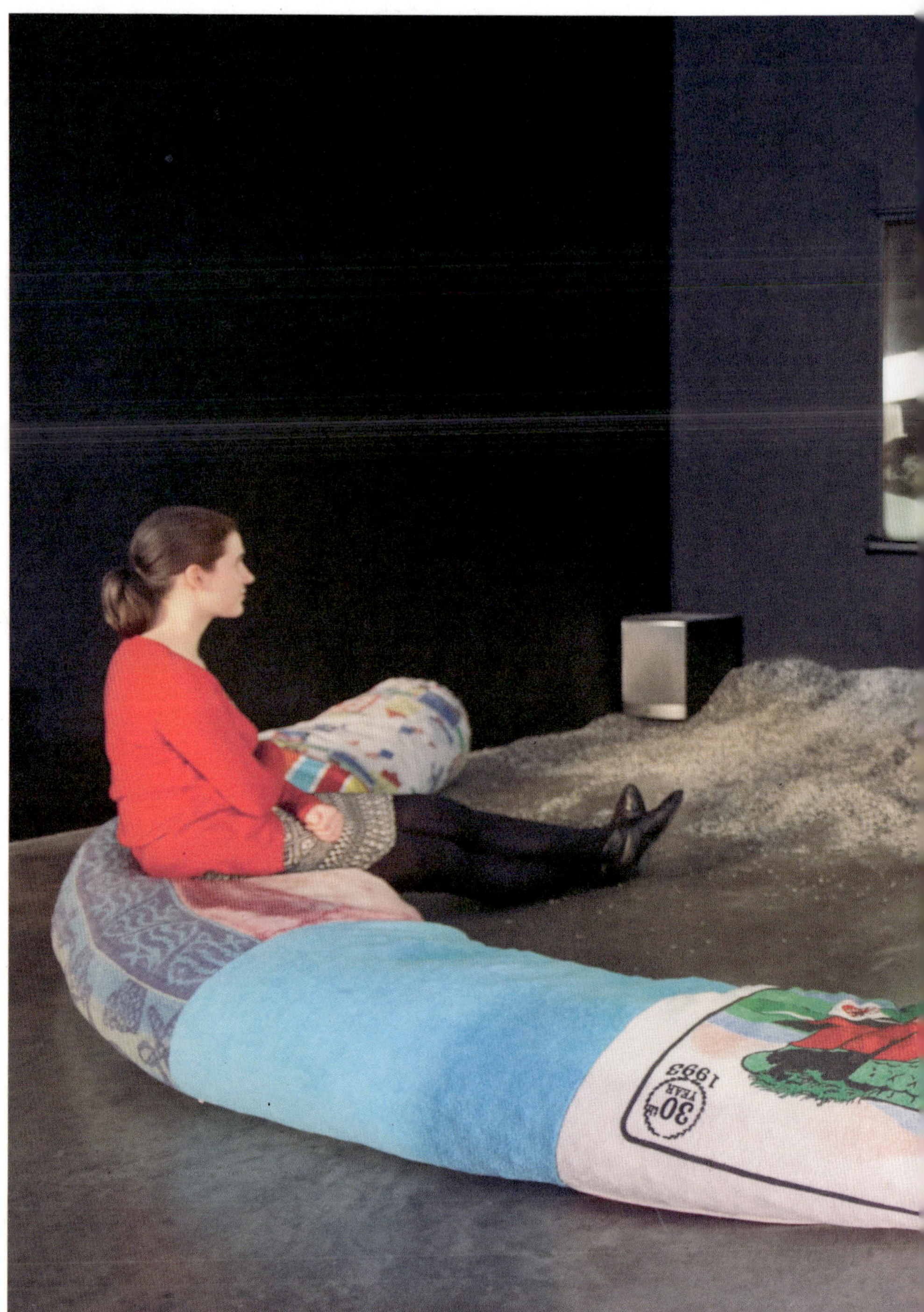

Installation view, ICA Philadelphia, 2015

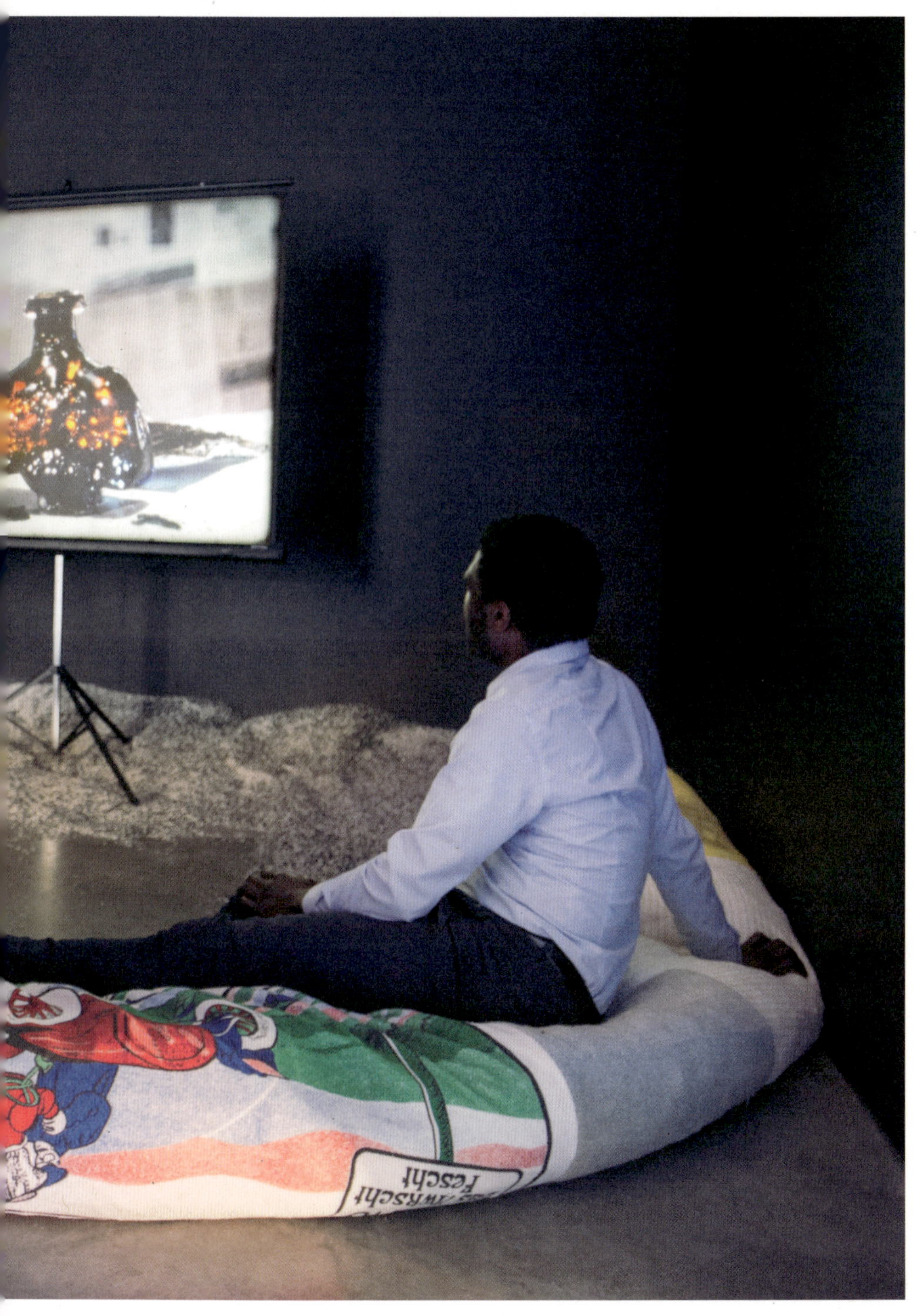
Fescht

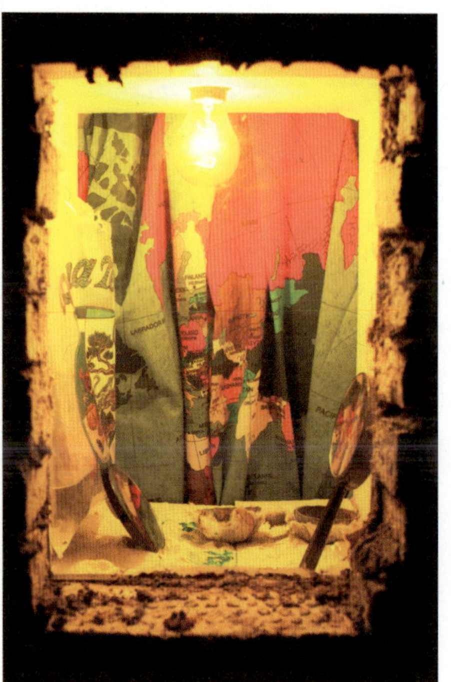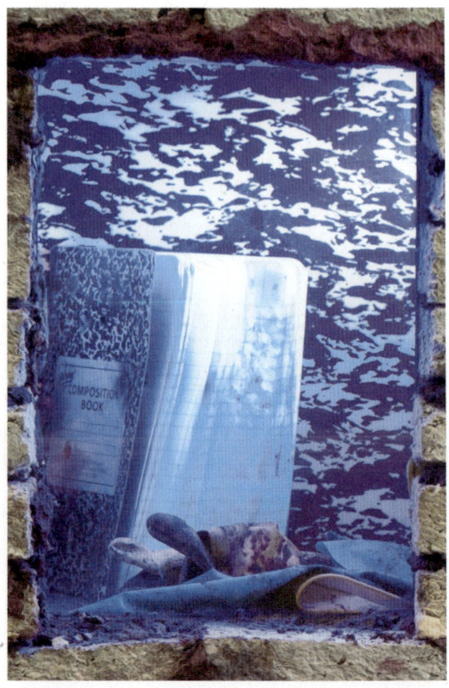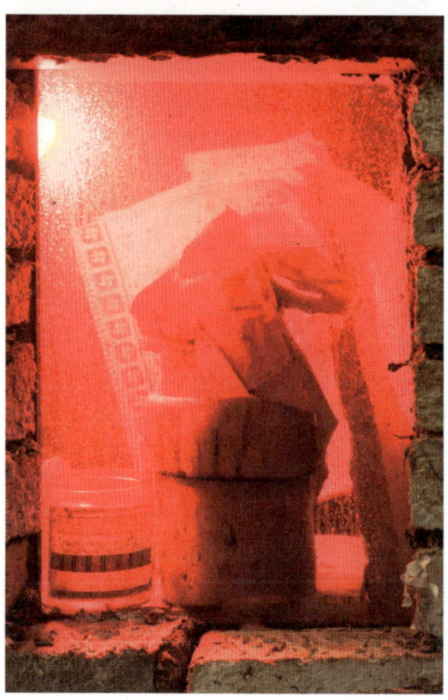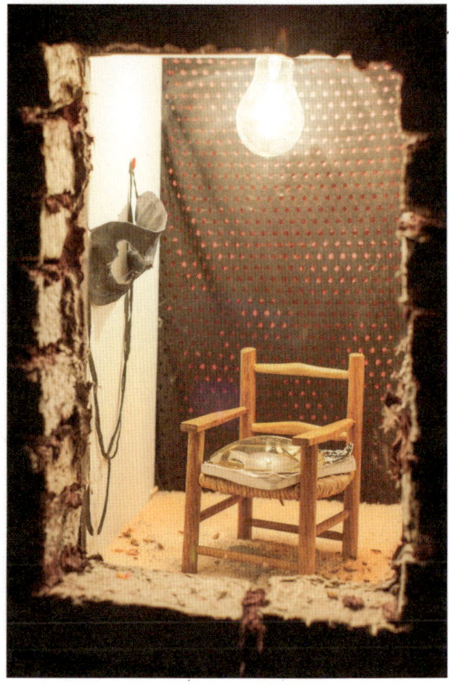

The Night Times Press Bar (details), 2015; installation views, ICA Philadelphia, 2015

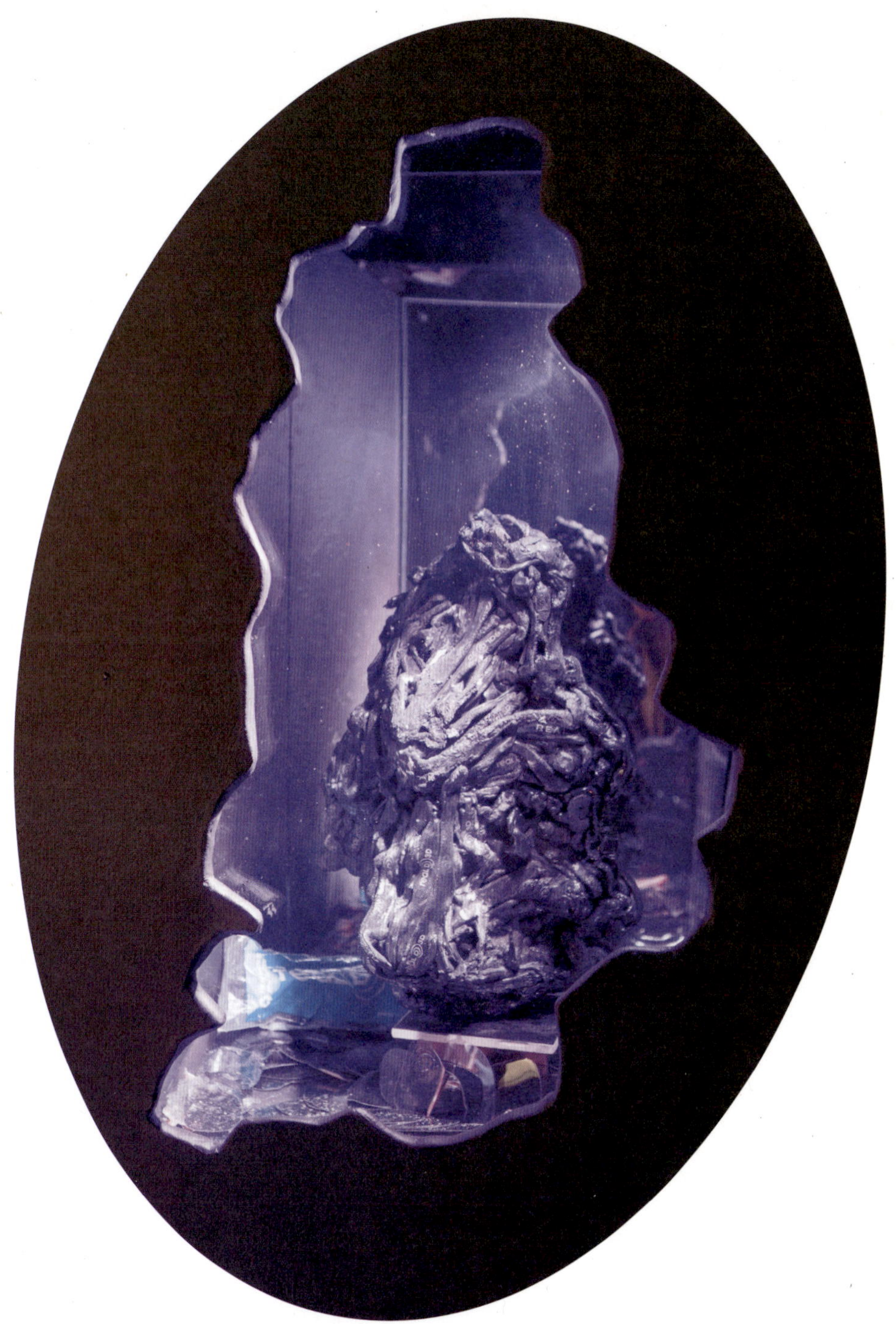

Blind Bottle 3D, 2015; installation view, ICA Philadelphia, 2015

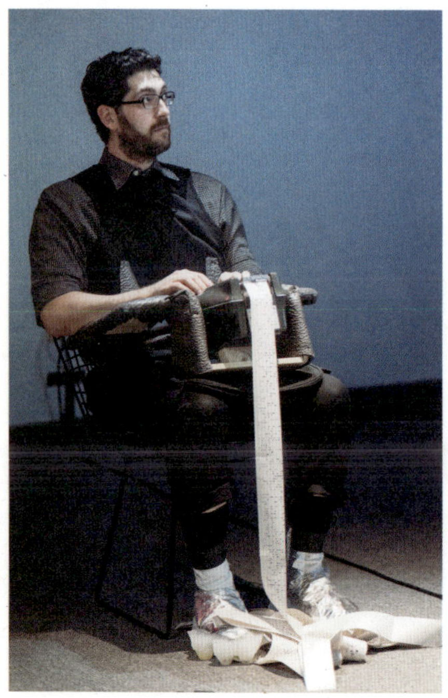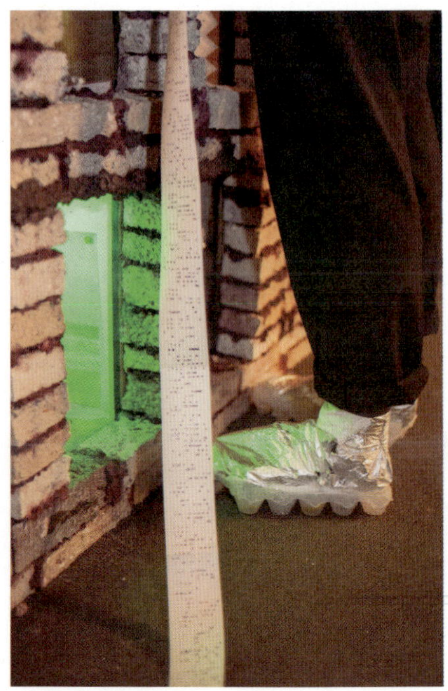

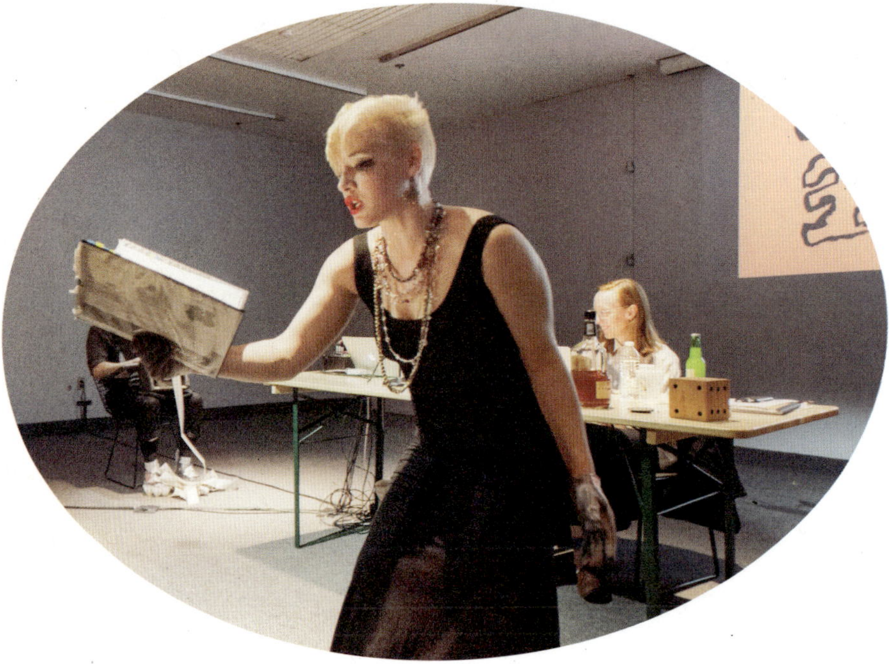

Performance of *Les Bouteilles de la Table Ronde* at ICA Philadelphia, 2015

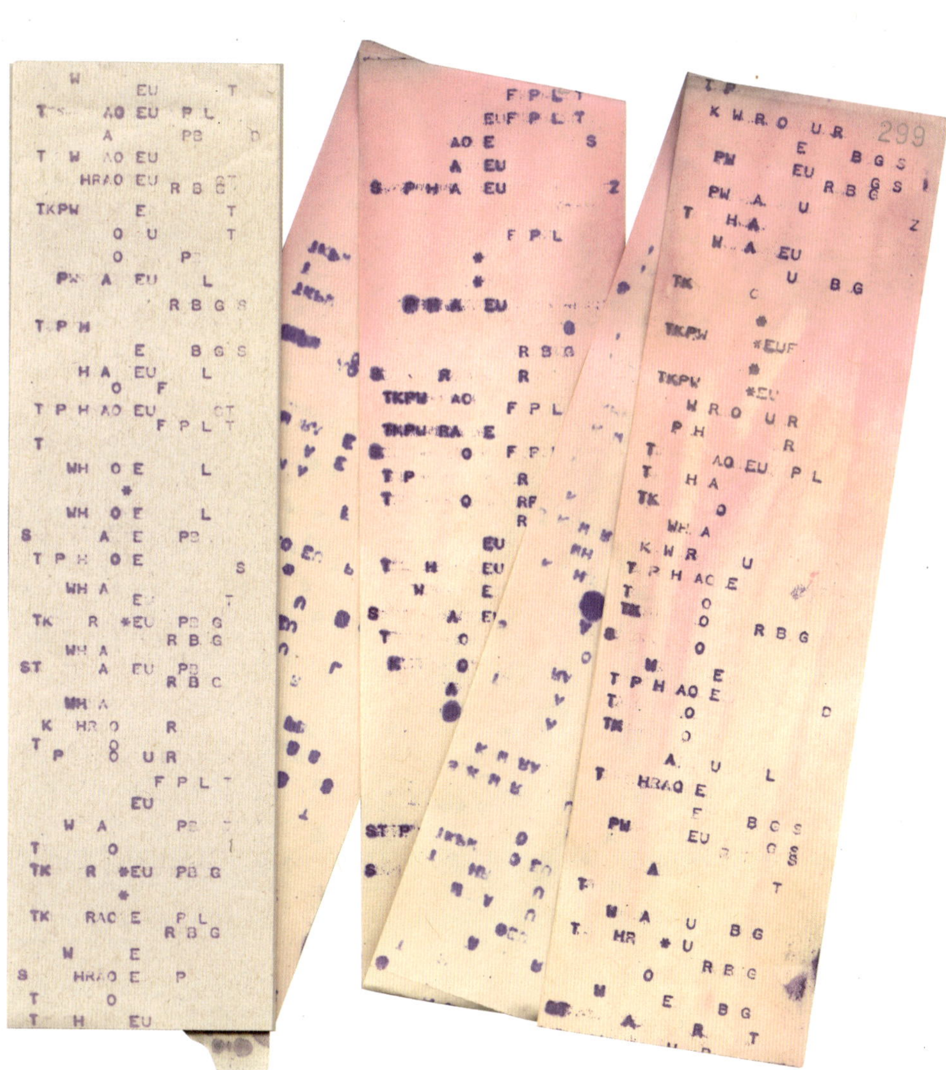

Dream stenography by Jim Hopper, 2015, ICA Philadelphia, 2015

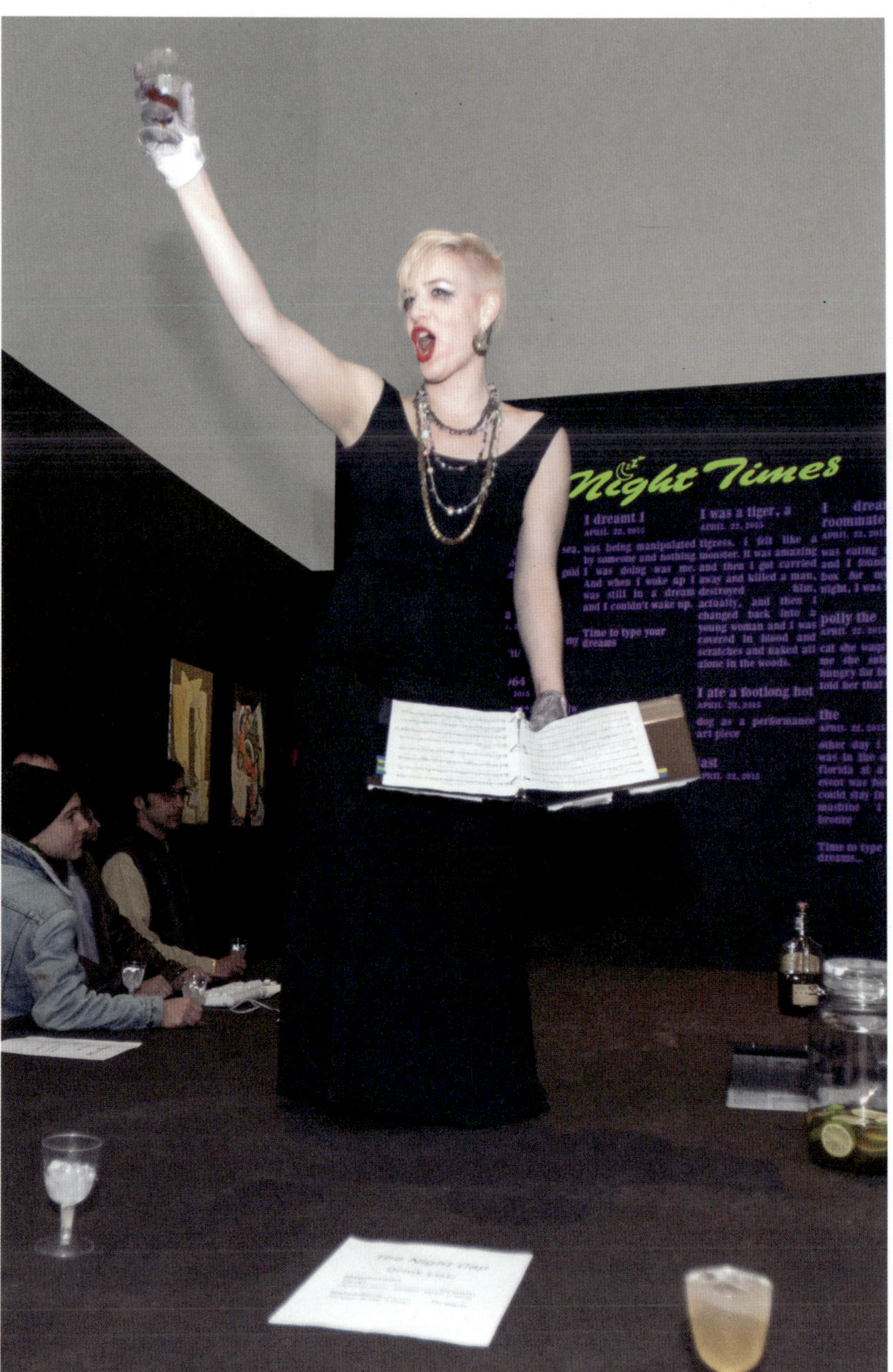

Lauren Pearl Eberwein performs *Les Bouteilles de la Table Ronde*, ICA Philadelphia, 2015

Night Times

sea
SEPTEMBER 9, 2016
I have dreamed that I was at the shore of the sea. I can not find the right direction to go back home.

I
SEPTEMBER 11, 2016
had a dream that tuition was cheap.

I dreamt
SEPTEMBER 17, 2016
that I was looking for a washroom. I walked through a changing room and a shower area. No toilet. I found another washroom but the toilets were all strange and dirty. I had to keep searching … so I didn't wet my bed.

looking for prisms
SEPTEMBER 17, 2016
in farmers fields with radar mounted on a space shuttle.

had purple and turquoise hard
SEPTEMBER 18, 2016
shelled growths on my toes, when I smeared them off the thin shells broke and clear liquid came out and it stung like hell.

Time to type your dreams…

thin candied shells
SEPTEMBER 18, 2016
as the enamel of my teeth became a thousand little shards in my mouth as I clenched by anxious jaw.

I
SEPTEMBER 20, 2016
had a dream that I was lost in a mushroom forest where the mushrooms were as big as skyscrapers and fireflies are as big as birds.

I used to
SEPTEMBER 21, 2016
dream that I was climbing a very long staircase to the top of a circus tent where I would sit and watch what was going on below. I was an observer ever taking part.

I dreamed that I
SEPTEMBER 21, 2016
was studying all night long, because I was full of energy, and I had a baby but that did not keep me from studying.

Time to type your dreams…

I
SEPTEMBER 21, 2016
dreamt he fucked my wife.

sometimes I dream when I'm
SEPTEMBER 21, 2016
awake. I dream that my grandfather is alive even though I fly home for his funeral later today. Blackbird is playing this Gallery. It's beautiful. I really loved by grandfather.

in
SEPTEMBER 21, 2016
my dreams my home is no longer my home. I am whole and alone.

I dreamt a spider bit
SEPTEMBER 21, 2016
the back of my leg (subsequent stings like a sewing machine).

I
SEPTEMBER 22, 2016
had to drive the old Astrovan on a long journey by myself and I was afraid. My dad said I'd be OK. The Astrovan was white and tall.

Time to type your dreams…

I was on
SEPTEMBER 22, 2016
stage with Scorpions. But my guitar had no strings.

I bought an old house
SEPTEMBER 22, 2016
and when I went in, things were sort of crumbling apart and really destroyed from age. I started freaking out, wondering what I had done, but then I climbed the stairs and got to this attic space that was full of super cool and old furniture and objects. I remember thinking I could really make something from this shithole.

I was
SEPTEMBER 23, 2016
cuddling a cat and wondering why cats always frighten me. Its warmth was rejuvenating.

Geoffrey Farmer
SEPTEMBER 27, 2016
knocked over all of the glasses in the cupboard. All my co-workers, which included David Lee from the Good Wife, were pissed.

Time to type your dreams…

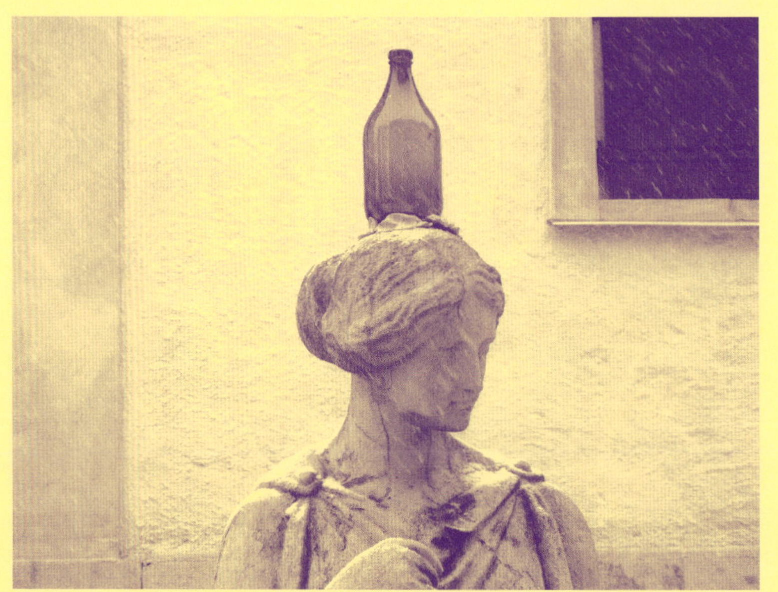

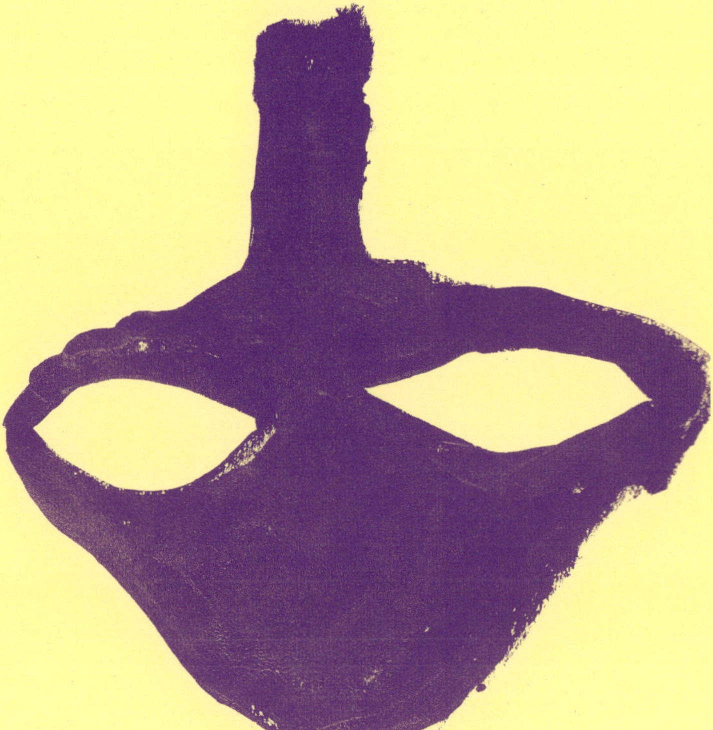

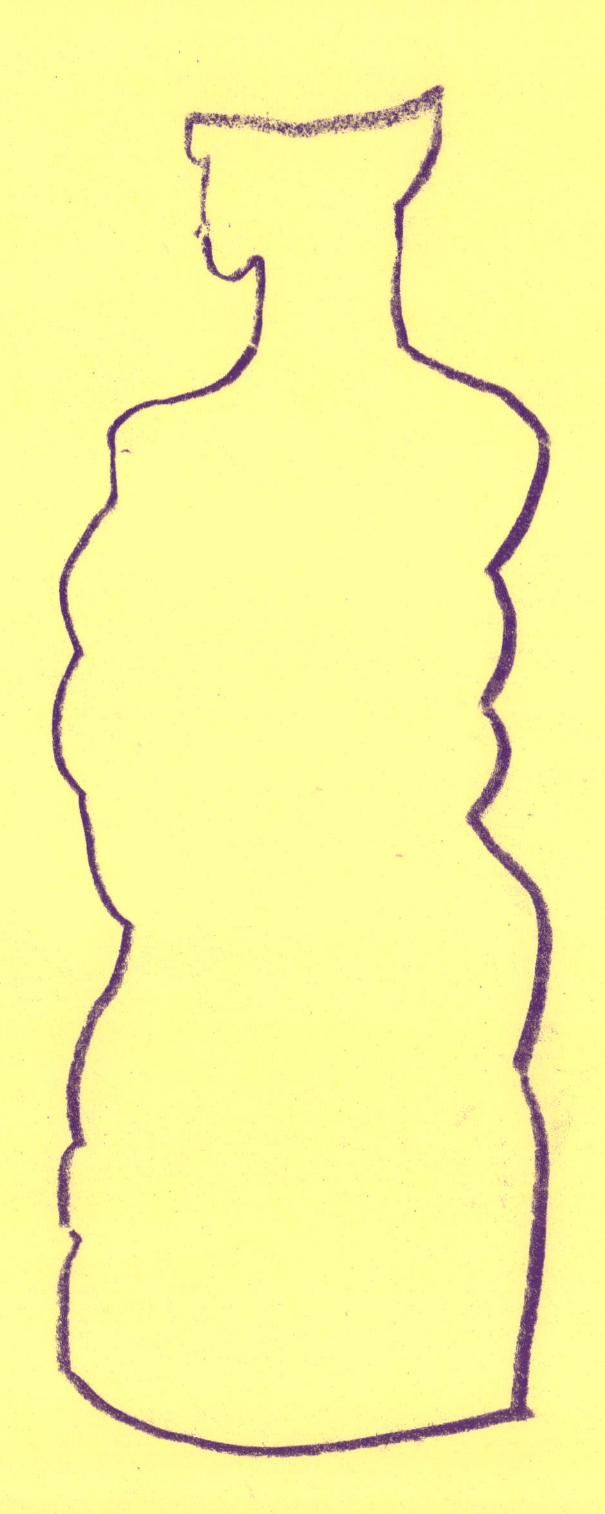

Night Times

I dreamed about
SEPTEMBER 27, 2016
you again last night. I still love you.

poetry
SEPTEMBER 28, 2016
I dreamt I was writing a book of poetry. I dreamt I was writing a book of poetry. I dreamt I was writing a book of poetry. I dreamt I was writing a book of poetry. I dreamt I was writing a book of poetry. I dreamt I was writing a book of poetry. I dreamt I was trying to burn a book of poetry. I dreamt I was trying to burn a book of poetry. I dreamt I was trying to burn a book of poetry. The little book of poetry won't burn. The little book of poetry won't burn. The little book of poetry won't burn.

I dream about
SEPTEMBER 28, 2016
people I have no business dreaming about, or even thinking about for that matter.

Time to type your dreams…

I was
SEPTEMBER 29, 2016
looking for a missing lid. Meanwhile my friend duplicated and I was looking for her missing half. I found her at an unusual wedding happening at the Belkin Art Gallery.

In real life
SEPTEMBER 29, 2016
my cat was peeing in the house and I was really mad. Then I had a dream and my cat played a key role in it, at one point, she was hanging off the curtains and she said in a small whiney voice, "look over there." And there was another cat where she was pointing with her paw. And the next day, in real life once again, I saw that the neighbour's cat WAS coming into our apartment through the window so my cat was rightfully peeing.

Time to type your dreams…

I actually
SEPTEMBER 29, 2016
did cut my finger off, not a dream, reality.

Im am falling
SEPTEMBER 29, 2016
and the screaming in my throat finds its way to my arms as it turns me into a blur of grey, a smear, a streak of ink crashing down against a cityscape. This is me, falling, not apart, just down.

you didn't want me anymore
SEPTEMBER 30, 2016
and when I woke up I felt more free than I have felt in years. And you weren't in my bed anymore but you called me later. Still.

Time to type your dreams…

a wedding
SEPTEMBER 30, 2016
I once dreamed that me and my family were at a wedding. I remember looking at my sister in her blue dress when I felt the sensation of my teeth beginning to fall out. I looked down at the table where my teeth had fallen and saw only rice crackers, the round pale lumpy ones. I looked back at my sister and suddenly her hair was pulled back in an uncomfortably tight bun.

where
SEPTEMBER 30, 2016
the grasslands meet jungle, I run with a man who shifts between human and tiger form. My hand meets skin and fur alternatively as I run my hand across him.

I had a
SEPTEMBER 30, 2016
dream that I was the only person who was real in the world and everyone around me was acting.

Time to type your dreams…

Night Times

I had a
OCTOBER 2, 2016
dream that I was the only person who was real in the world and everyone around me was acting.

On the
OCTOBER 2, 2016
cusp of solving something, only to wake up and realize it doesn't really matter, whatever it was.

I gave birth to a
OCTOBER 4, 2016
baby girl in my parent's bathroom. My brother did not congratulate me.

My back has
OCTOBER 4, 2016
been hurting lately, so last night when I was sleeping, each time I had to roll over – which was a lot – I dreamed that I had to make a journal entry, like an accountant, and each roll I had to credit $400 and debit $400 to two different accounts, but I could never quite tell which accounts I was debiting and crediting. One was my back, but I couldn't see the other.

Time to type your dreams...

Last night
OCTOBER 5, 2016
I dreamt that I was flying over the surface of an ocean but I dove down and swam forever down til the water turned navy black and I swam through a city of sharks by the ocean floor and I never needed to come up for air and noen of them hurt me, we just admired each other in silence and swam.

I dreamed
OCTOBER 5, 2016
I was back in that big old house, you know, the one with many rooms...

I had
OCTOBER 6, 2016
a dream that ladybugs invaded my window sill. I ended up vacuuming it all, but they kept on booming uncontrollably.

I dreamt that
OCTOBER 6, 2016
I was in mangroves and sea water. It was sunny and clear. Some creatures came to attack us and I didn't know how to protect us but somehow we got away in clear glass tubes that skirted along the water's surface. I woke up on a rock after that.

Time to type your dreams...

my dream
OCTOBER 7, 2016
I'm always being chased.

I was sitting
OCTOBER 7, 2016
there silently, I was sitting just watching and feeling the energy around me. Others' energy and my own, the trickling of water running down my back, the wind finding the cracks in my clothes – gusting through my sinuous lungs, but I had no mouth to exhale, so he breathed for me, his lips pressed against mine...

Yesterday I dreamt
OCTOBER 7, 2016
that I was being chased by a woman holding a scorpion.

About encountering the adolescenthood crush
OCTOBER 7, 2016
again – a juvenile yet profound attachment, the subject that symbolized security, the feeling to be relished, the wish to be special.

Time to type your dreams...

dreaming about Paul who
OCTOBER 7, 2016
has left us. Till we meet again.

Time to type your dreams...

Chocolate...
OCTOBER 8, 2016
covered everything – the ground, the trees, the clouds. Everything bad in the world was OK again. Then I woke up. Everything was covered in shit.

Bucky
OCTOBER 8, 2016
my cat had a twin. I spent much time trying to tell which one was Bucky.

Falling
OCTOBER 8, 2016
always falling. Again and again.

I dreamed that
OCTOBER 11, 2016
members from the band Radiohead were trying to burn my house down, but Lapis Lazuli, who is a character from the cartoon Steven Universe, saved me, what a relief.

Time to type your dreams...

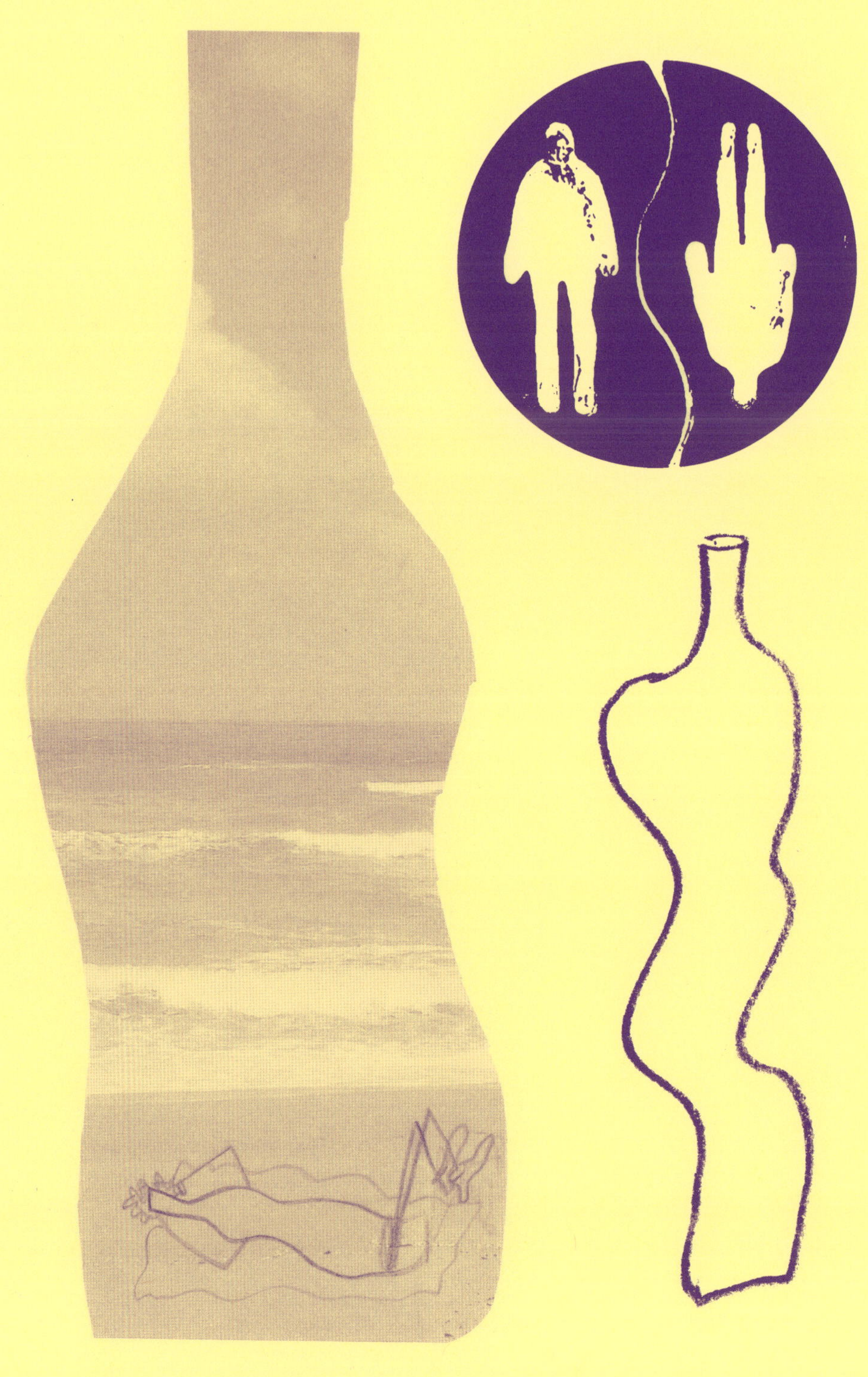

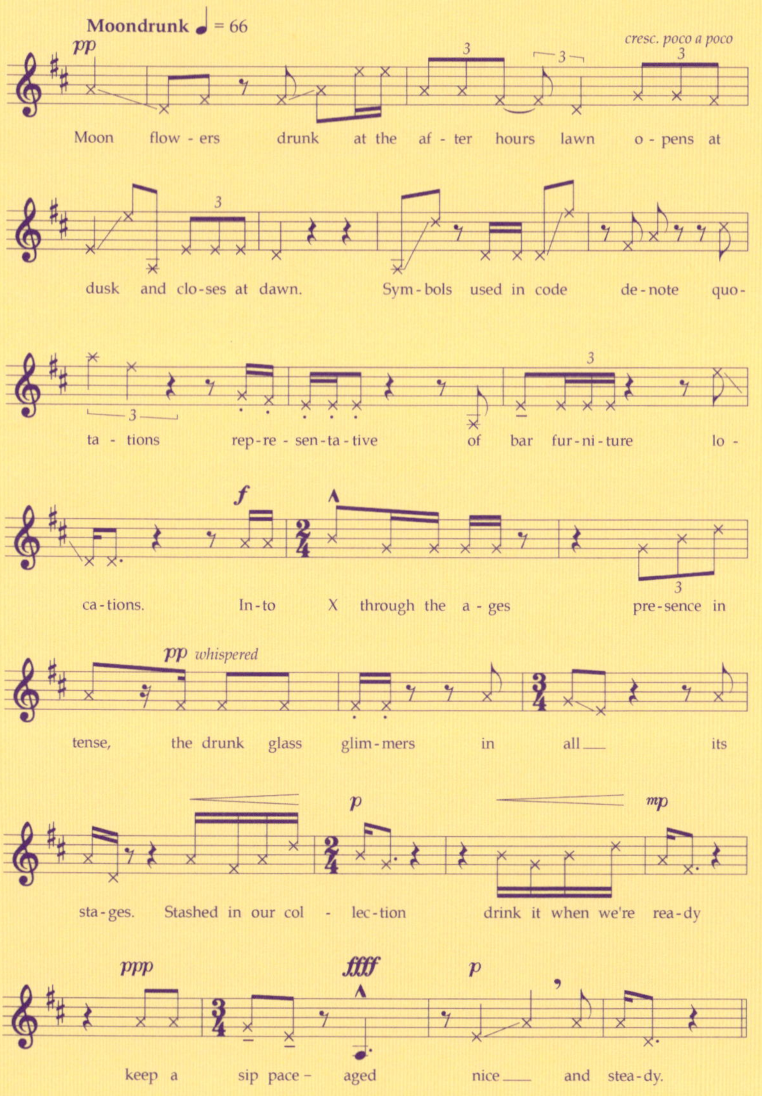

Moondrunk ♩ = 66
pp
cresc. poco a poco
3
3
3
Moon flow - ers drunk at the af - ter hours lawn o - pens at
3
dusk and clo - ses at dawn. Sym - bols used in code de - note quo -
3
3
ta - tions rep - re - sen - ta - tive of bar fur - ni - ture lo -
f
2/4
3
ca - tions. In - to X through the a - ges pre - sence in
pp whispered
3/4
tense, the drunk glass glim - mers in all___ its
p
mp
2/4
sta - ges. Stashed in our col - lec - tion drink it when we're rea - dy
ppp
ffff
p
3/4
keep a sip pace - aged nice___ and stea - dy.

Night Times

I had a
OCTOBER 11, 2016

dream last night that I wrapped a dead bird in foil but the foil started to move like the bird was breathing. I opened the foil and the bird flew out.

I
OCTOBER 11, 2016

dreamed an orca jumped over my boat and told me to jump in the water and get a ride. It then took me to a beautiful island full of peaceful people and animals living in harmony!

I dreamed
OCTOBER 11, 2016

that I was in my friend Dante's kitchen in Ottawa. We were talking and I brought up the fact that my friend Kay had just organized a music festival. I looked up the lineup and it was a lot of people I didn't recognize, but also Lucinda Williams and Morrissey. Dante didn't know Lucinda Williams but he really hates Morrissey so I told him he was there. He asked me why Kay would invite him and I said I didn't know. We both laughed about it.

Time to type your dreams...

Cookie
OCTOBER 11, 2016

Lyon was having a breakdown, remembering a past lesbian lover. She was unstable and scaring her caregiver, also her bedroom was a disaster.

I
OCTOBER 12, 2016

kept running and running, being followed by a number of people I've never met. I don't remember them either. I was scared and my family was running next to me, at some point we are reached by our persecutors and I don't know why, I grab a gun from my father's pants and shoot him in the head. I wake up to the drowning guilt of the dream as it mixes with the conscious guilt of my father's suicide.

I mushroom was growing out
OCTOBER 13, 2016

of my temple. It was the size of a loonie and the colour of my skin but then got grey at the end. I couldn't pull it off, attached like a skin tag. I spent all that time looking in the mirror.

Time to type your dreams...

We have to leave
OCTOBER 15, 2016

We were all in the grocery store late and it was a 30 minute walk home and there was something very important to do in the morning. I try to get everyone to leave but no one listens.

I was in a grocery store
OCTOBER 15, 2016

and realized I could fly. I just floated over the aisles and my mom couldn't find me. It was very exciting and I can still fly in my dreams whenever I remember to.

Stranded
OCTOBER 16, 2016

I dreamt that I was stranded on an island surrounded by water. I wanted to jump onto a nearby platform but there was a reptile-like creature swimming around, apparently this reflects some sort of helplessness and isolation in my waking reality.

Time to type your dreams...

War
OCTOBER 16, 2016

I was fighting the red army and I got shot in the knee. The last thing I knew was that I was in the hospital bed with my leg and arm amputated. And then I woke up.

I dreamed that I was
OCTOBER 16, 2016

having a baby but after the baby was born the doctor told me to be careful and I didn't understand until I looked at the baby. The baby was made from cooked chicken and then I realized that I was hungry and I started to eat the chicken. I'm a vegetarian so this dream was disturbing on so many levels.

Adopting a Dog
OCTOBER 16, 2016

I dreamt of adopting a stray, it was the last dog at a shelter's open house. I knew it was meant for me and she knew I was meant for her. I worried that I had no food bowl for her and that my husband was not going to be happy. But that face...

Time to type your dreams...

Night Times

I dreamed
OCTOBER 19, 2016
it was my best friend's birthday but I somehow forgot about it. All I could think of on short notice was the fact that she really likes crabs. So in a video game called Yo-Kai Watch, I caught a rare crab and sent her a picture of it, and that was the extent of the birthday celebration.

I'm running around
OCTOBER 19, 2016
an oval dirt track in a wooded rural area, accompanied by an old friend. There are many deer standing in the centre of the oval and many rabbits sitting on the track. When my friend and I approach the rabbits, they grow wings and fly out of harm's way. I decide they are flying foxes (all while being aware in the dream that flying foxes are bats and that the creatures in the dream are rabbits). I round the track again and the rabbits fly away one more time.

Time to type your dreams...

Wax sculpture
OCTOBER 19, 2016
I was in a boarding school and was not allowed to leave. The one attractive blonde man who seemed to be the least abusive member of the staff was my only friend. He then tried to pour boiling wax over me to make a sculpture.

I dreamt that my friend
OCTOBER 19, 2016
ran up to me and told me, "Girl, you really need to put on some deodorant!"

Last night I dreamt
OCTOBER 19, 2016
that I was walking a Golden Retriever. It was perfect.

alien
OCTOBER 19, 2016
invasion/colonization was rumoured to be imminent – government was taking what was described as preventative measures. Making mandatory pre-scriptions for mood/intel-lect inhibiting medica-tions. Social media was being monitored to sup-press and potential upris-ings. Mercenary groups were forming to fight the alien colonizers by word of mouth.

Time to type your dreams...

I dreamed I was late
OCTOBER 20, 2016
for my incense making class.

I was in the
OCTOBER 21, 2016
Yukon and it was flooded everywhere from Polar ice melting.

I dreamt we were
OCTOBER 22, 2016
on T's houseboat and her neighbours were dressed in red and white and I had to poo and she asked I keep the toilet bowl clean.

I dreamt I
OCTOBER 23, 2016
was learning how to drive stick shift in a parking arcade. I turned a corner and found a KFC stall. I woke up craving popcorn chicken.

I'm running around
OCTOBER 30, 2016
an oval dirt track in a wooded rural area, accompanied by an old friend. There are many deer standing in the centre of the oval and many rabbits sitting on the track. When my friend and I approach the rabbits, they grow wings and fly out of harm's way. I decide they are flying foxes (all while being aware in the dream that flying foxes are bats and that the creatures in the dream are rabbits). I round the track again and the rabbits fly away one more time.

Time to type your dreams...

There was a massive rain
NOVEMBER 1, 2016
storm which was flooding my apartment through a squishy hole in my window.

I dreamed
NOVEMBER 1, 2016
it was my best friend's birthday but I somehow forgot about it. All I could think of on short notice was the fact that she really likes crabs. So in a video game called Yo-Kai Watch, I caught a rare crab and sent her a picture of it, and that was the extent of the birthday celebration.

I had a
NOVEMBER 2, 2016
dream that a man stabbed me in the wings and it hurt so badly I woke up. I was in pain until I realized I don't have wings, my shoulders hurt instead.

Time to type your dreams...

2 shots of pulpy prickly pear juice

35 drops energy elixir :
fermented white ginseng
green tea extract
rhodiola root
guarana seed tincture

Bach remedy for the secretary :
2 drops gentian
2 drops Oak

squeeze of lime

top up with mineral water

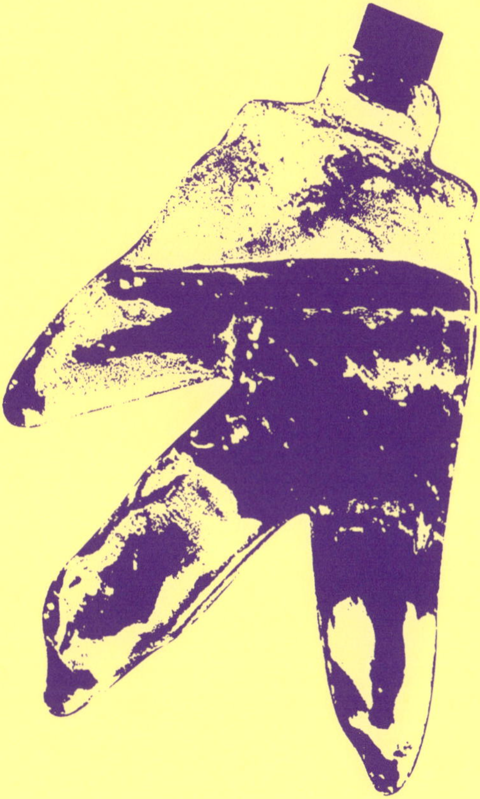

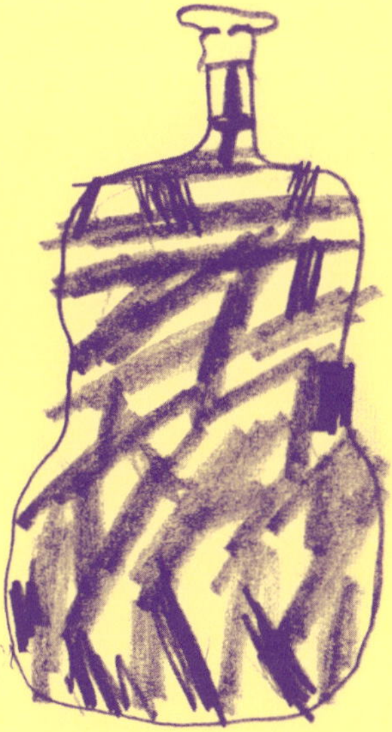

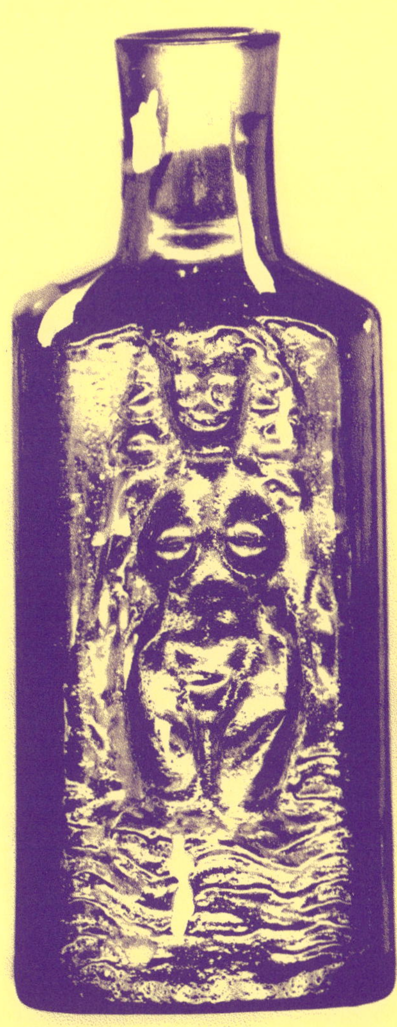

Night Times

I dreamt I showed
NOVEMBER 3, 2016

up late to lecture and wasn't wearing any clothes...

A group of
NOVEMBER 3, 2016

buffalo were singing "Larger than Life" by the Backstreet Boys.

we were looking at tomatoes
NOVEMBER 3, 2016

trying to pick them, we grabbed them off the ground instead.

there was a couple
NOVEMBER 3, 2016

hat murdered each other lying in our apartment, each in sleeping bags wriggling around. I watched them and wondered why they were there.

I dreamt that I could
NOVEMBER 3, 2016

enter a different dimension with each new tone I heard.

Time to type your dreams...

I dreamed that I was
NOVEMBER 4, 2016

earning to drive, and all was going pretty well, I was driving along, but then I started to shrink in the seat. I kept shrinking down gradually until first my hands couldn't reach the steering wheel and then my feet couldn't reach the pedals. It was awful.

I was dating a
NOVEMBER 4, 2016

friend of mine. It was great.

I found two kittens
NOVEMBER 4, 2016

and after we made sure our dogs weren't going to eat them we decided to adopt them. After awhile, they grew up and it turned out they were raccoons but we still thought that was cool. My cousin and I bought ferret leashes for them at the pet store. But a week later the small one died because no one knew how to take care of raccoons. People started spreading a rumour that my dad had poisoned them because he hated them. I was worried the whole time about contracting rabies.

Time to type your dreams...

I dreamed that my girlfriend
NOVEMBER 5, 2016

and I had a fight that resulted in breaking up. It was sad.

A ball
NOVEMBER 6, 2016

fantastical things occurred where creatures of many varieties and shapes and sizes jumped about on trapeze lines, listening to Bono, yelling in inordinate speech patterns. I was there, staring, starting, staring and all I heard was the siren. The sirens of an ambulance. Why? Why? Why? My alarm ended it. Homer Simpson in a nuclear power plant ended it.

I dreamt that
NOVEMBER 6, 2016

world had flooded, and fish were slowly swimming by (notably, a giant sturgeon). I began to panic as I was running out of oxygen. I woke with a sudden start and realized I was facedown, and couldn't breathe because my face was in the pillow.

Time to type your dreams...

I was sleeping and a
NOVEMBER 9, 2016

person was hding in my kitchen. I wanted to wake up, hide or fight back, but I couldn't do anything but sleep.

I was walking through
NOVEMBER 9, 2016

a hallway. A light in the end. I try to keep walking, but no end. And the light was just so attracted. I felt heart-attack.

The
NOVEMBER 9, 2016

first nightmare I can remember I was visiting my friend's house and saw the wicked witch of the west through their bedroom window. I tried to hide under the desk but she came in with a broom to set me on fire.

Time to type your dreams...

Night Times

Nightmare
NOVEMBER 10, 2016
the head of the suicide bomber after he exploded his vest, all that was left was the face of evil.

I dreamt of
NOVEMBER 11 2016
the lead singer of the spice girls was sitting on my boyfriend's lap and she grew a penis.

I had a
NOVEMBER 11 2016
dream that the head of the department was strangling me with white rubber gloves on.

Trump dreams
NOVEMBER 13 2016
dreamed that I fought off Donald Trump with a broken Coke bottle, and won.

I dreamed that I
NOVEMBER 13 2016
went to summer camp and met my ideal man. One day, when I was staring lovingly into his eyes, I noticed that he had the pupils of a goat. I then realized that he was a goat.

Time to type your dreams...

There was a
NOVEMBER 16 2016
First Nations carver making masks. He was planting grass, like a Chia Pet, as hair on the masks.

I dreamed there
NOVEMBER 16 2016
was a hand towel in the front passenger seat in a limousine.

I dreamed my
NOVEMBER 16 2016
house was made of paper and tape. It blew down.

I keep dreaming
NOVEMBER 17 2016
About people and places that are unfamiliar to me, yet they give me a sense of familiarity.

I was swimming in
NOVEMBER 17 2016
a lake and I gasped for air as I tired to find my friends, they were gone.

Time to type your dreams...

My teeth fell out
NOVEMBER 17 2016
when my mother told me she arranged a marriage.

I dreamt
NOVEMBER 17 2016
that I robbed a bank and then flew away.

I
NOVEMBER 17 2016
was trying to escape from Billy Zane's house. It was very big, with a disgusting garden.

The vault
NOVEMBER 17 2016
of the gallery I worked in looked like the inside of Costco. I had to climb a ladder on top of a table in the middle of an aisle. Only after pulling an artwork down did I recognize how dangerous it was.

I was a needle
NOVEMBER 17 2016
with a red ribbon bouncing through a pile of metal logs coated with rubber.

I dreamt I was being
NOVEMBER 19 2016
chased, I tried to get away, but my legs went weak and wouldn't support me.

Time to type your dreams...

In my hometown I was
NOVEMBER 20 2016
left alone at home and a burglar tried to get in, there was no way for me to stop him...

Waking up in a room
NOVEMBER 20 2016
with walls that are dripping with moisture. Peeling plaster much like the image in the Coen Brothers film called Barton Fink where the protagonist writer is holed up in a motel with high humidity and peeling wallpaper.

I dreamed of something vaguely familiar
NOVEMBER 20 2016
I felt that I was in a familiar place with familiar people but all I can remember is a chrome towel rail.

I dreamed
NOVEMBER 22 2016
that Jon Hamm kidnapped me and my roommate.

I dreamt I was
NOVEMBER 22 2016
driving a dirtbike down the PCH with my eyes closed, feeling my way around the curves of the road.

Time to type your dreams...

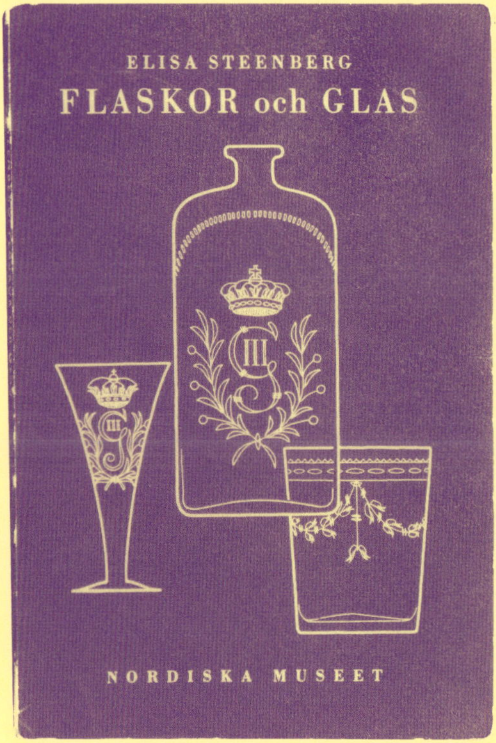

ELISA STEENBERG
FLASKOR och GLAS

NORDISKA MUSEET

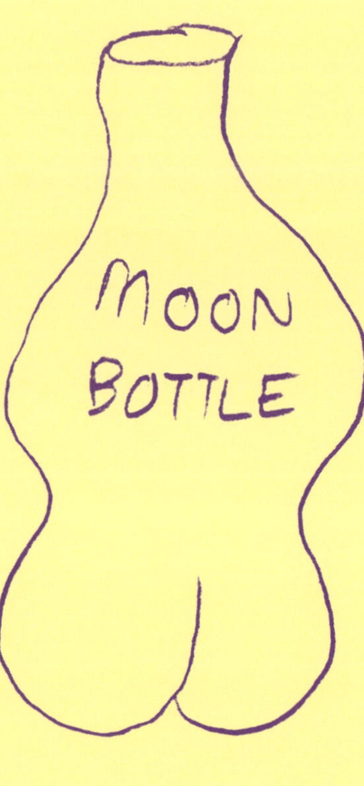

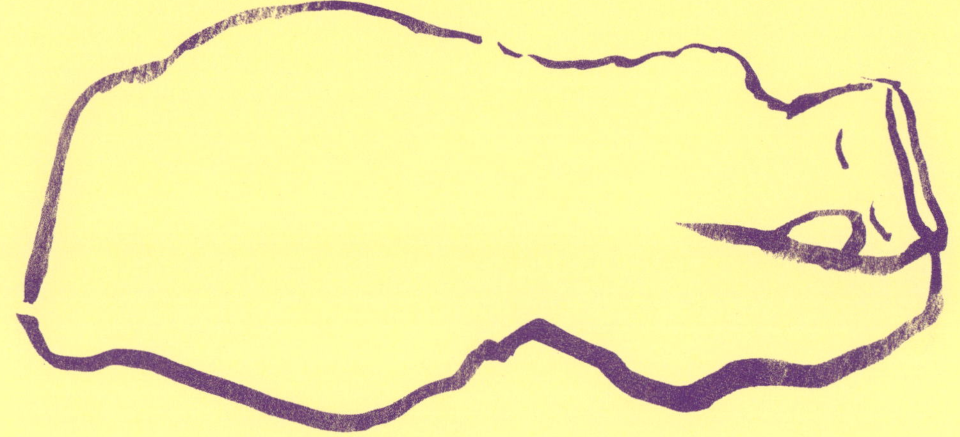

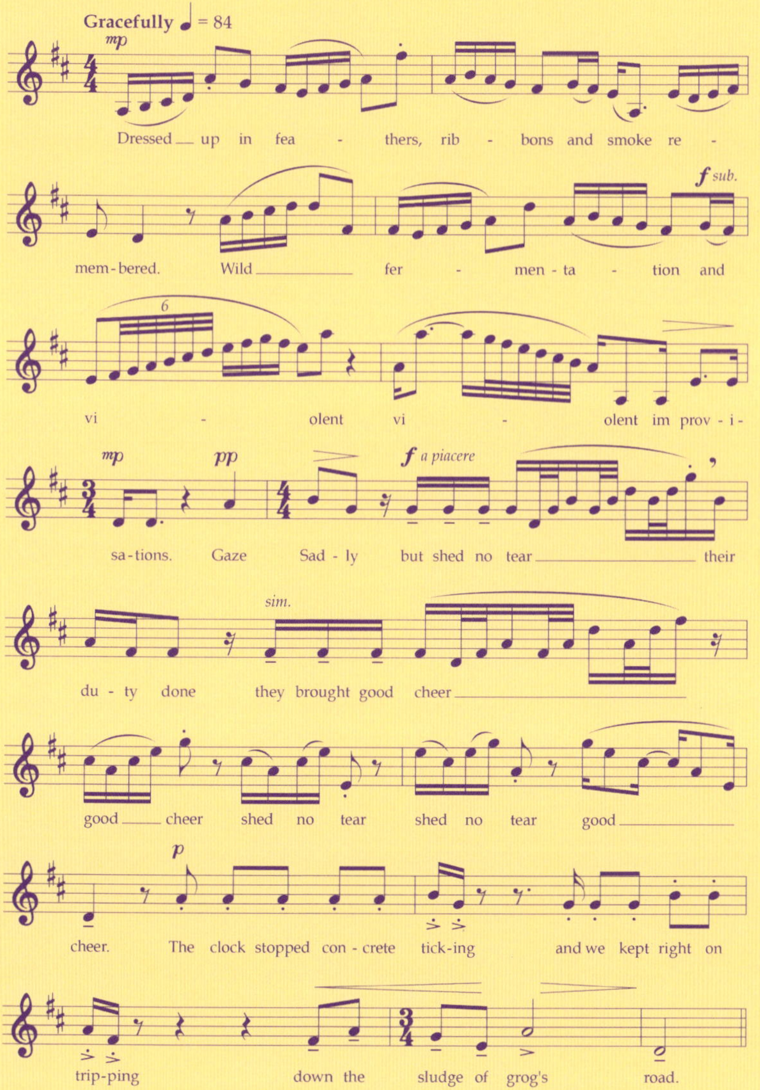

Gracefully ♩ = 84
mp
f sub.
6
mp
pp
f a piacere
sim.
p
Dressed up in fea - thers, rib - bons and smoke re -
mem - bered. Wild fer - men - ta - tion and
vi - olent vi - olent im prov - i -
sa - tions. Gaze Sad - ly but shed no tear their
du - ty done they brought good cheer
good cheer shed no tear shed no tear good
cheer. The clock stopped con - crete tick-ing and we kept right on
trip-ping down the sludge of grog's road.

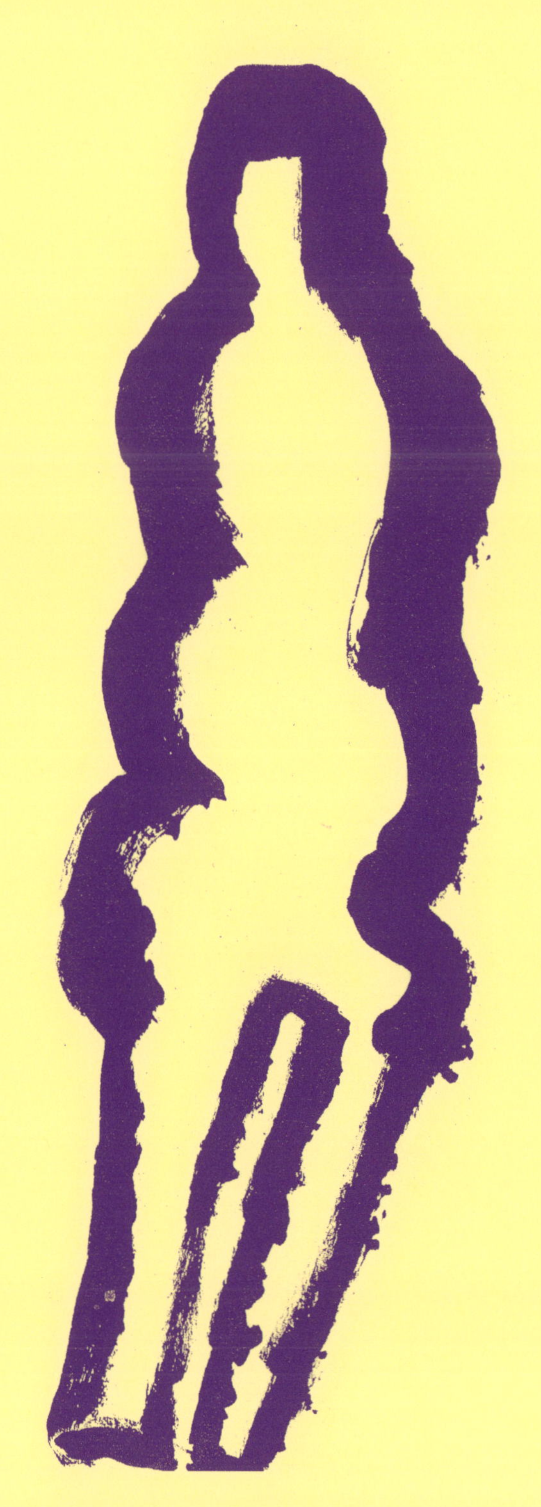

The
Last Waves

Belkin
Art Gallery

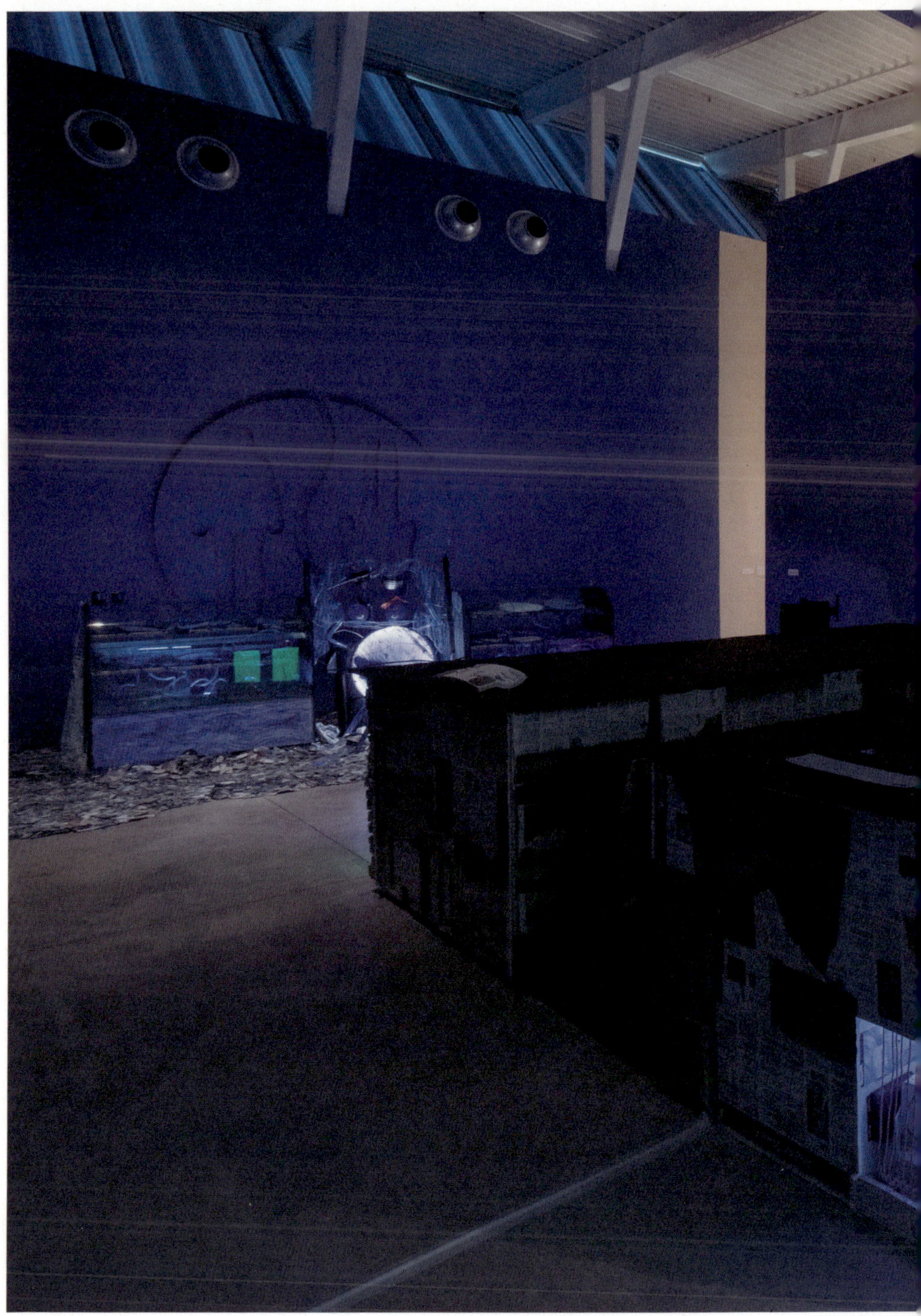

The Night Times Press Bar, 2015–16

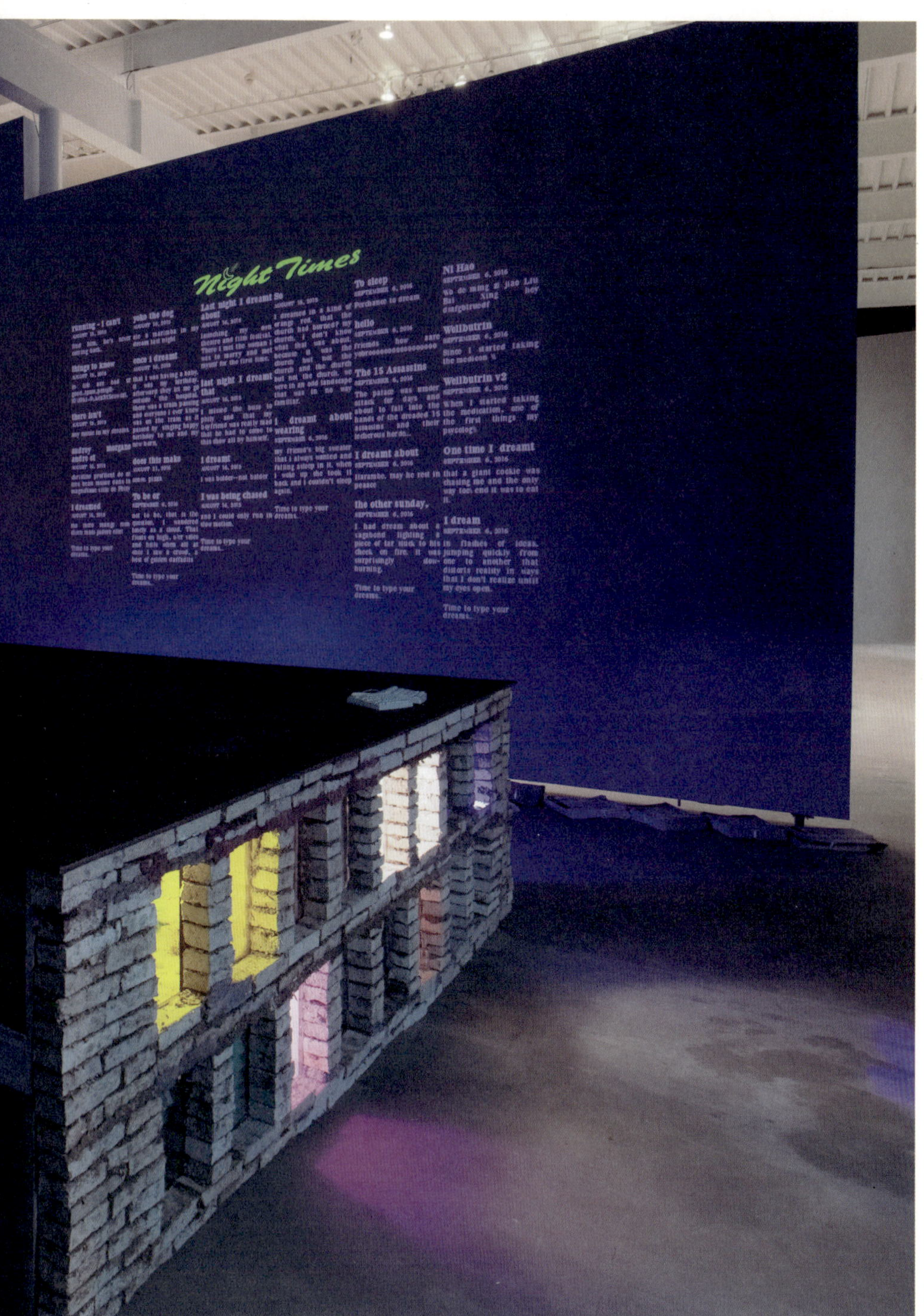

Installation view, Morris and Helen Belkin Art Gallery, 2016

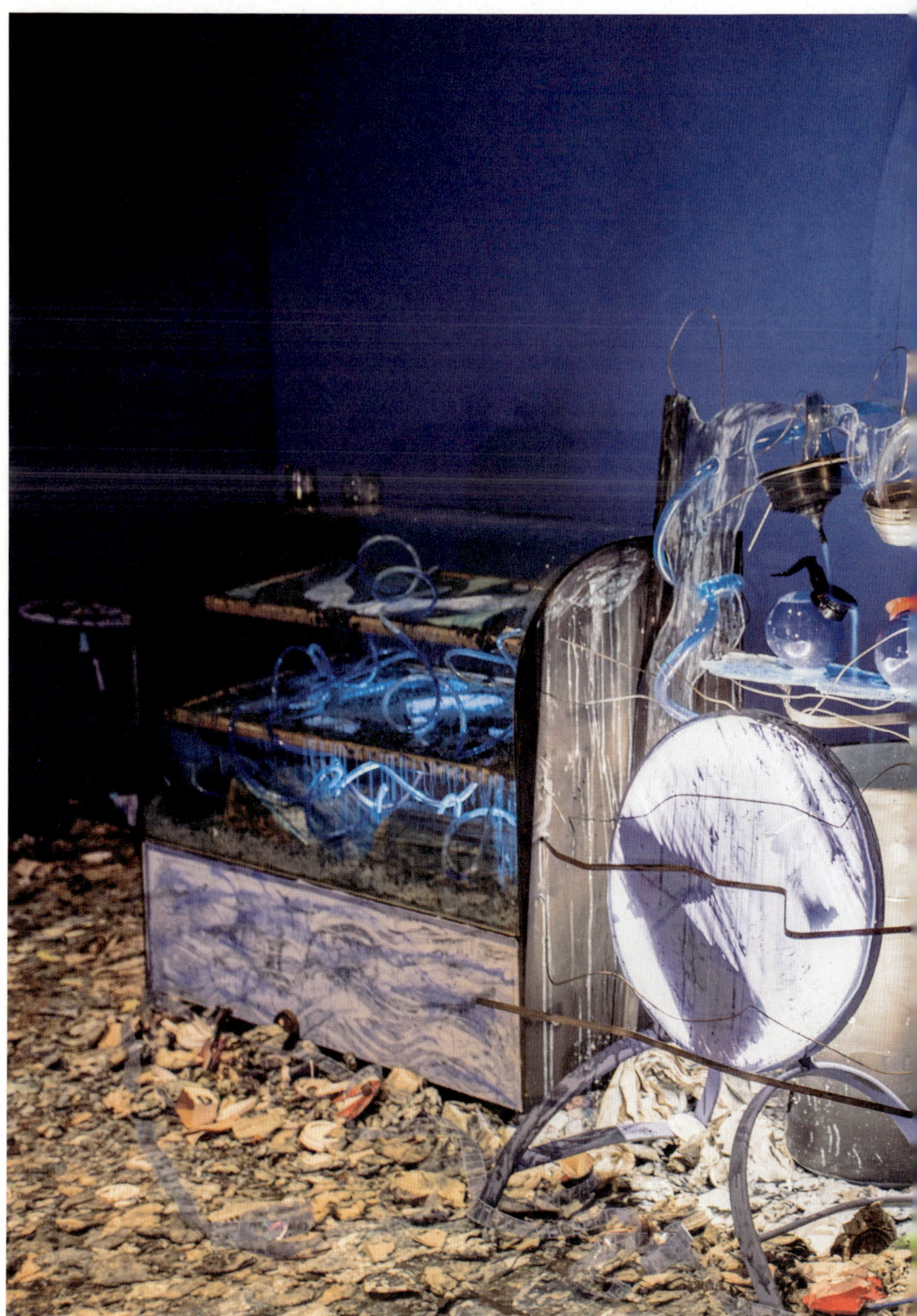

WAVES, 2016; installation view, Morris and Helen Belkin Art Gallery, 2016

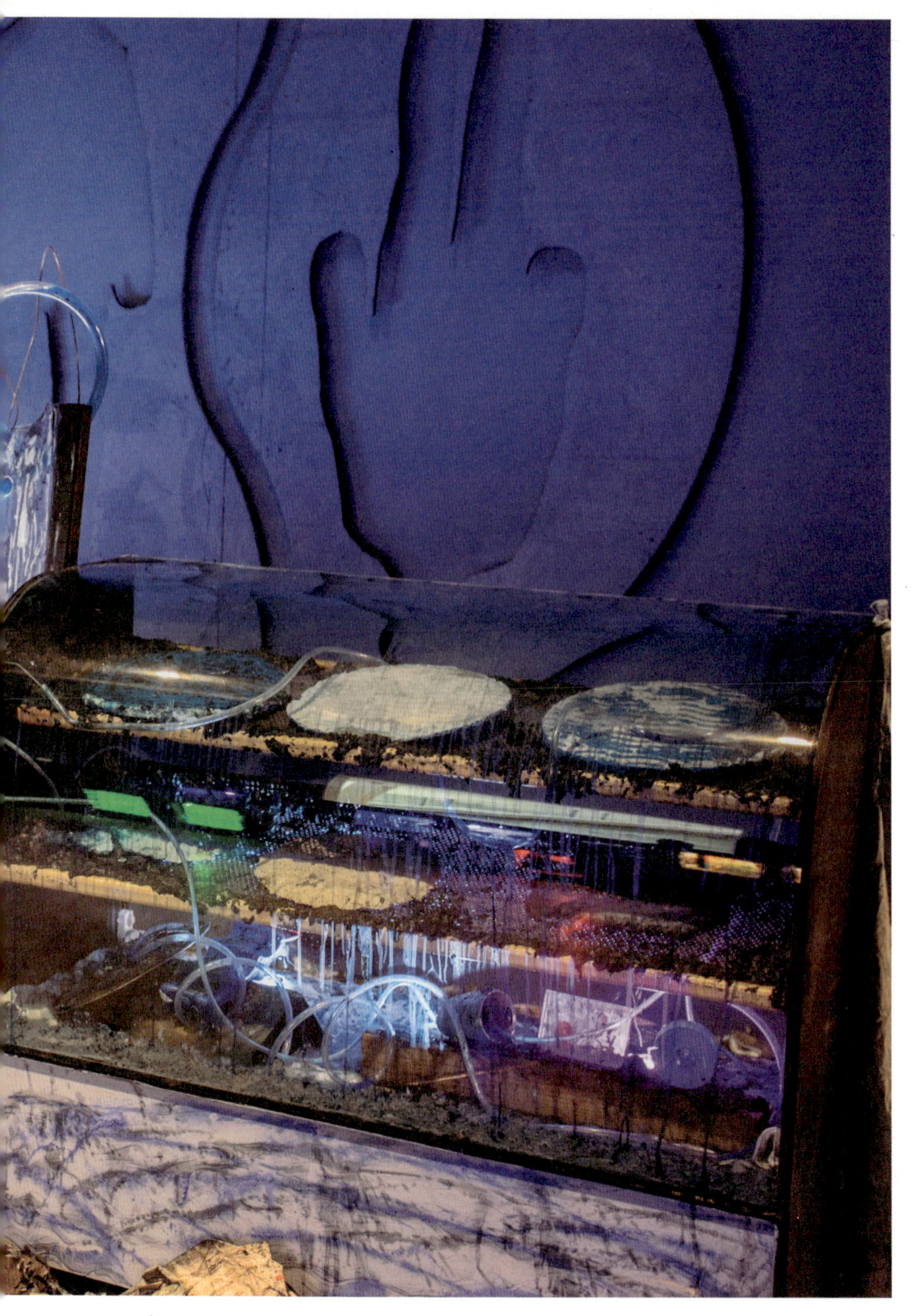

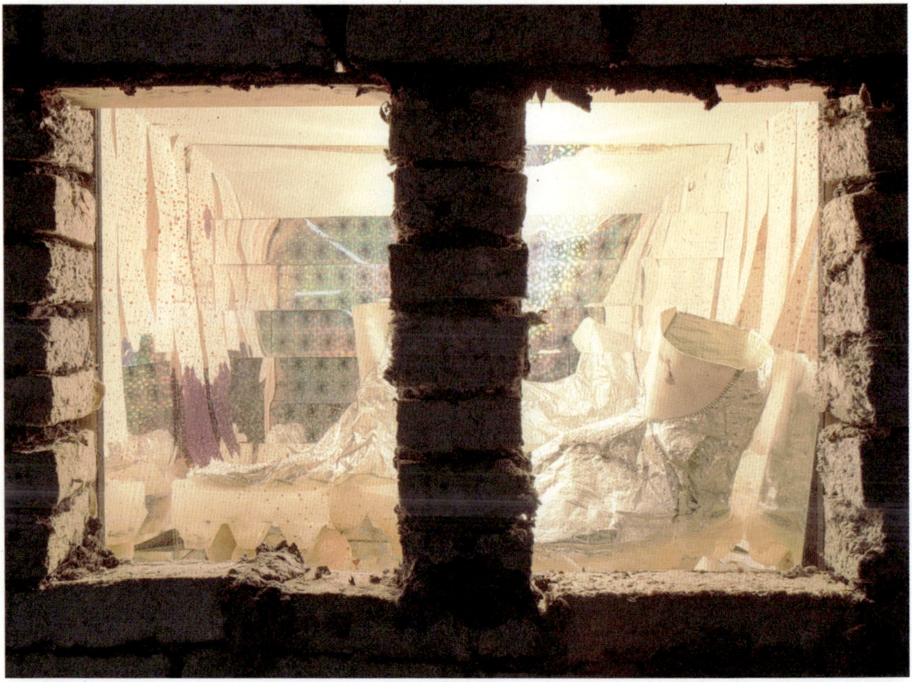

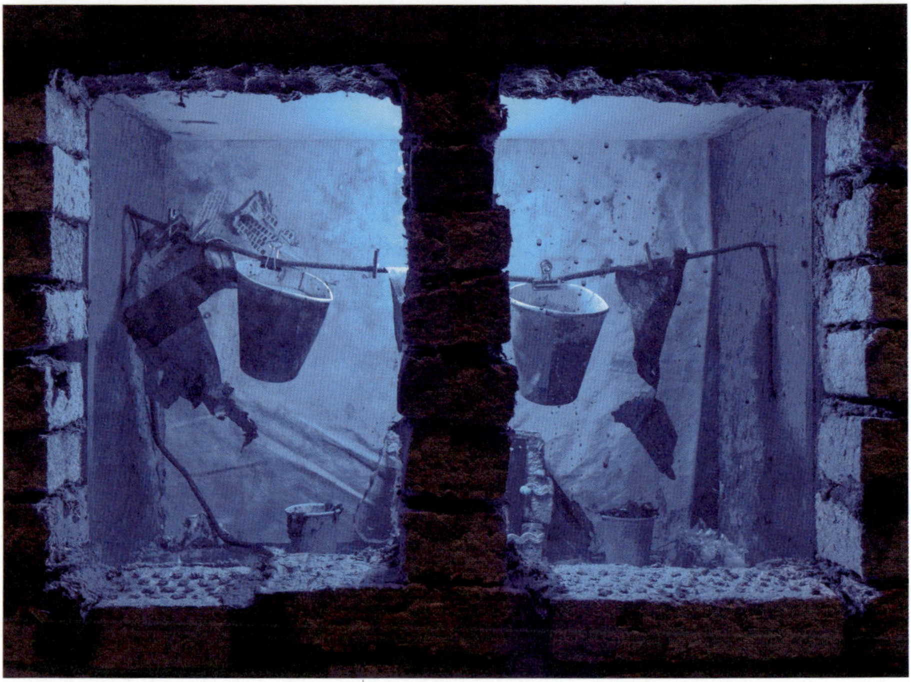

The Night Times Press Bar (details), 2015–16

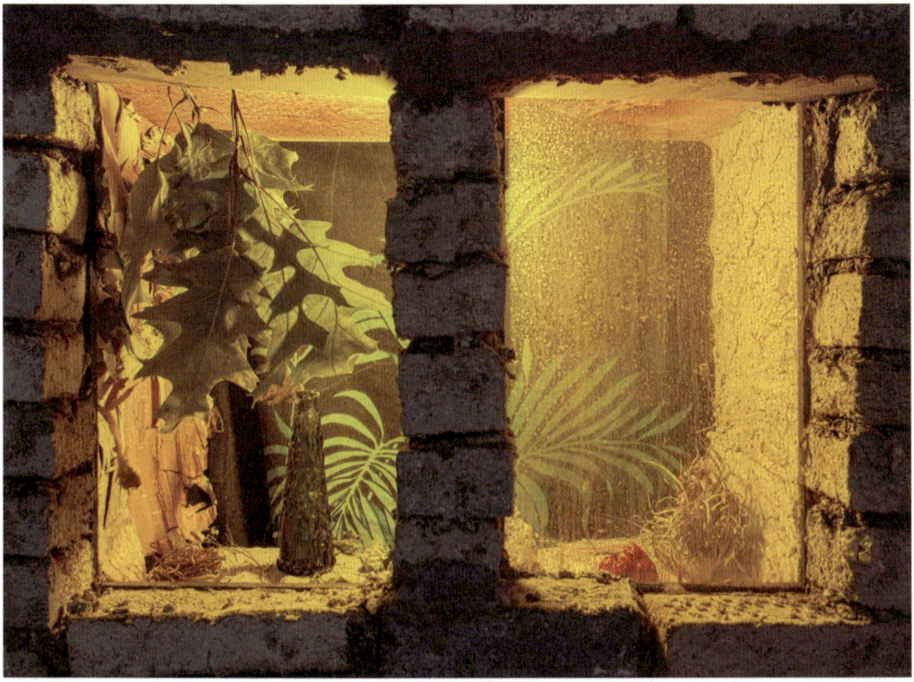

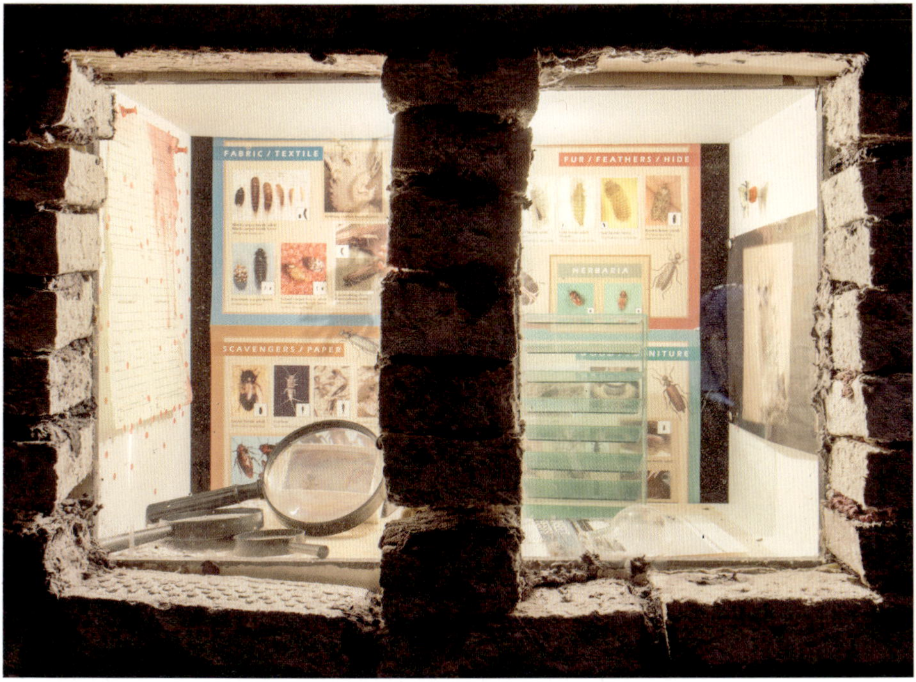

Installation views, Morris and Helen Belkin Art Gallery, 2016

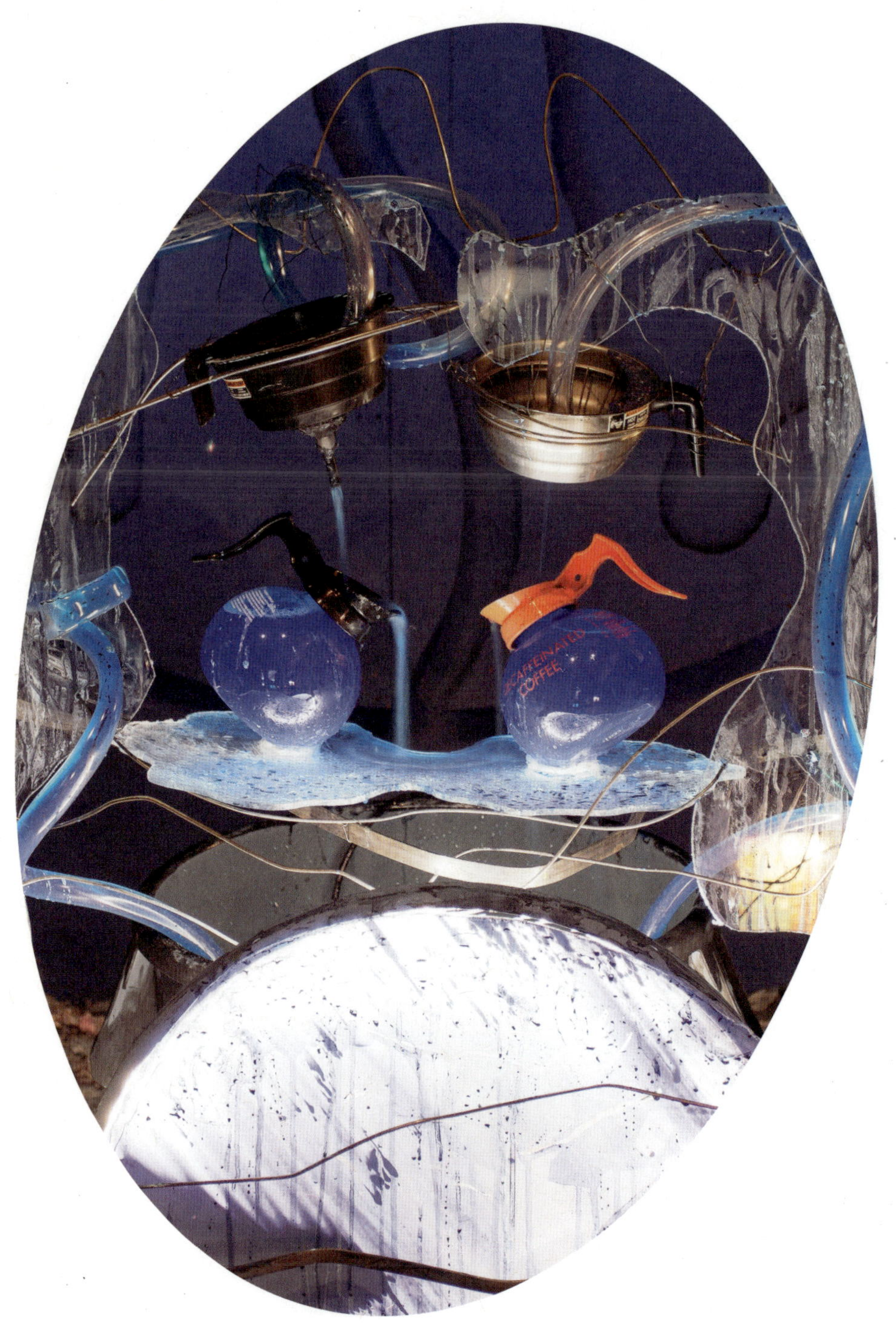

WAVES, 2016; installation views, Morris and Helen Belkin Art Gallery, 2016

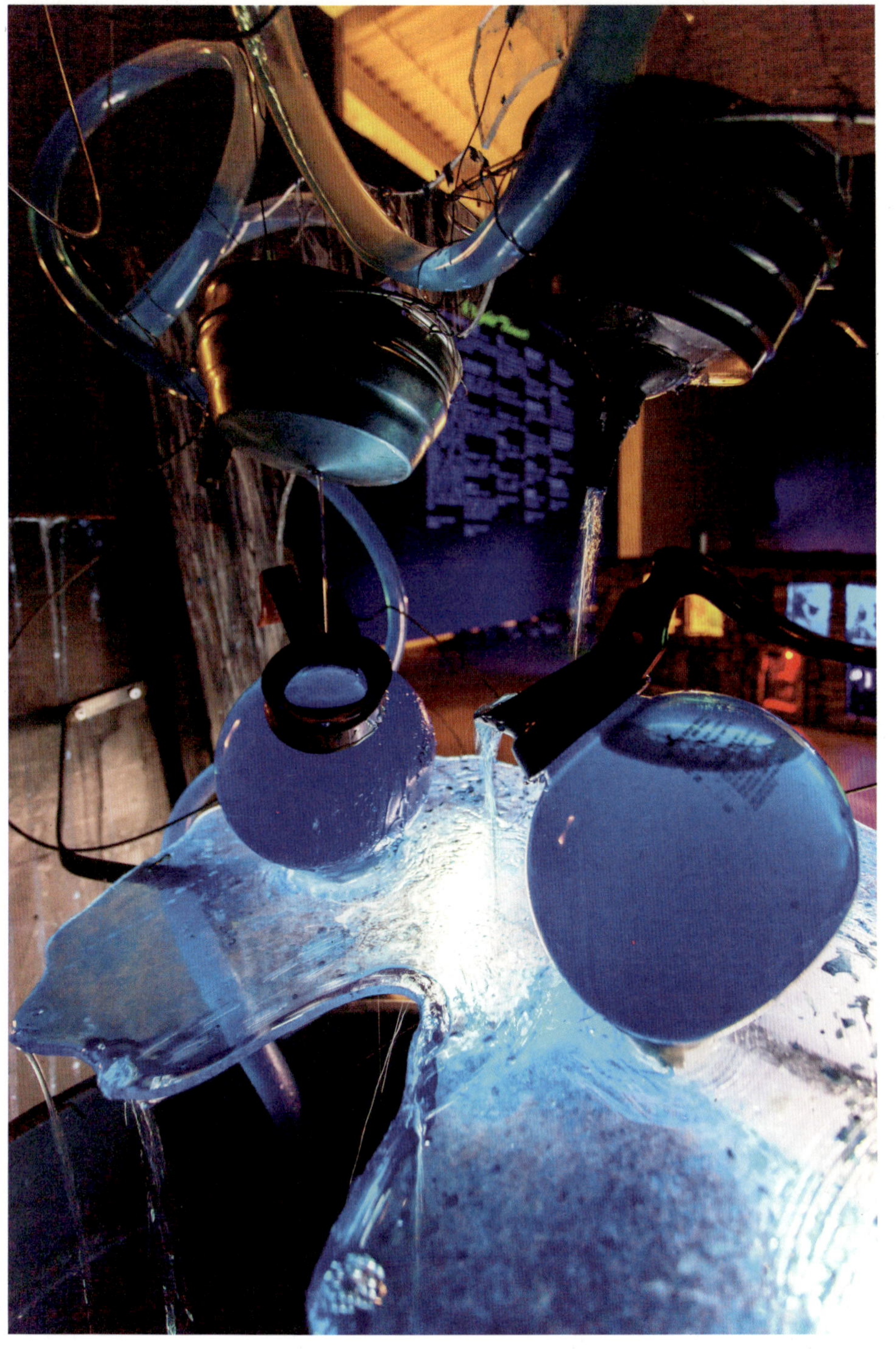

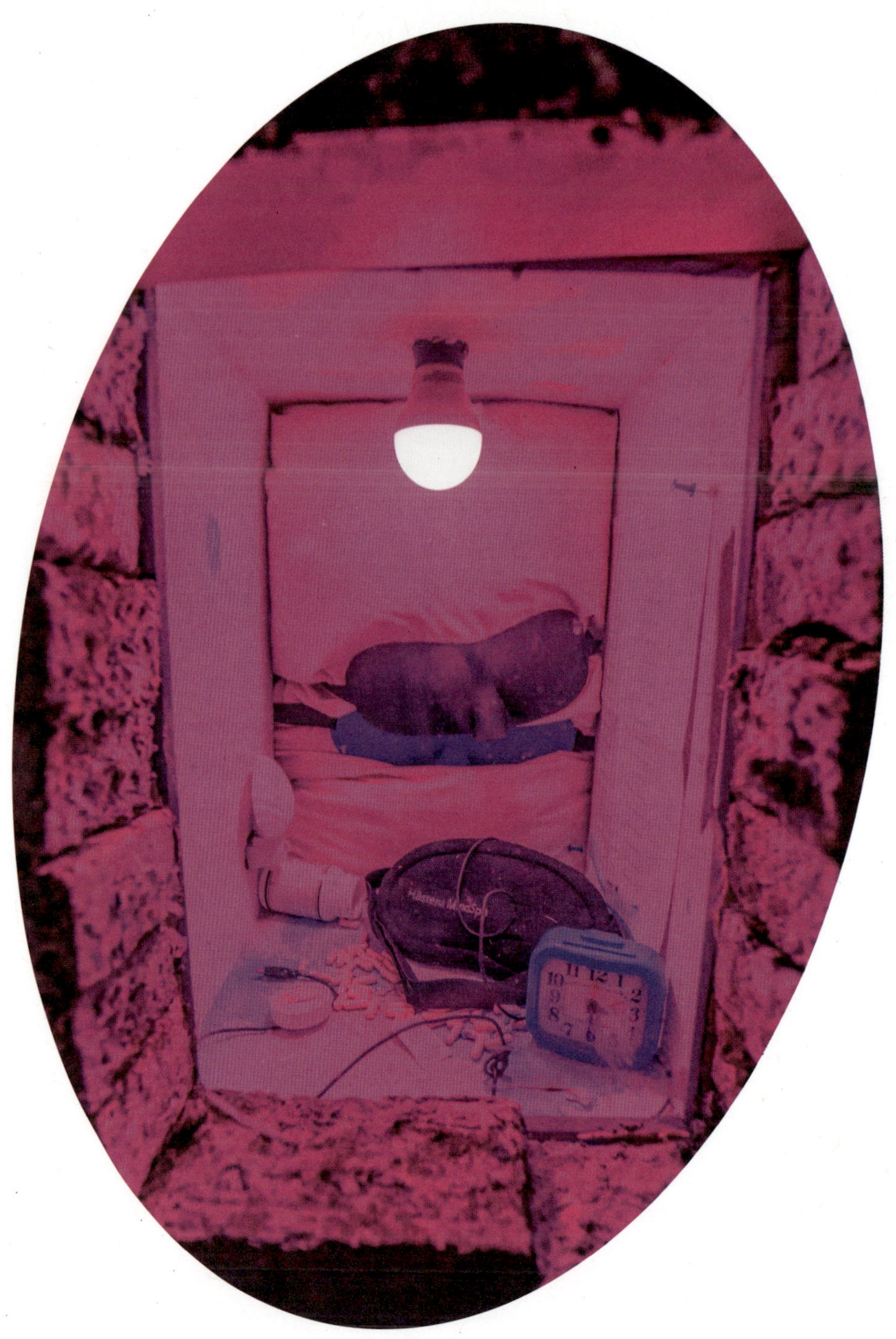

The Night Times Press Bar (details), 2015–16

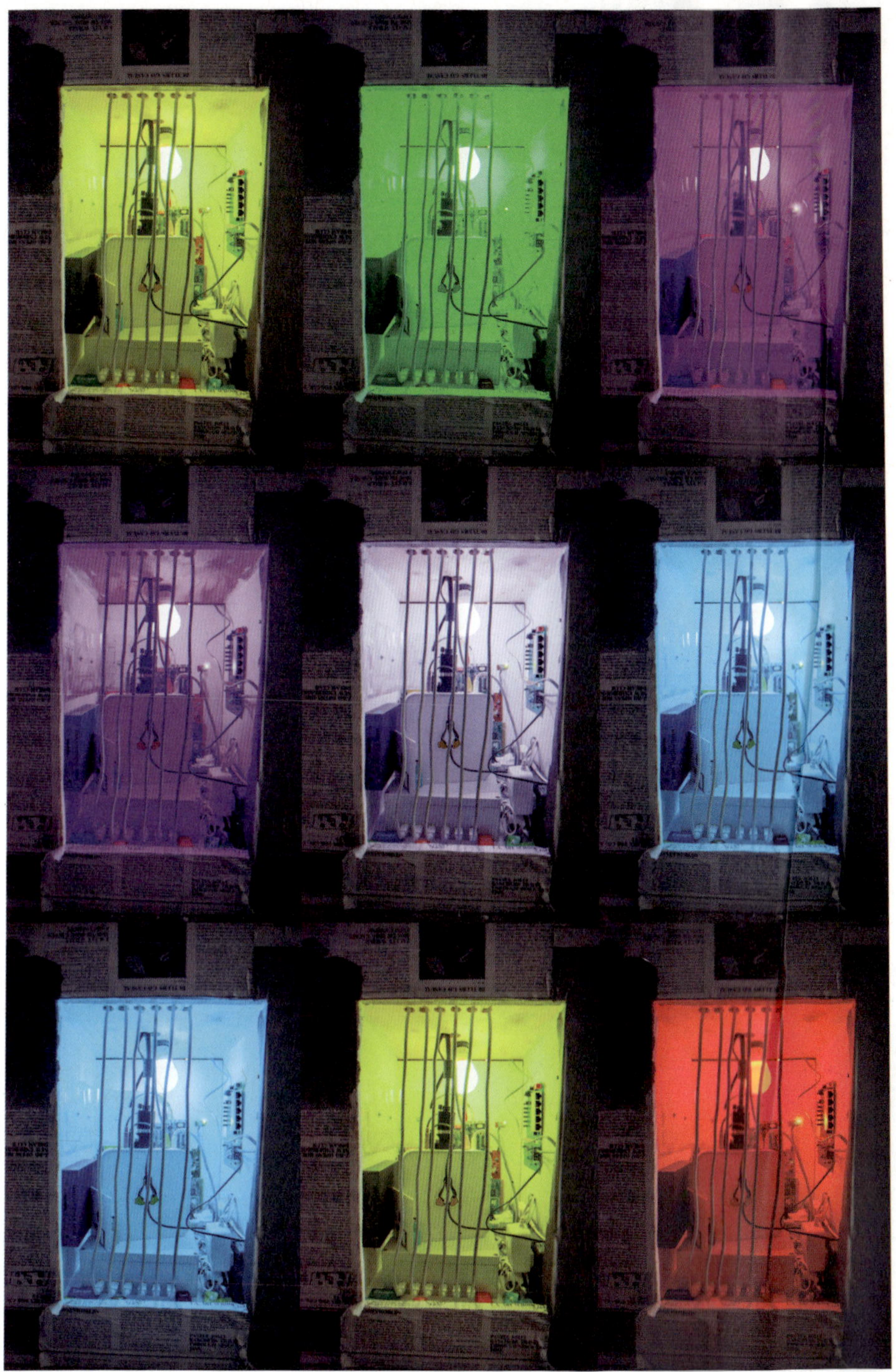

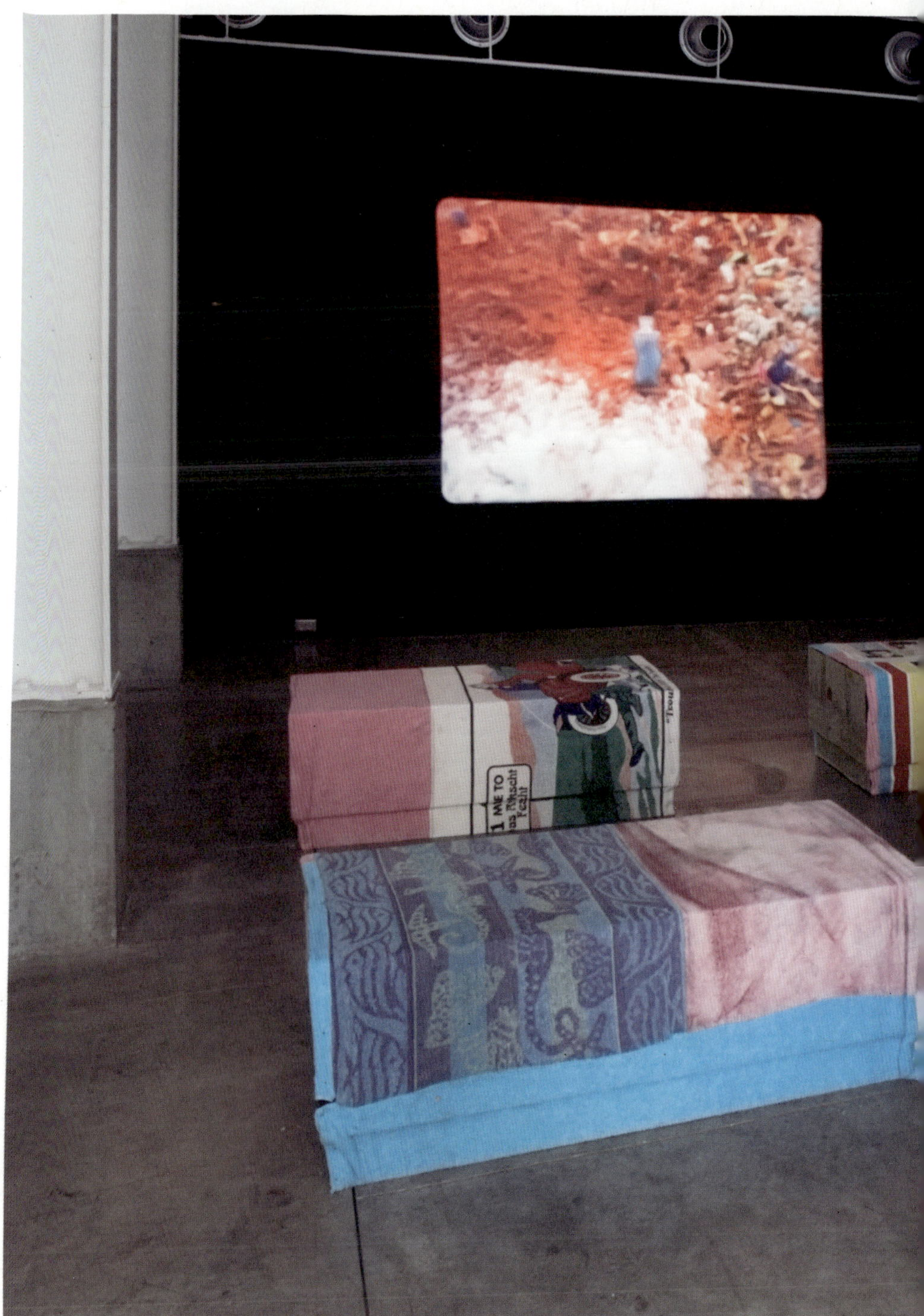

Installation view, Morris and Helen Belkin Art Gallery, 2016

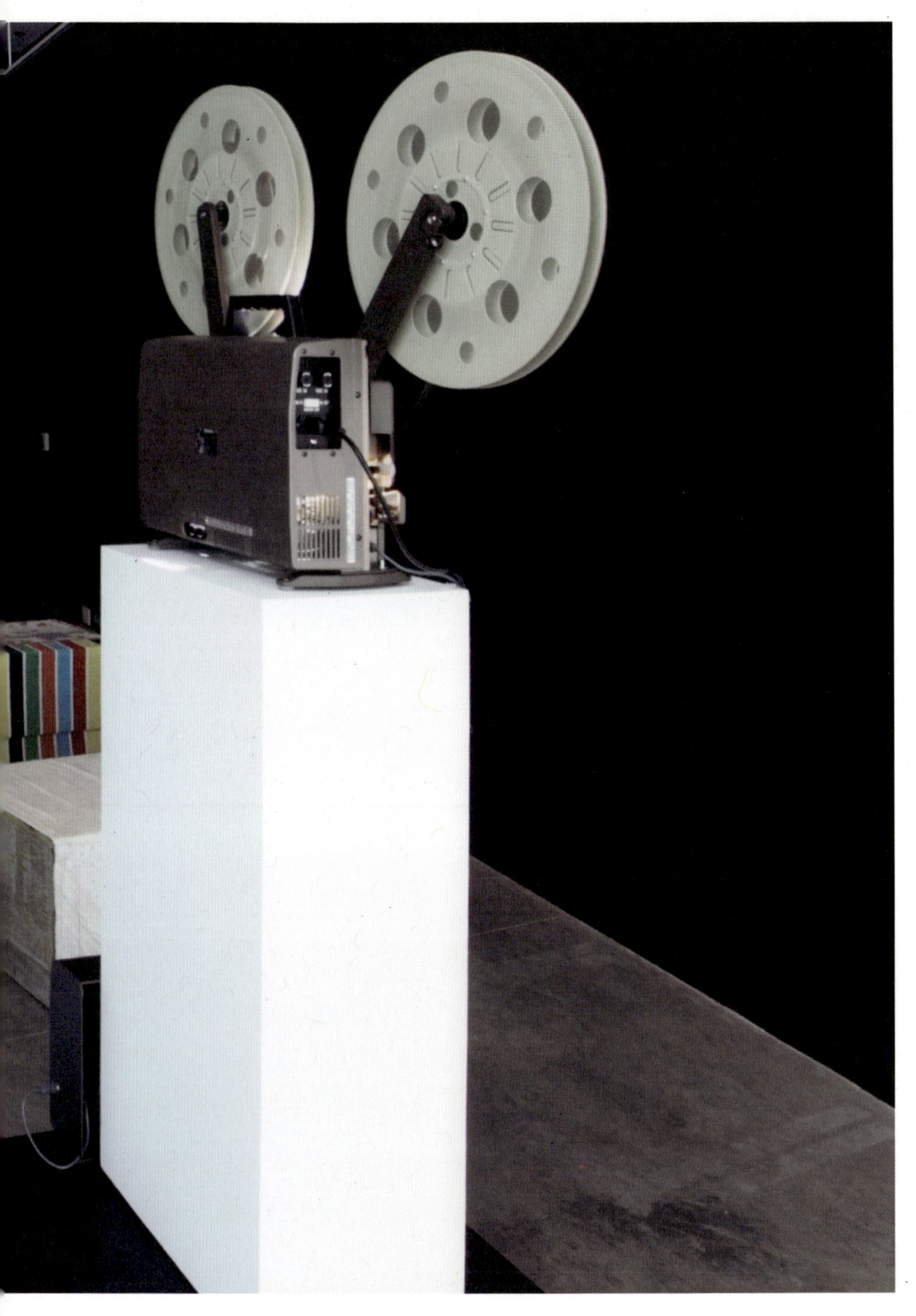

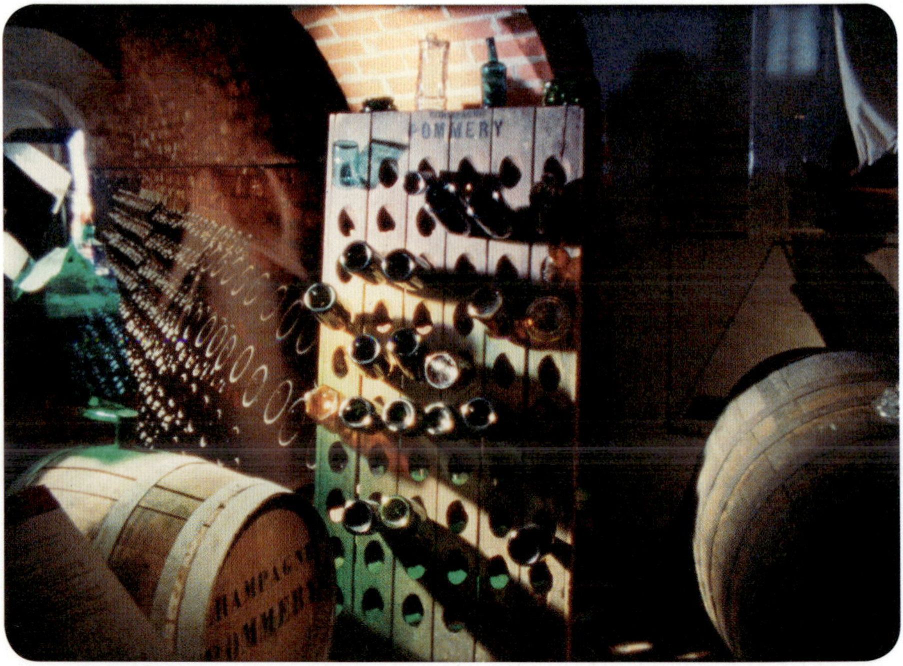

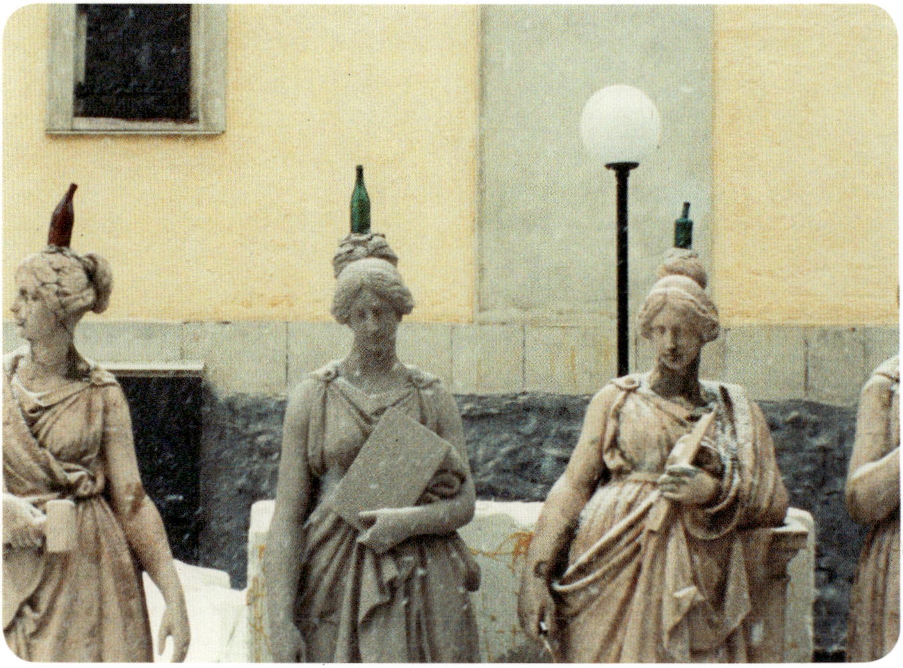

Bottles Under the Influence (film stills), 2012

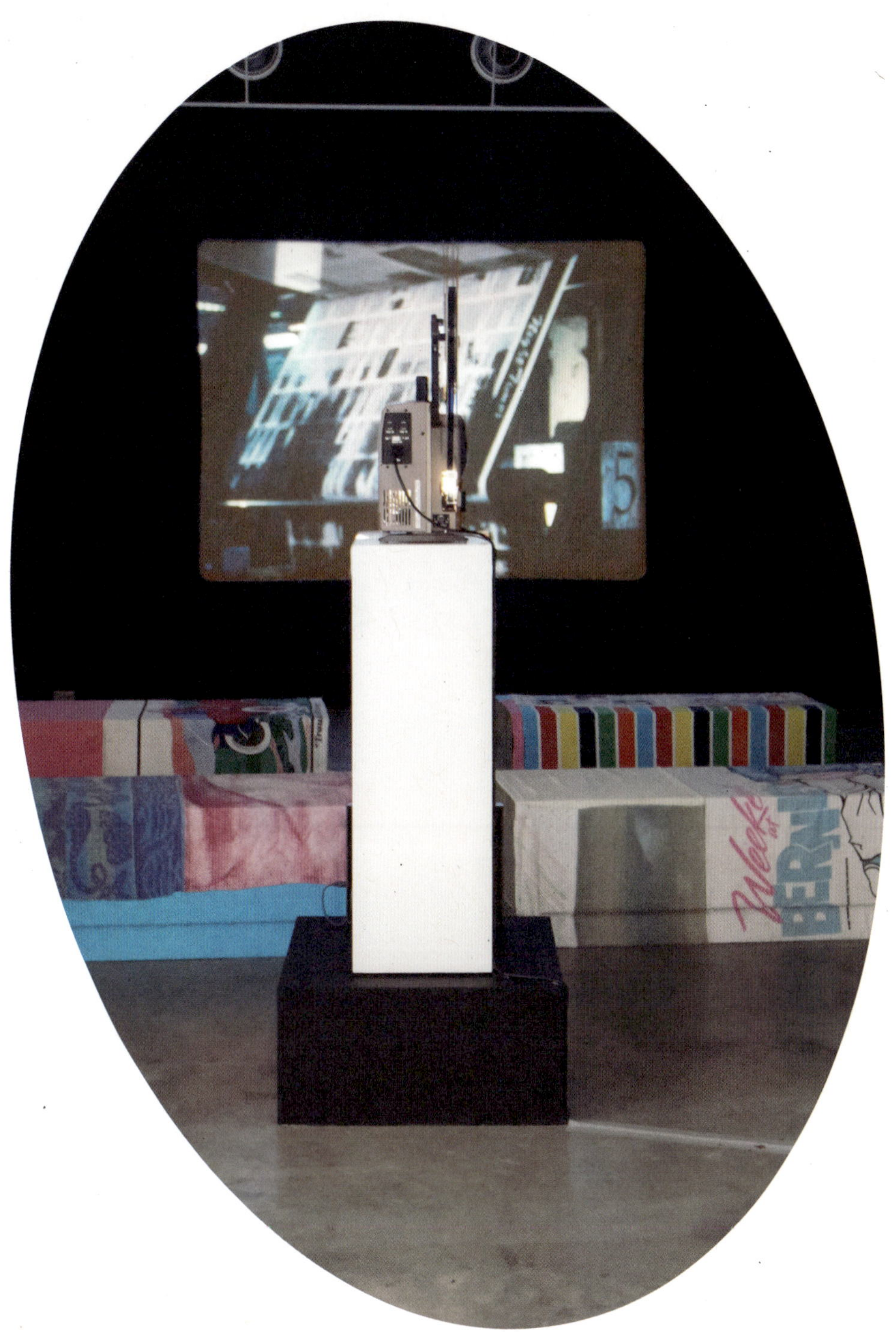

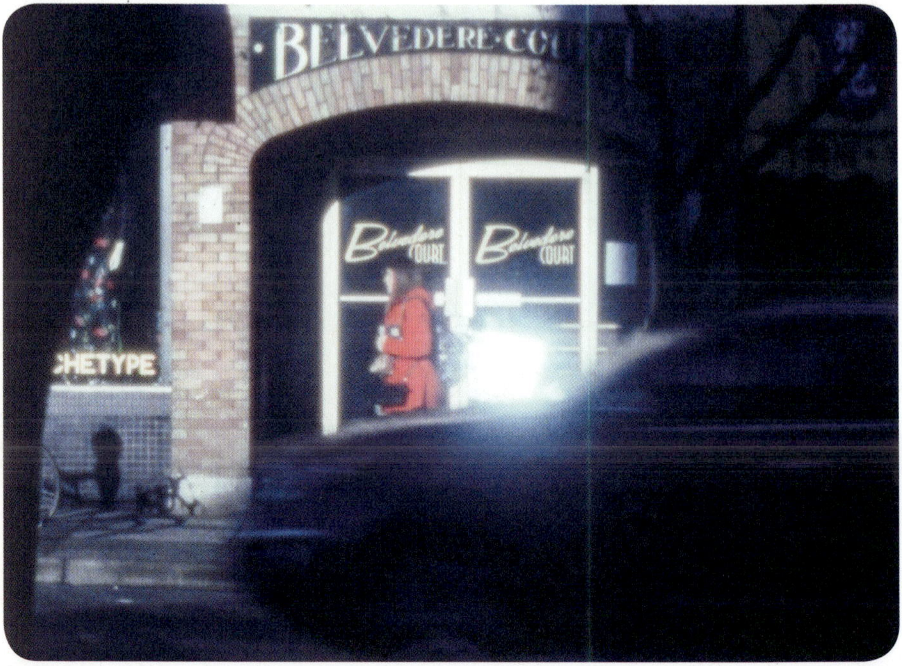

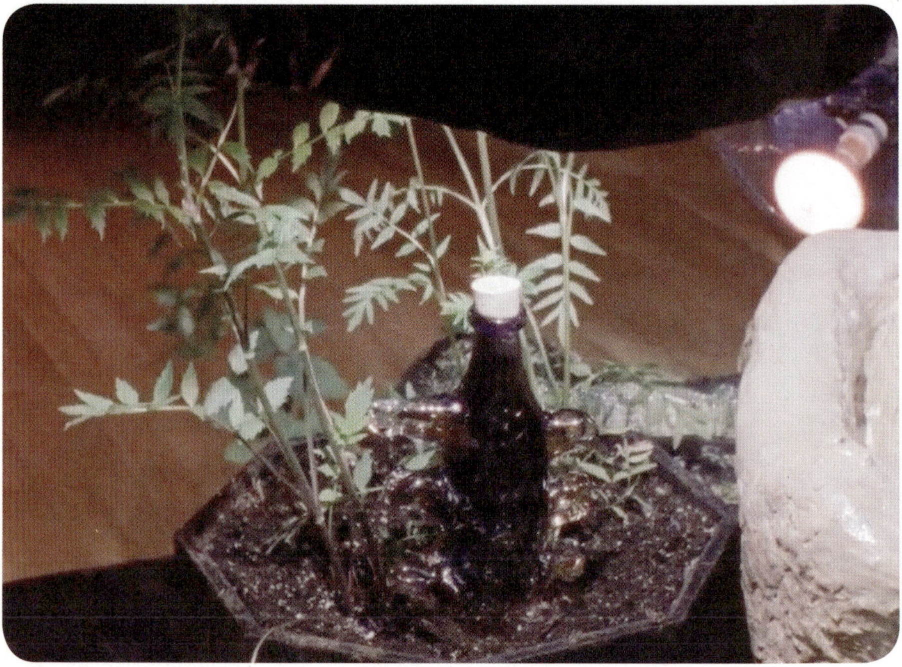

Consider the Belvedere (film stills), 2015

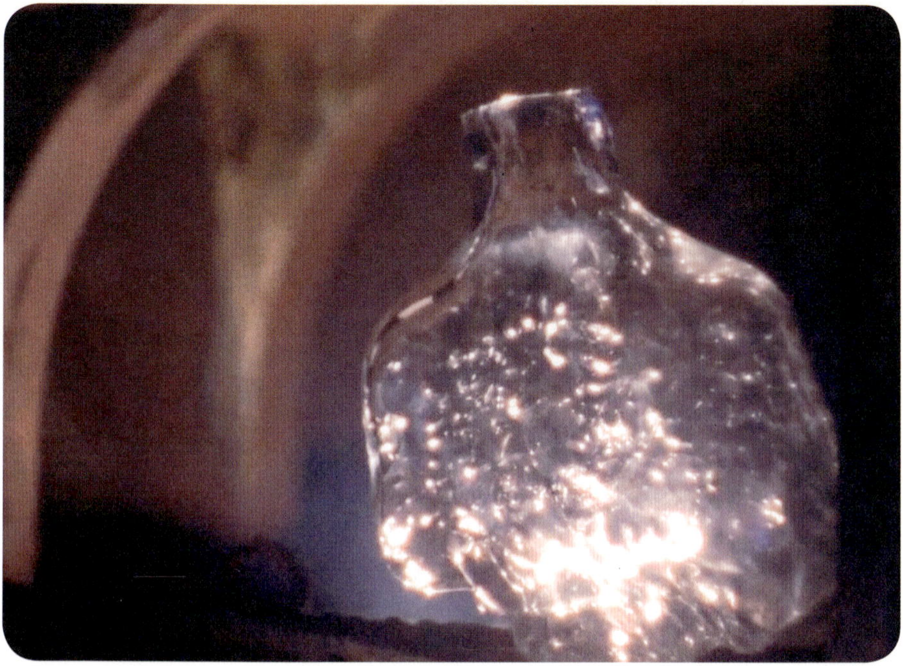

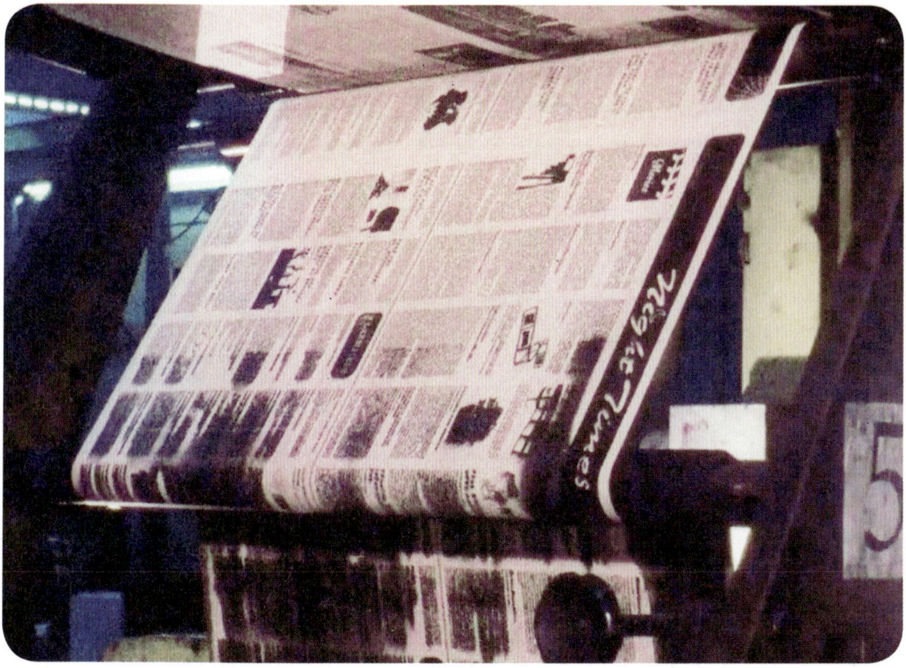

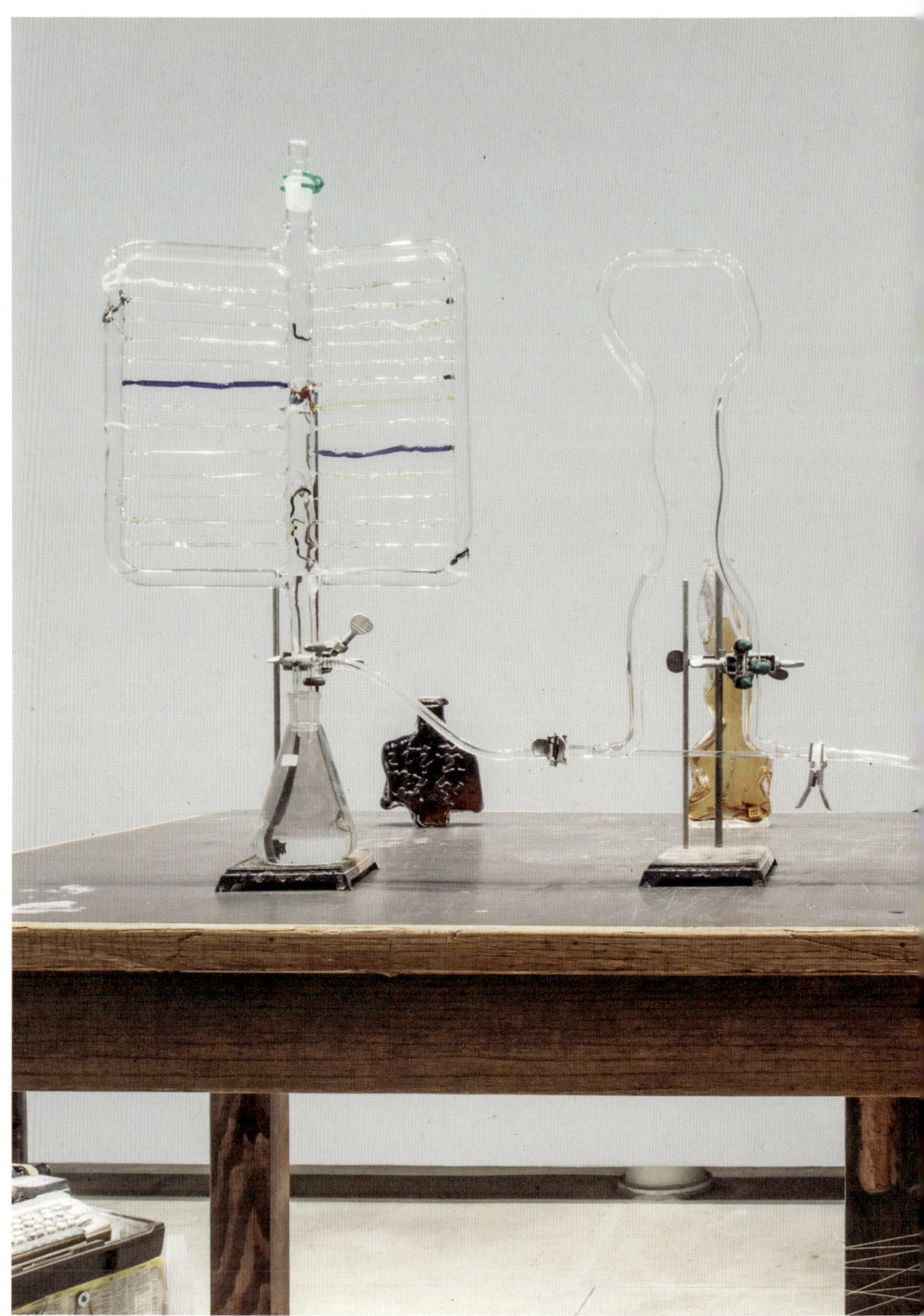

Communicating Vessels: Galactic Glass Healer, 2016

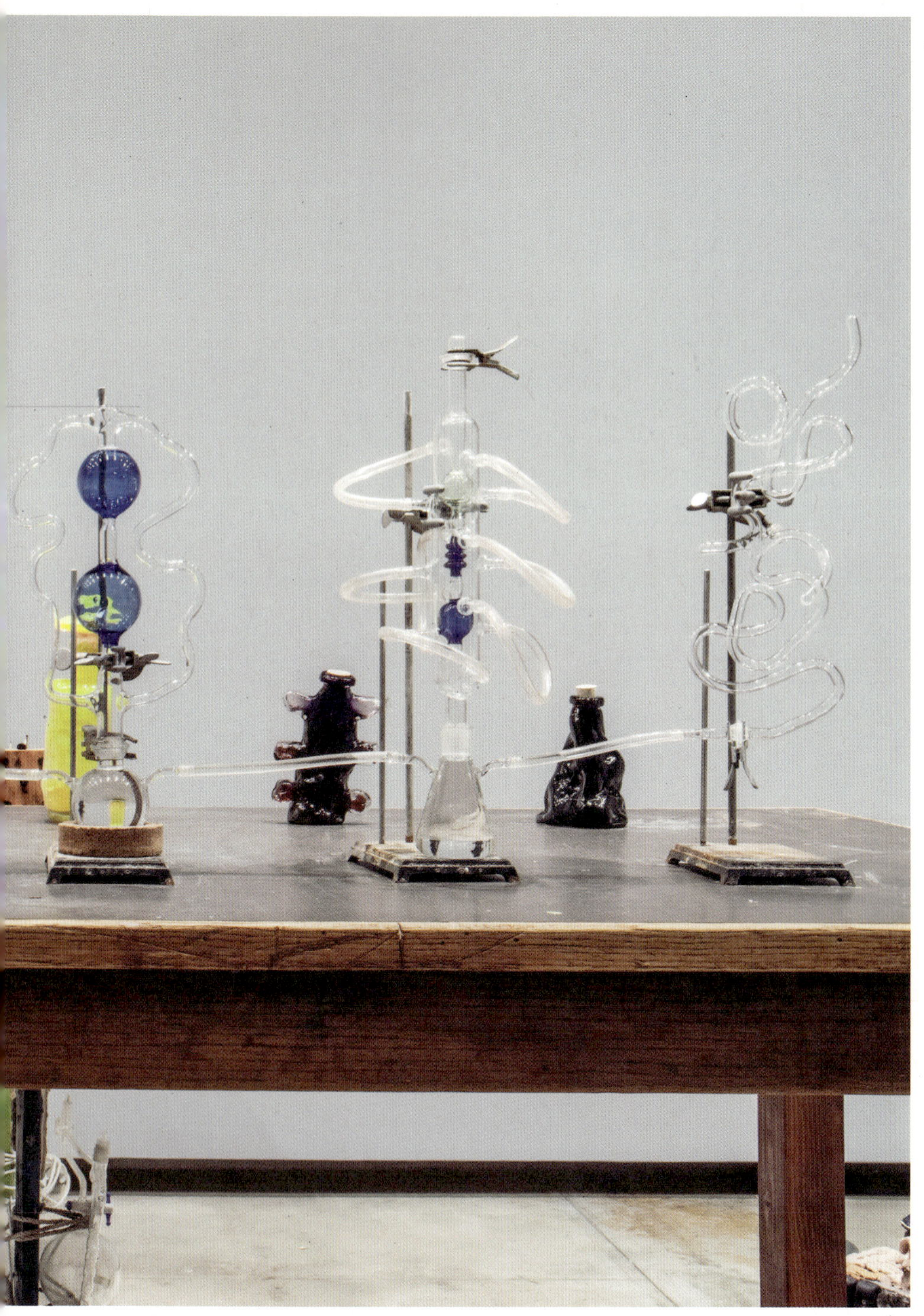

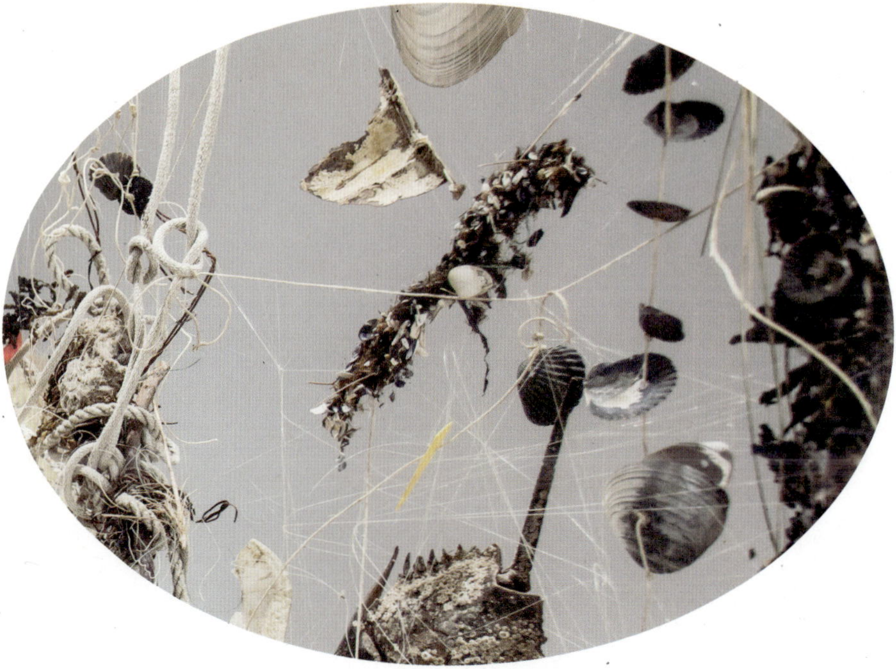

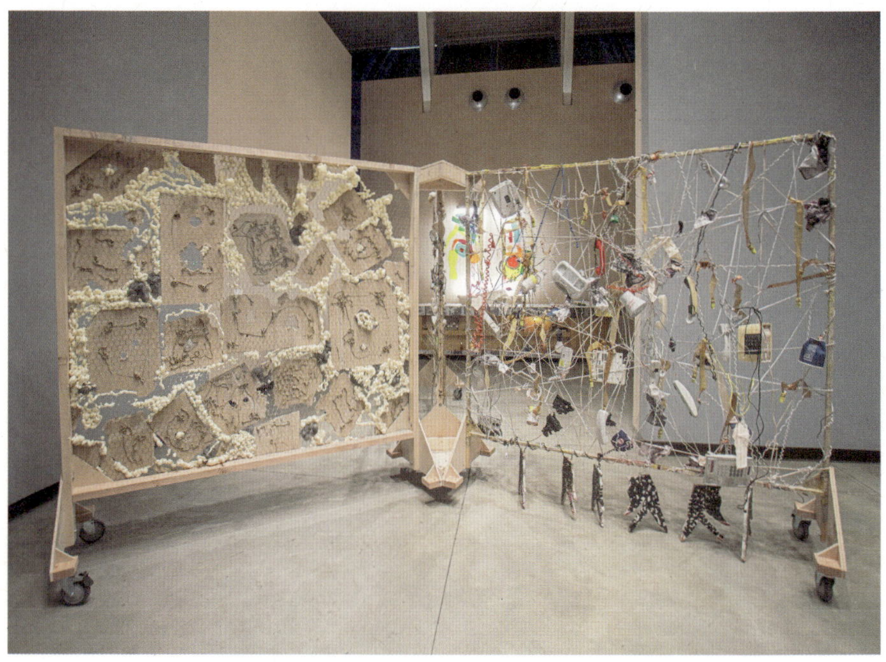

Beachcomber's Cucoloris (detail), *Exclusion* and *Secretary Cucoloris*, 2015–16
Installation view, Morris and Helen Belkin Art Gallery, 2016

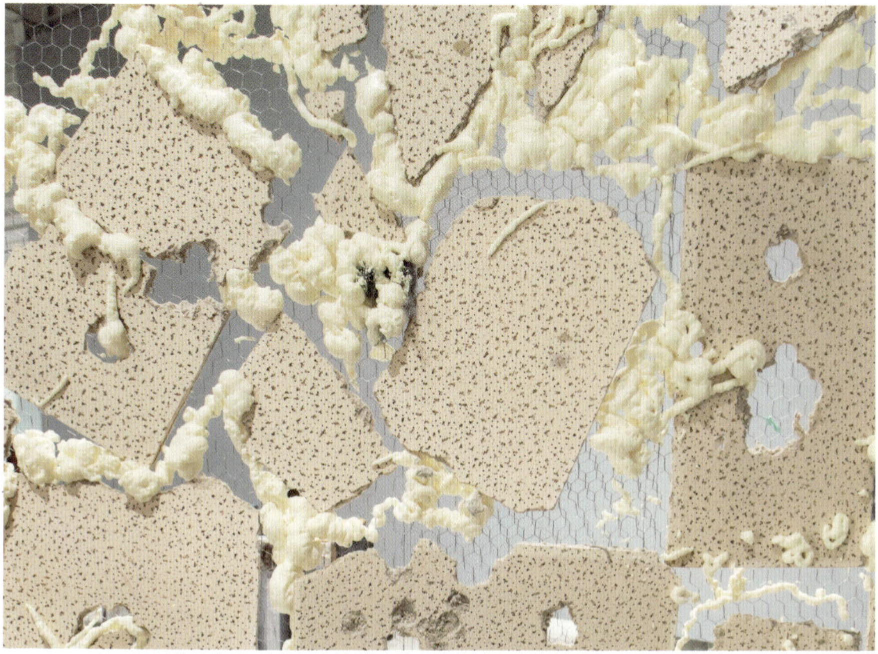

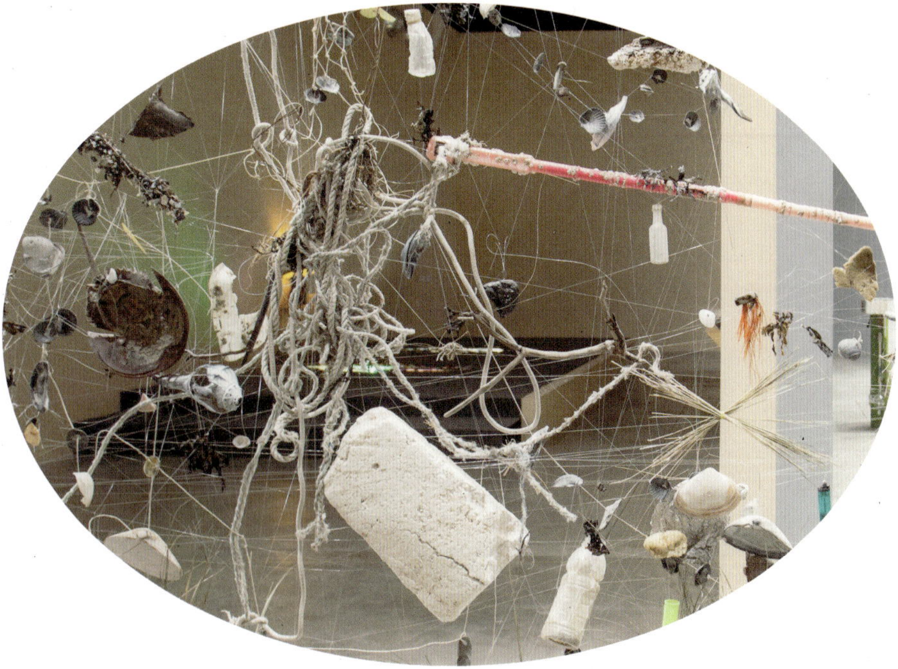

 Exclusion Cucoloris (detail), *Beachcomber's Cucoloris* (detail), 2015–16
Installation view, Morris and Helen Belkin Art Gallery, 2016

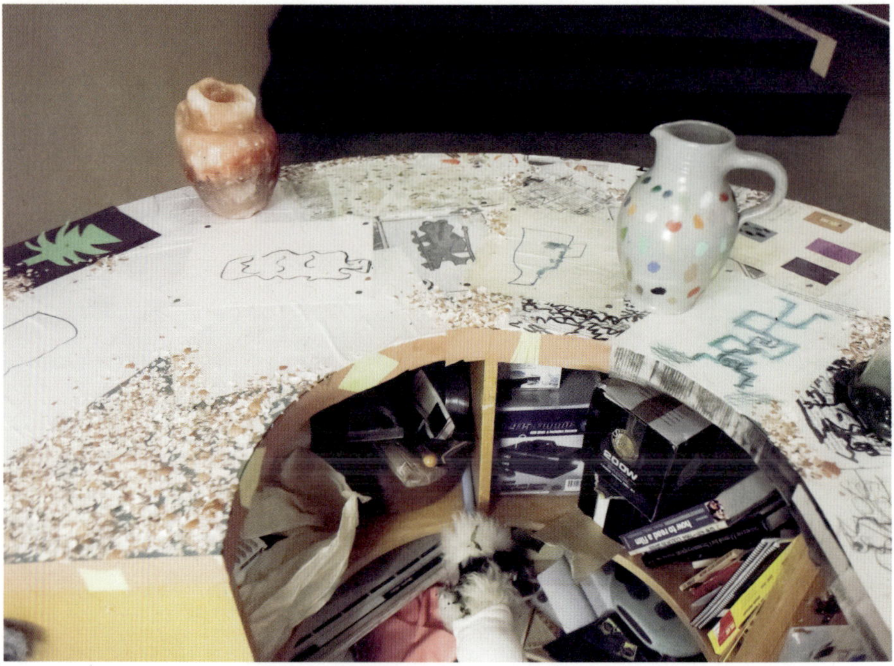

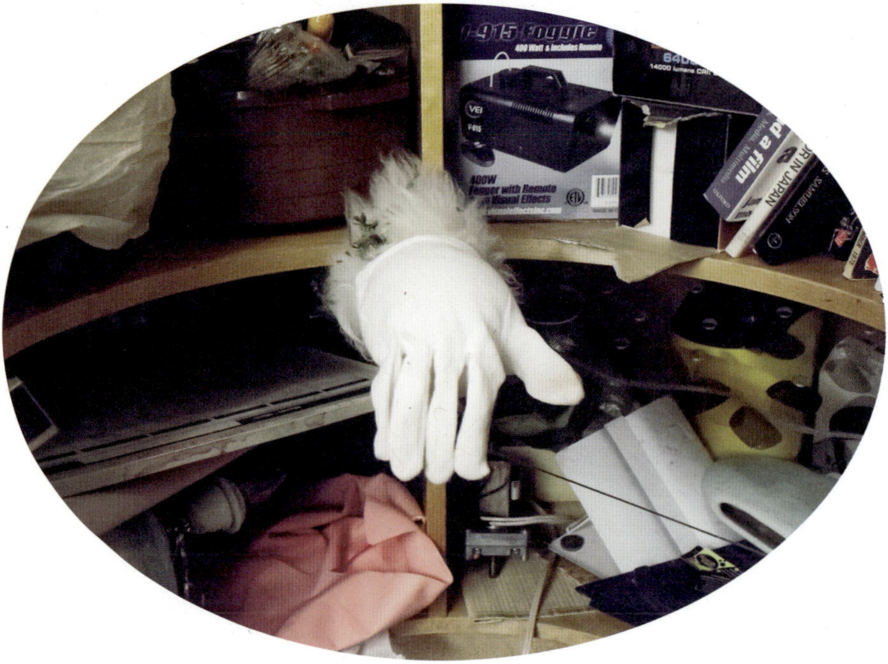

Hotel Reception Desk (details), 2016
Installation view, Morris and Helen Belkin Art Gallery, 2016

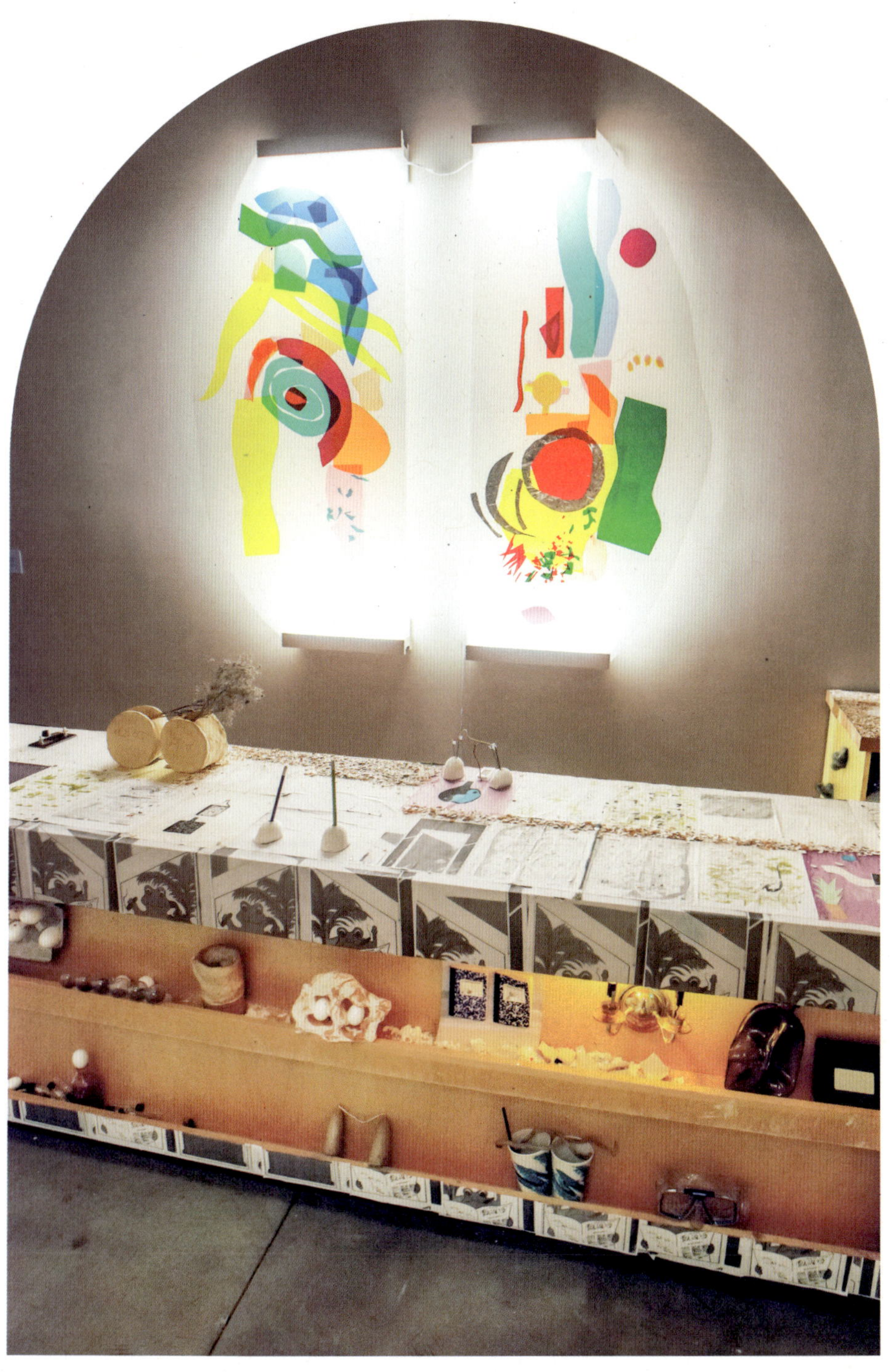

Receptionists, 2015–16 and *Hotel Reception Desk*, 2016
Installation view, Morris and Helen Belkin Art Gallery, 2016

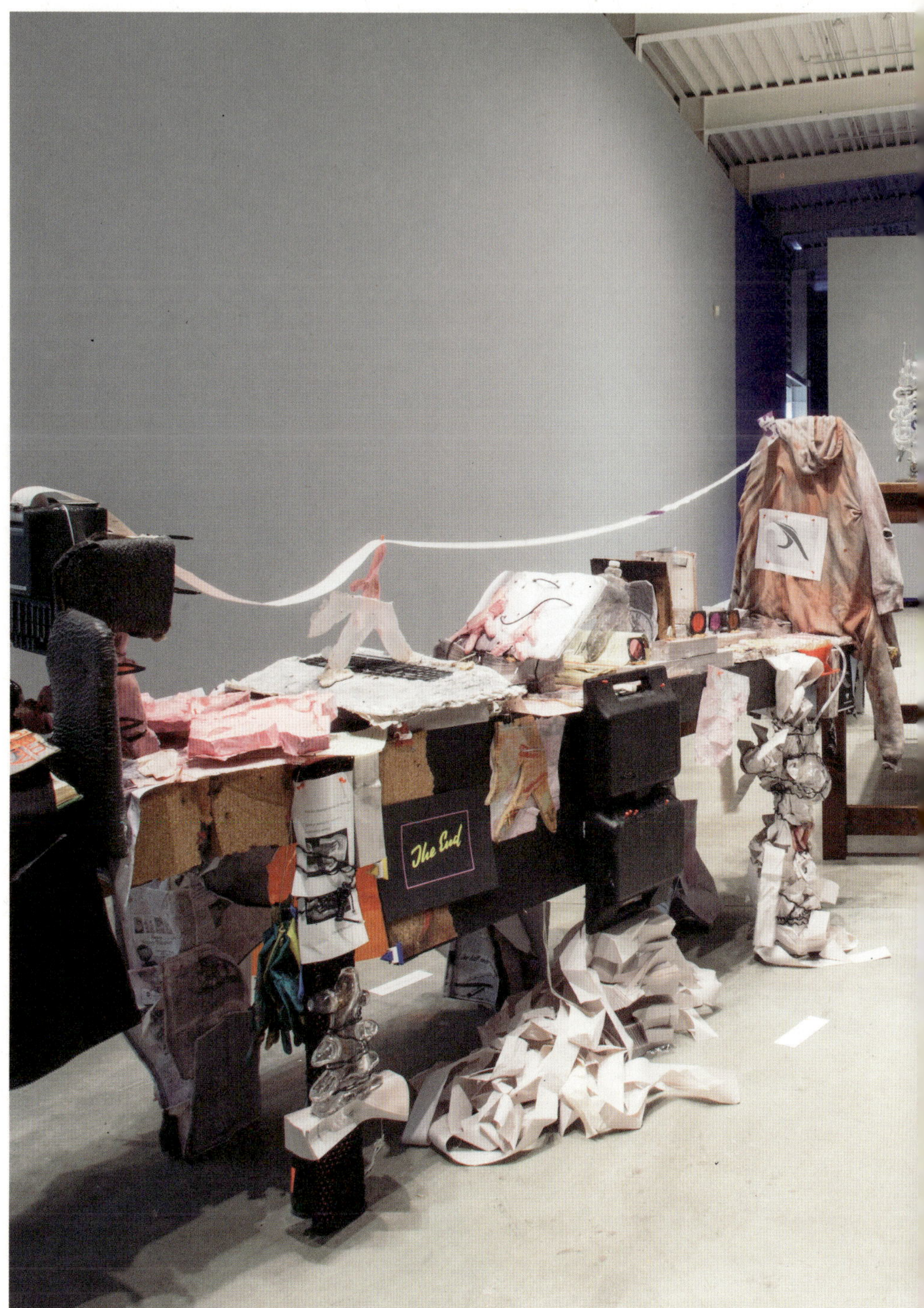

Installation view, Morris and Helen Belkin Art Gallery, 2016

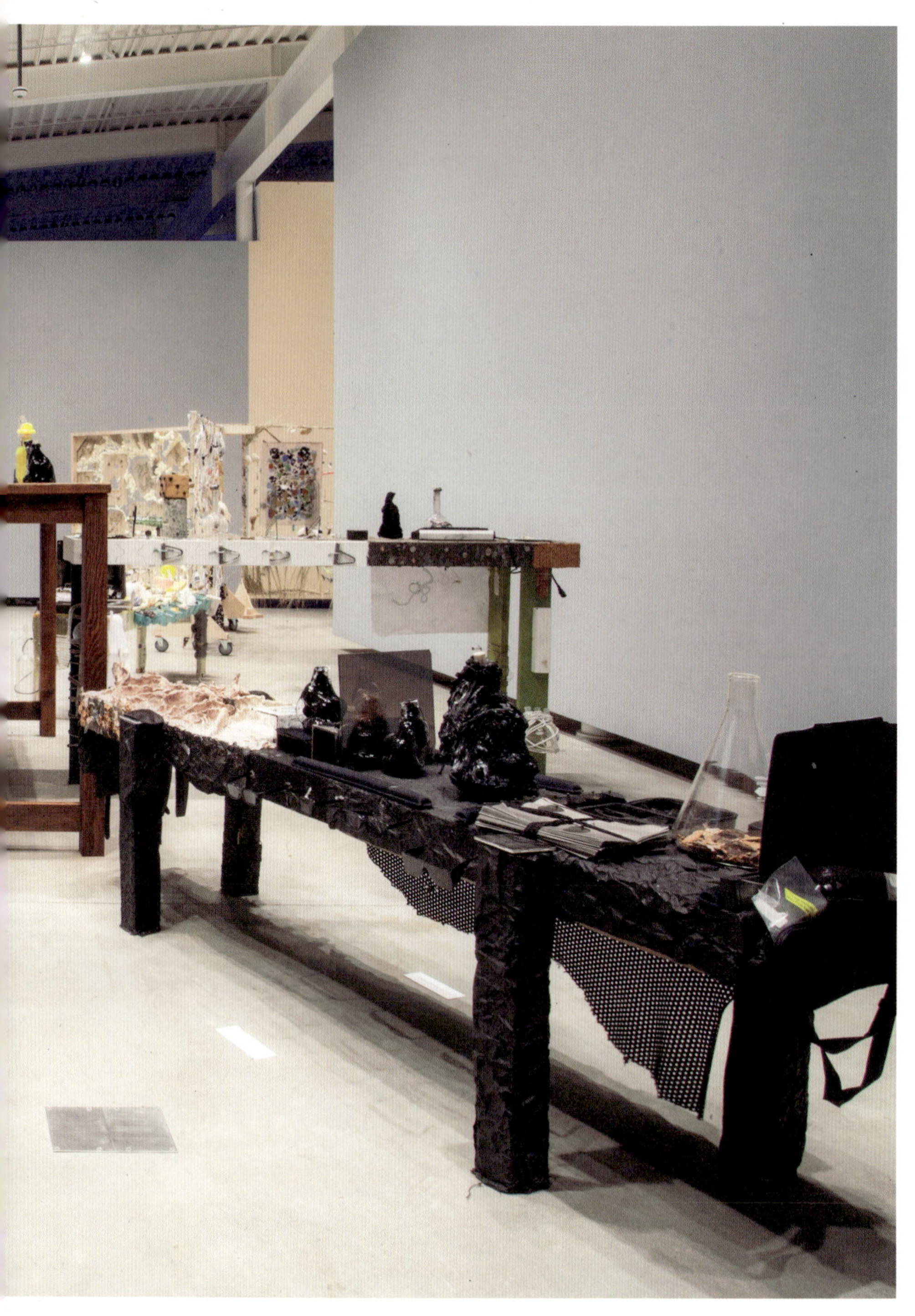

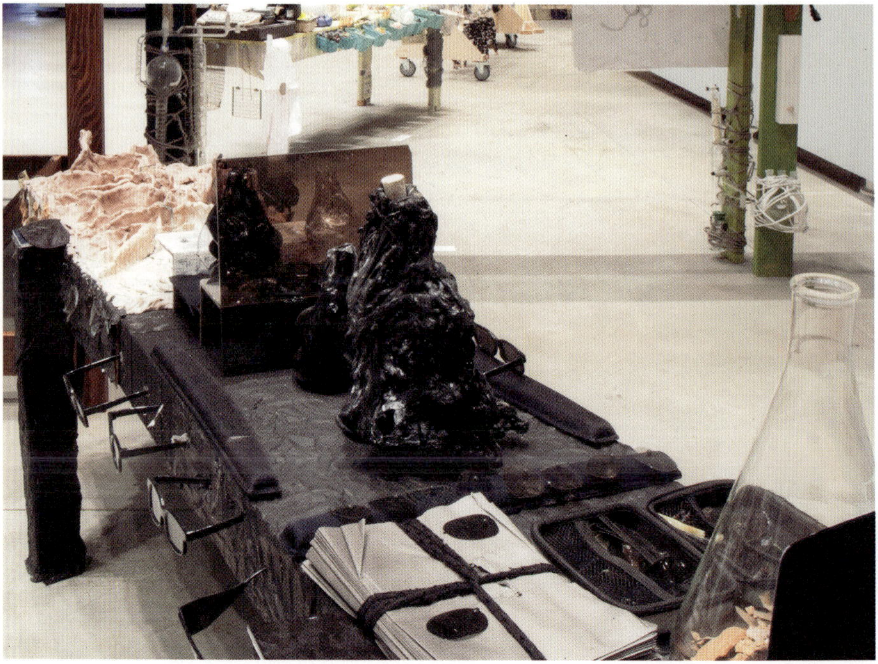

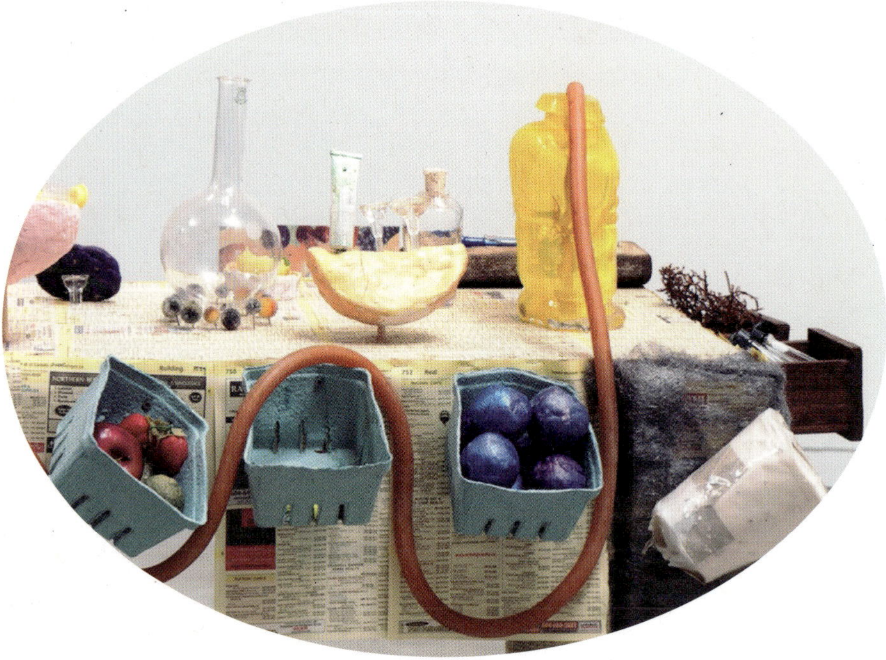

Blind Table (detail), *Pest Detective Table* (detail), 2015–16
Installation view, Morris and Helen Belkin Art Gallery, 2016

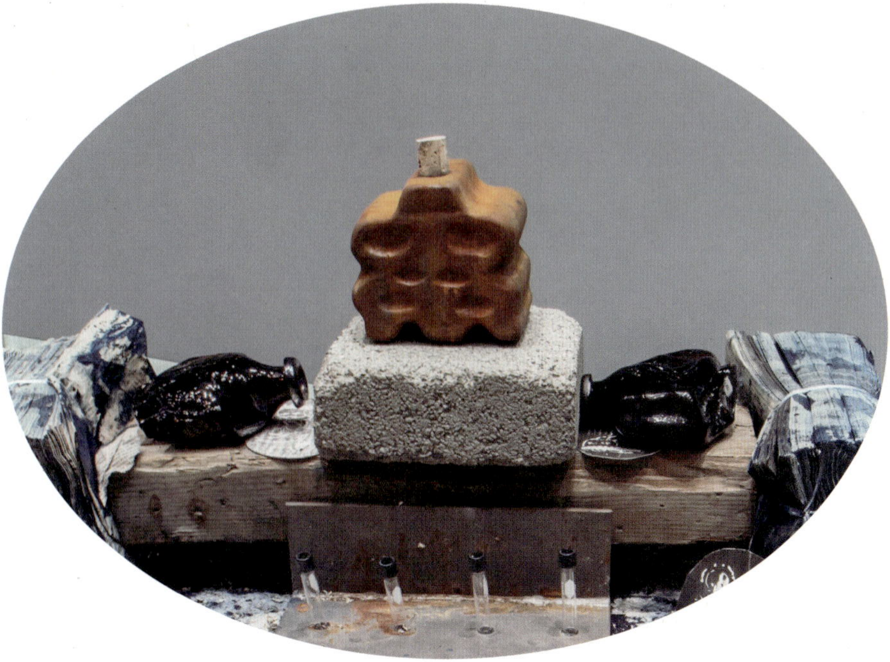

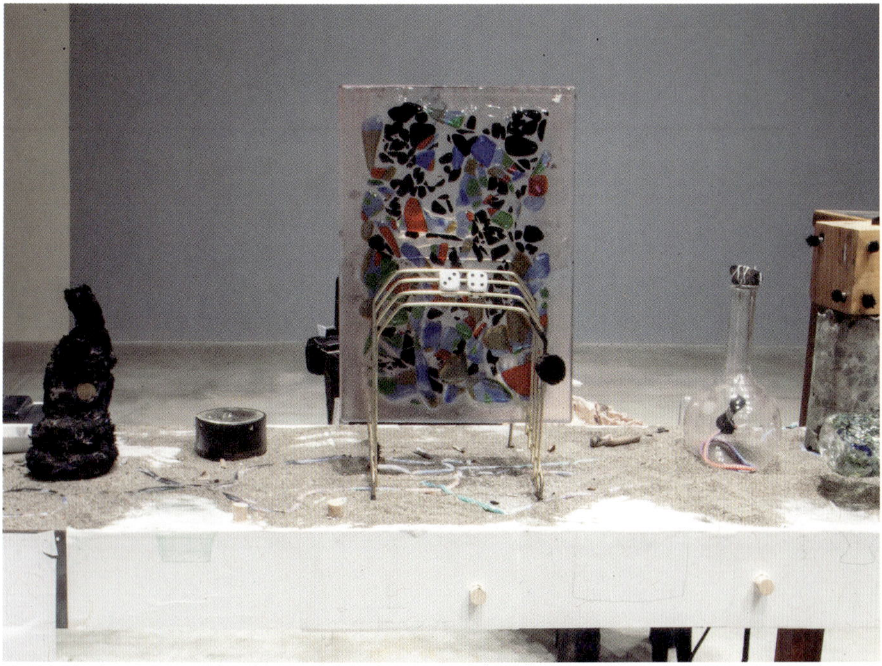

Newspaper/Boiler Room Table (detail), *Chance Table* (detail), 2015–16
Installation view, Morris and Helen Belkin Art Gallery, 2016

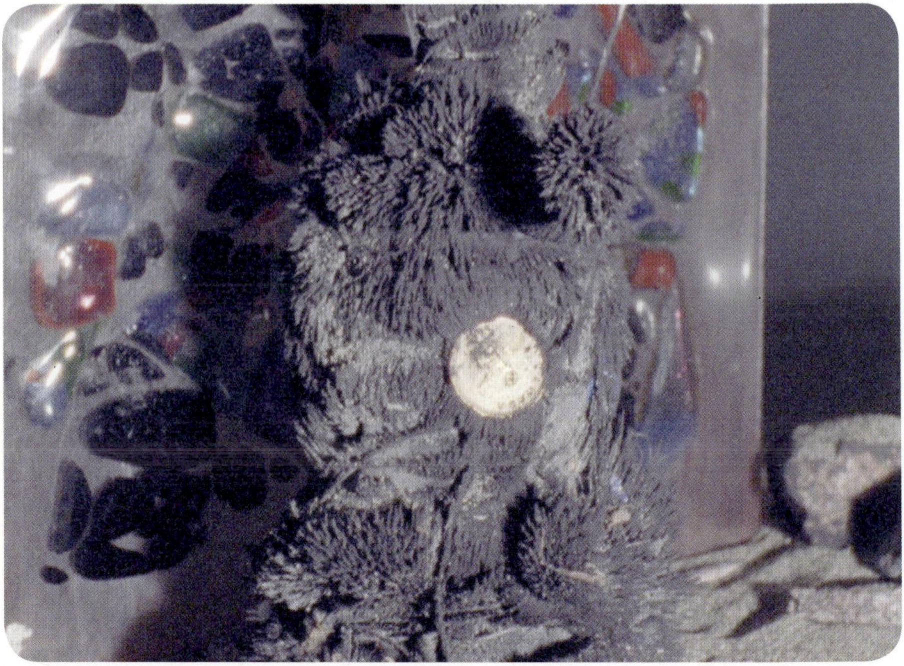

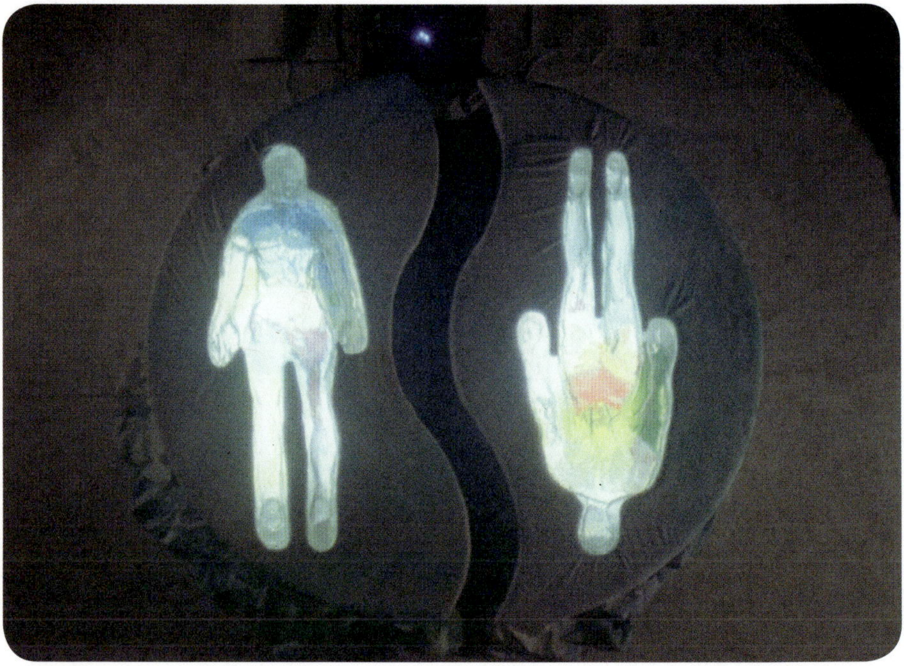

The Last Waves (stills from upcoming film), 2018–present

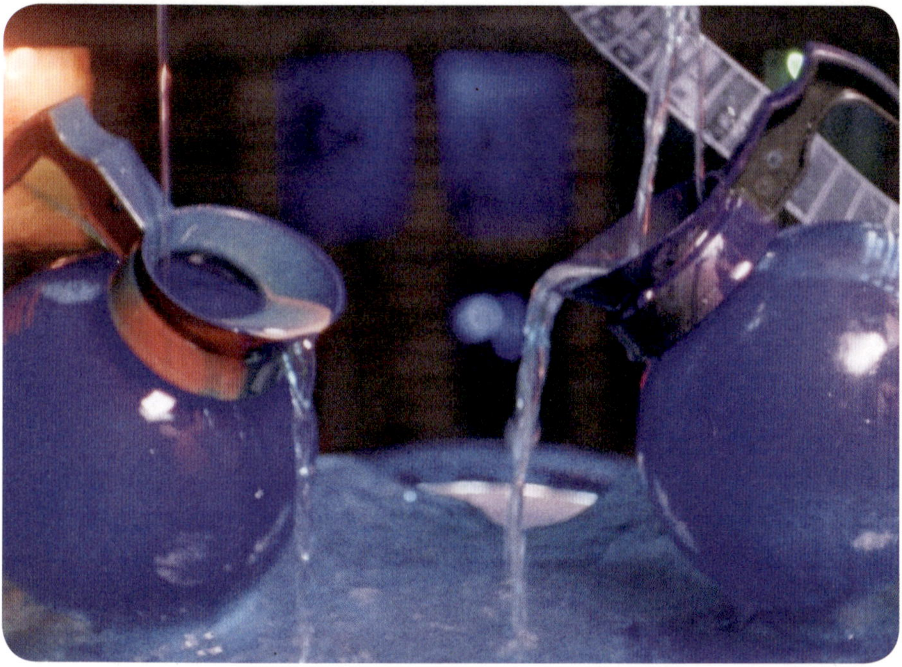

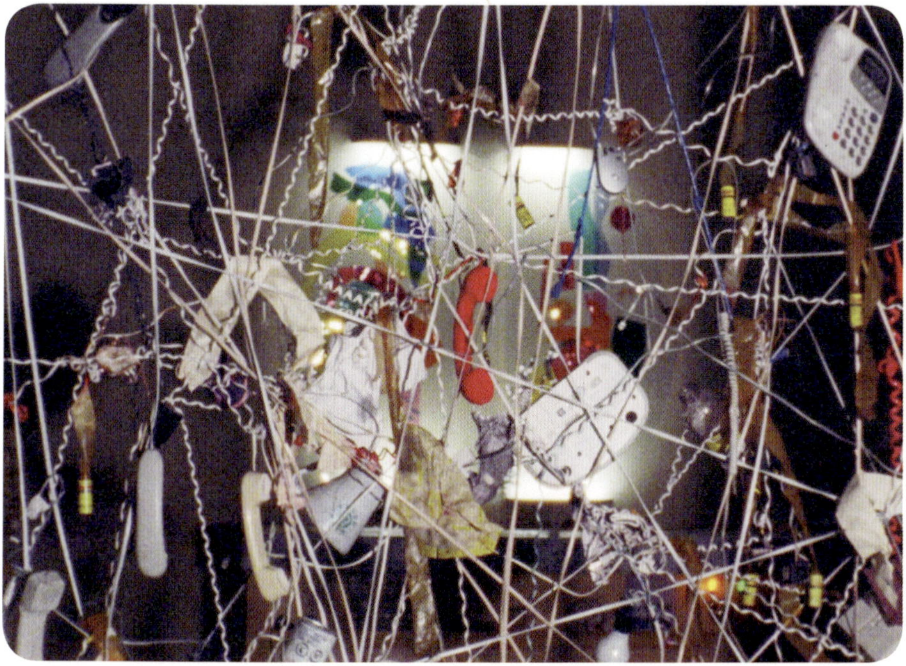

Belkin

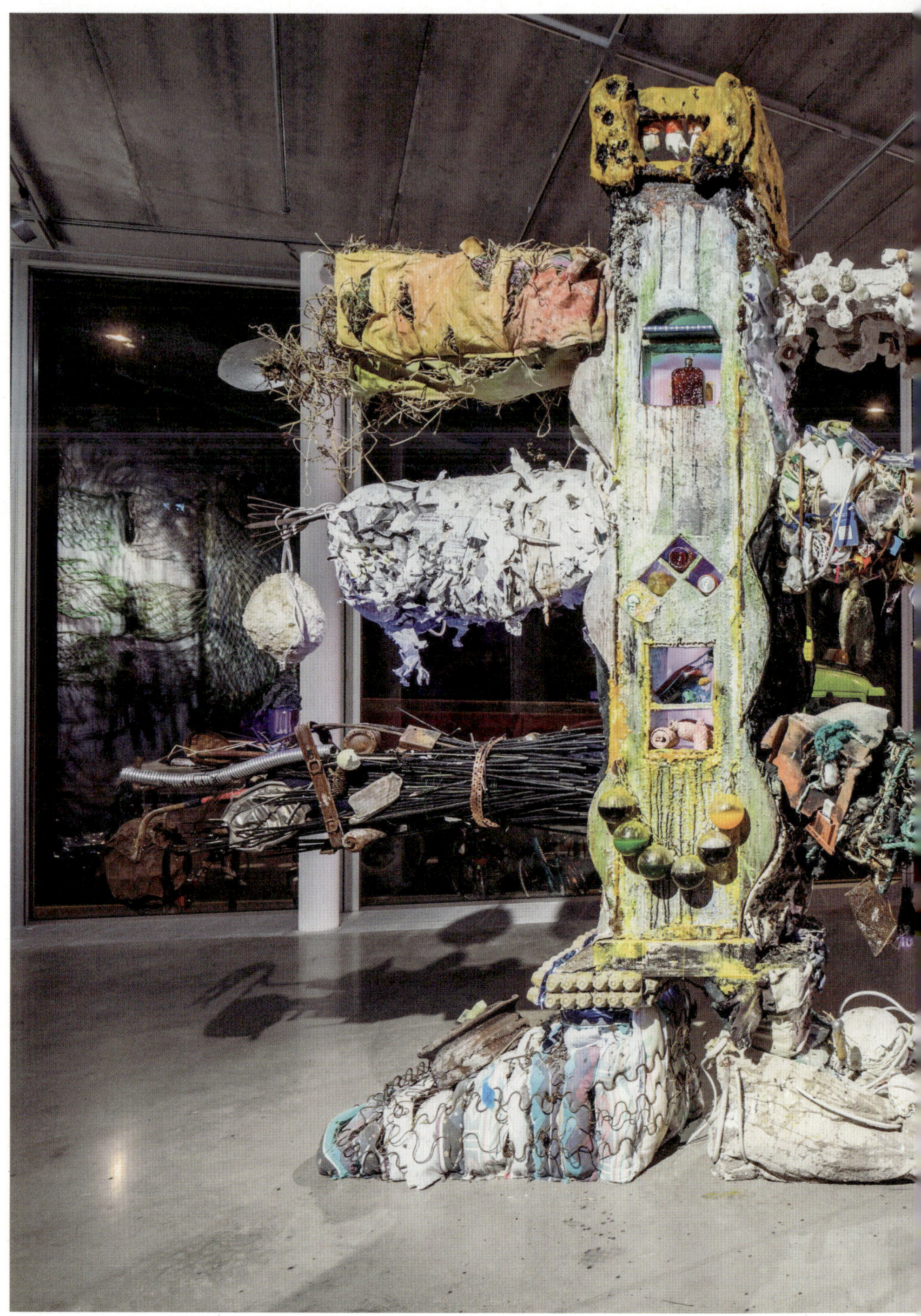

  The Old Hag, 2015–16; installation view, *Insomnia*, Bonniers Konsthall, Stockholm, 2016–17

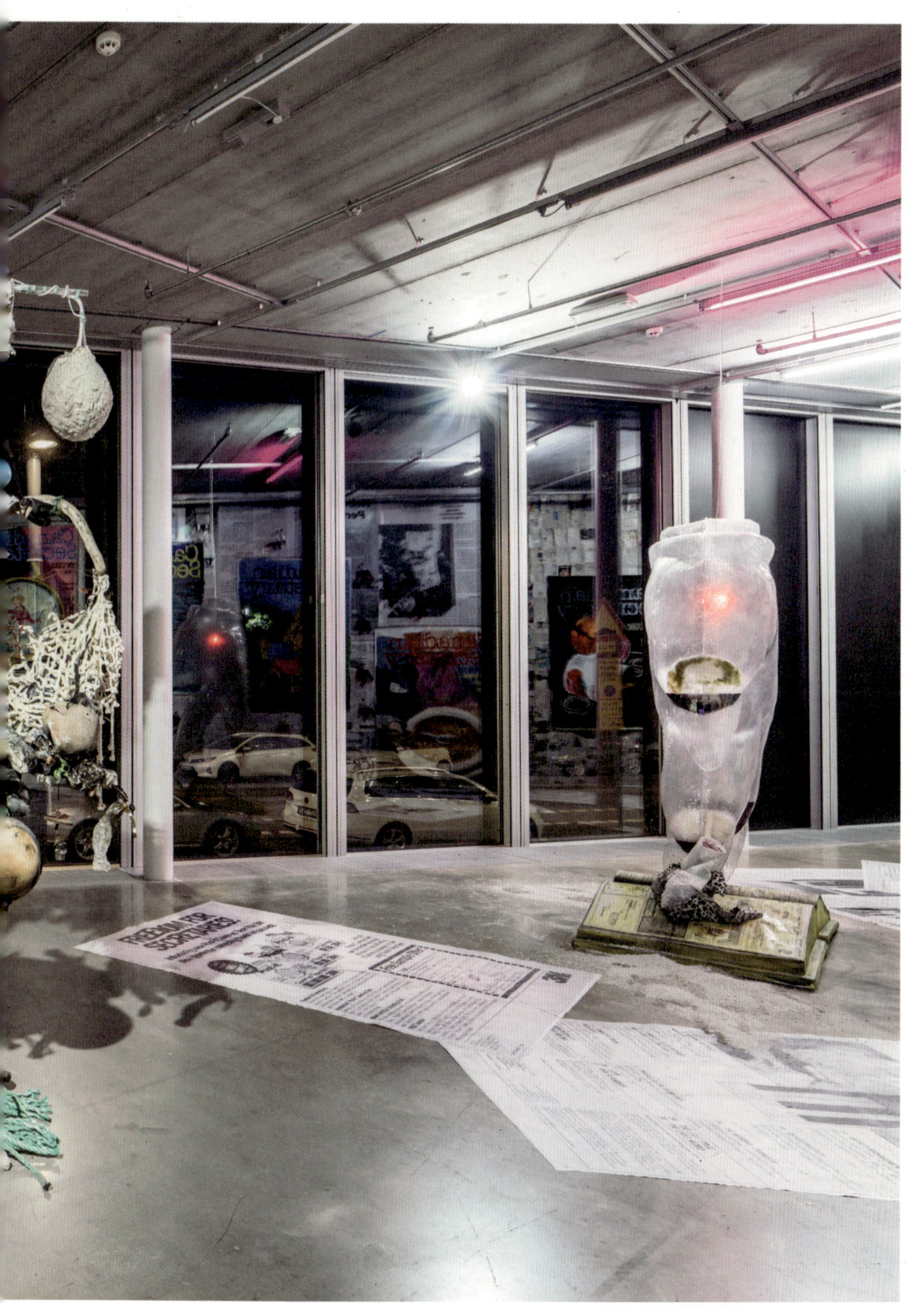

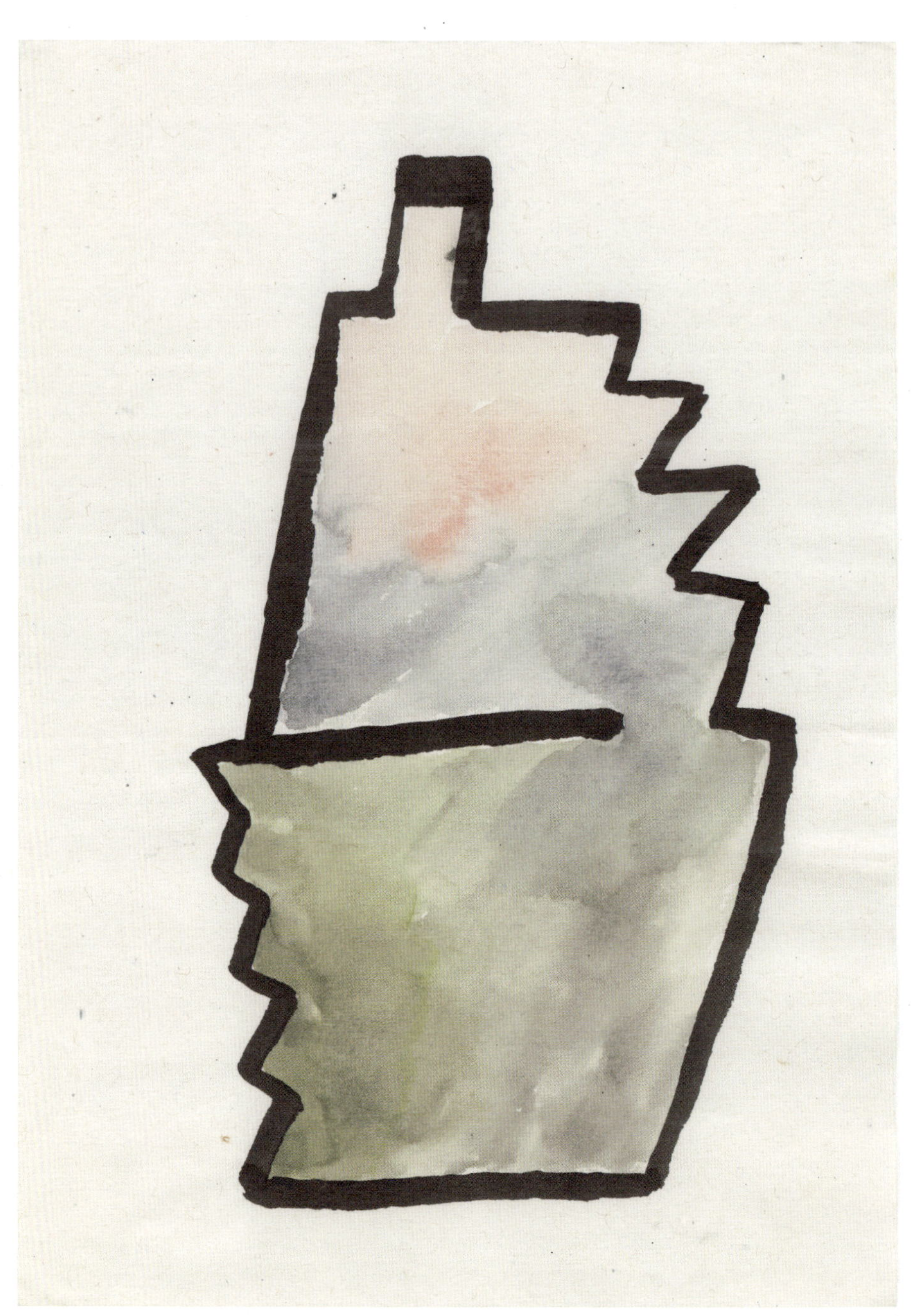

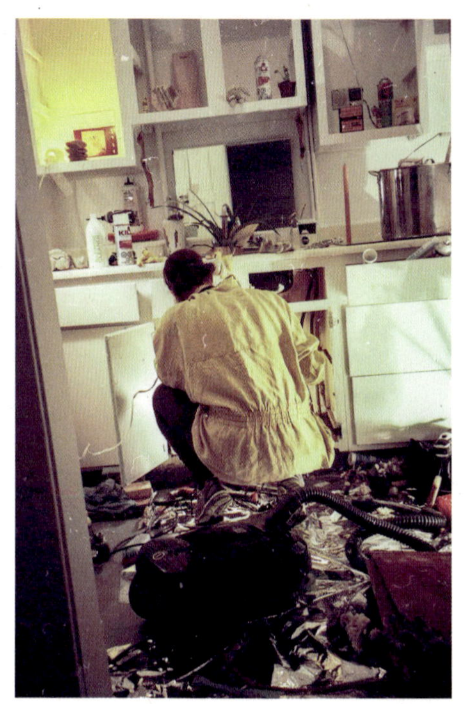
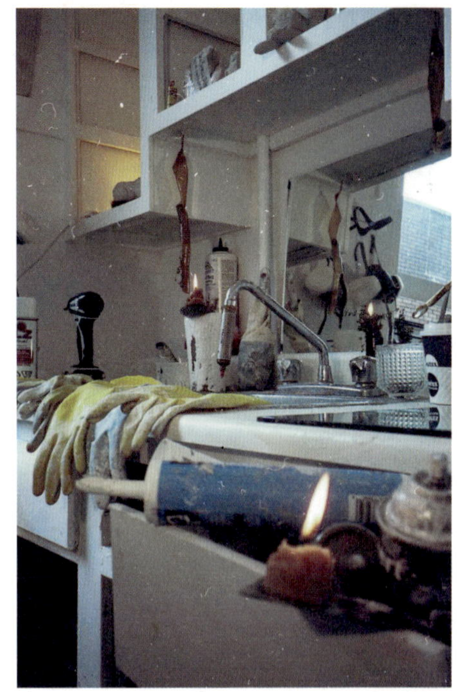
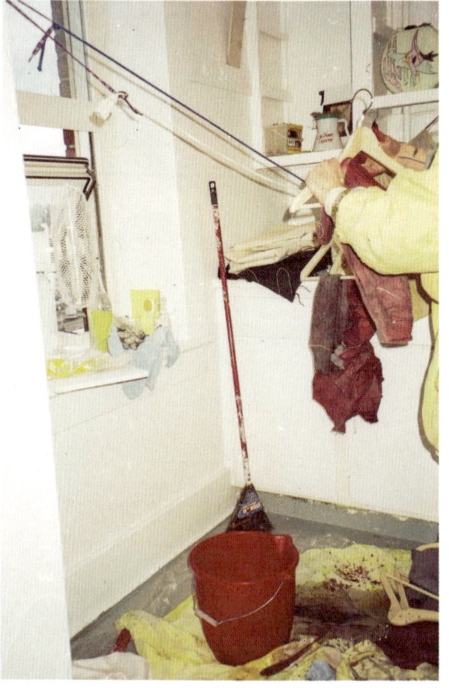
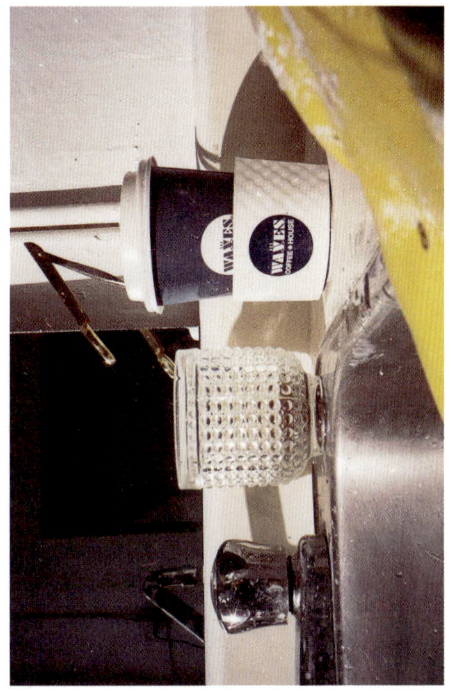

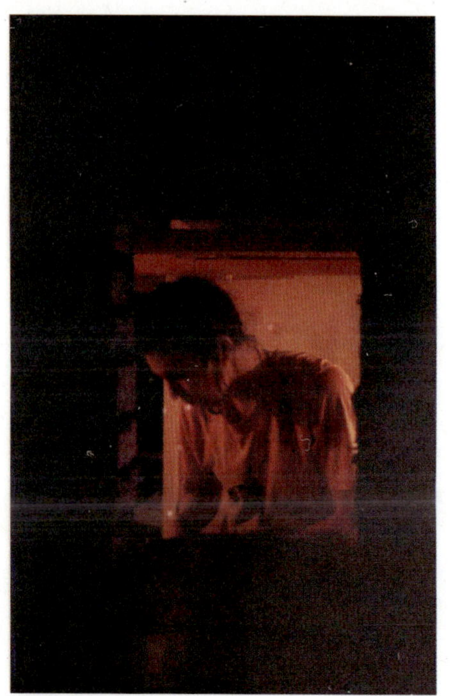
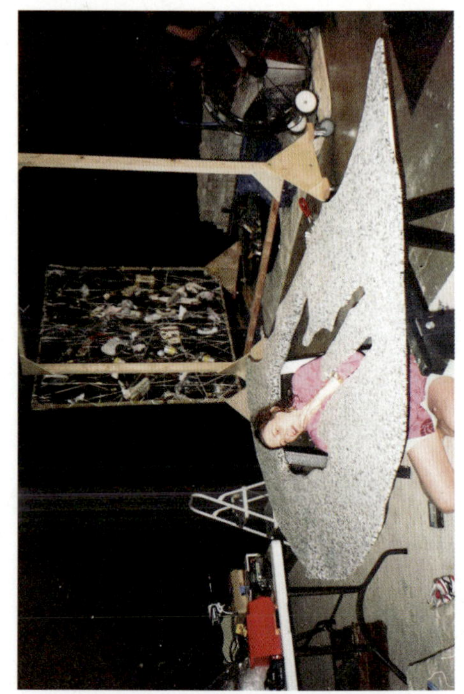
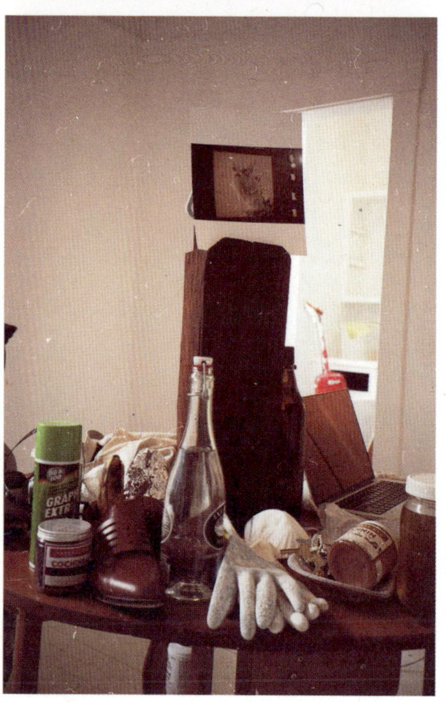
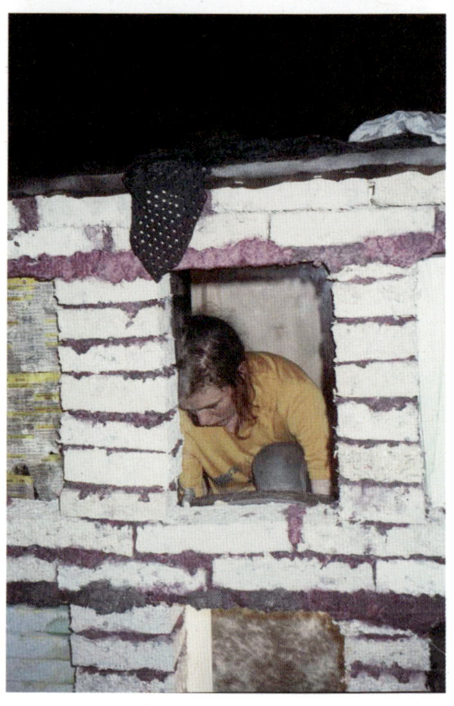

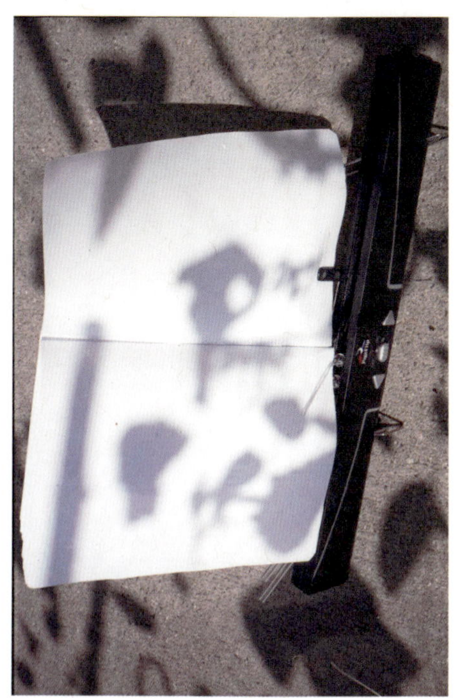
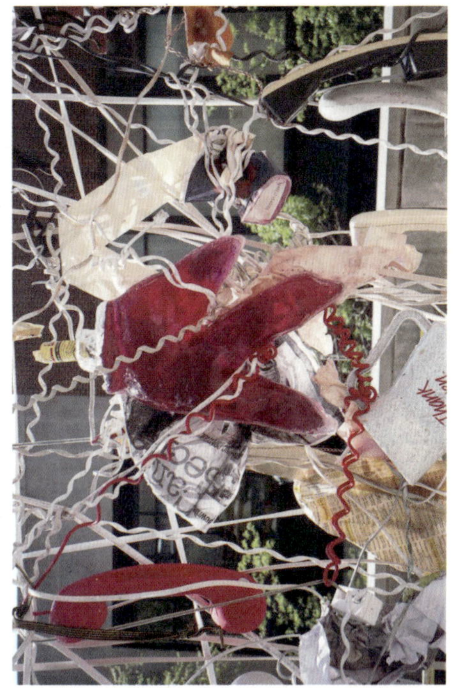
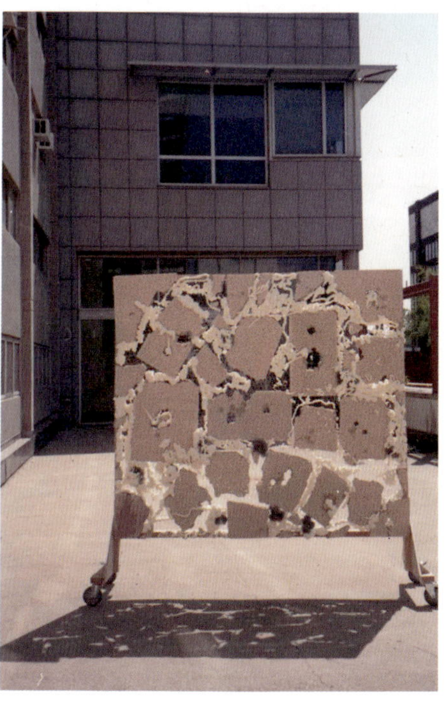
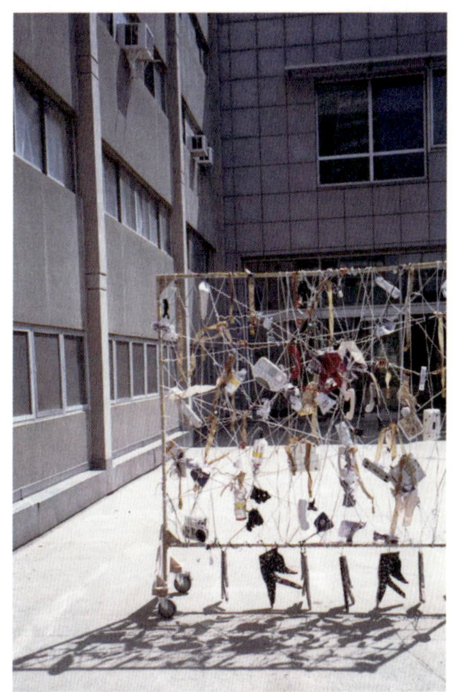

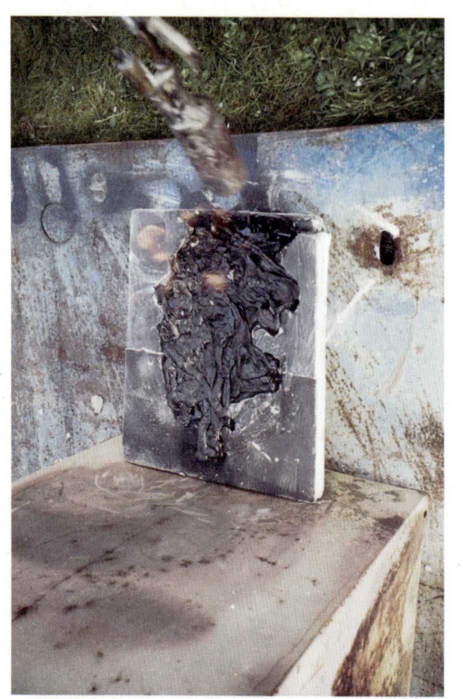
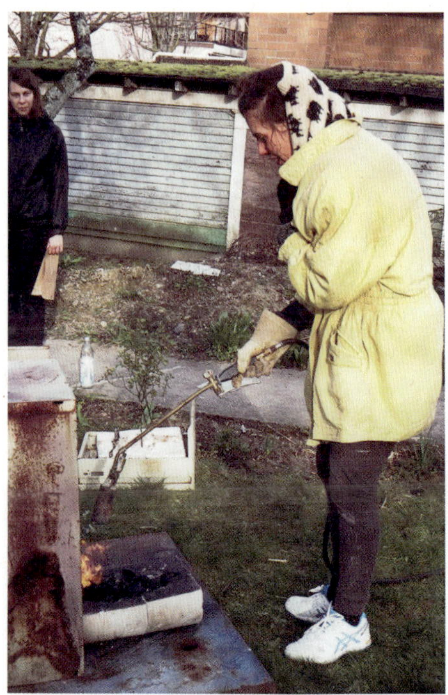
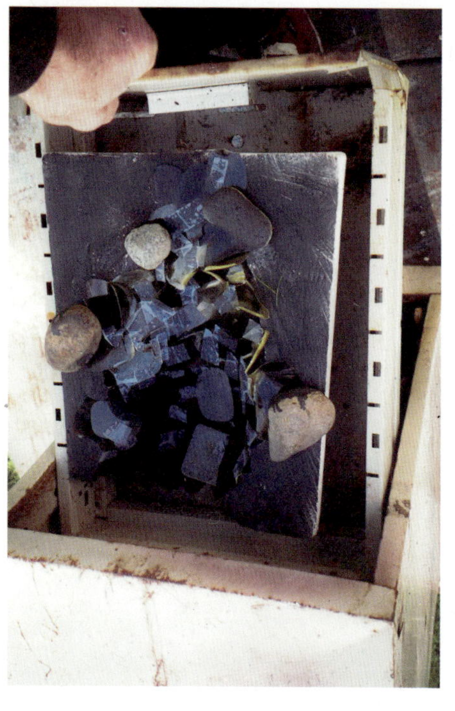
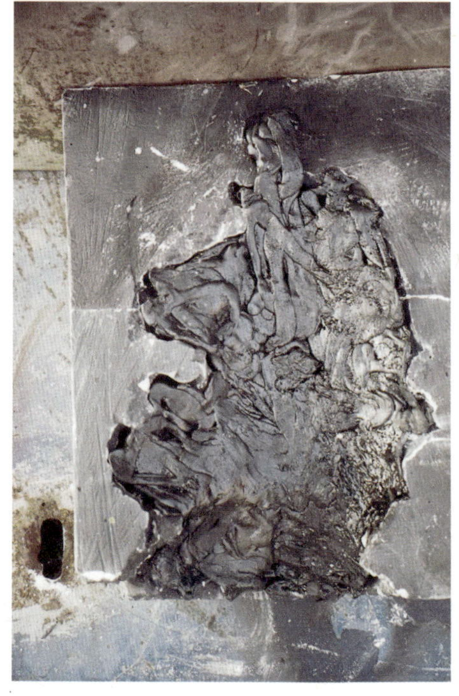

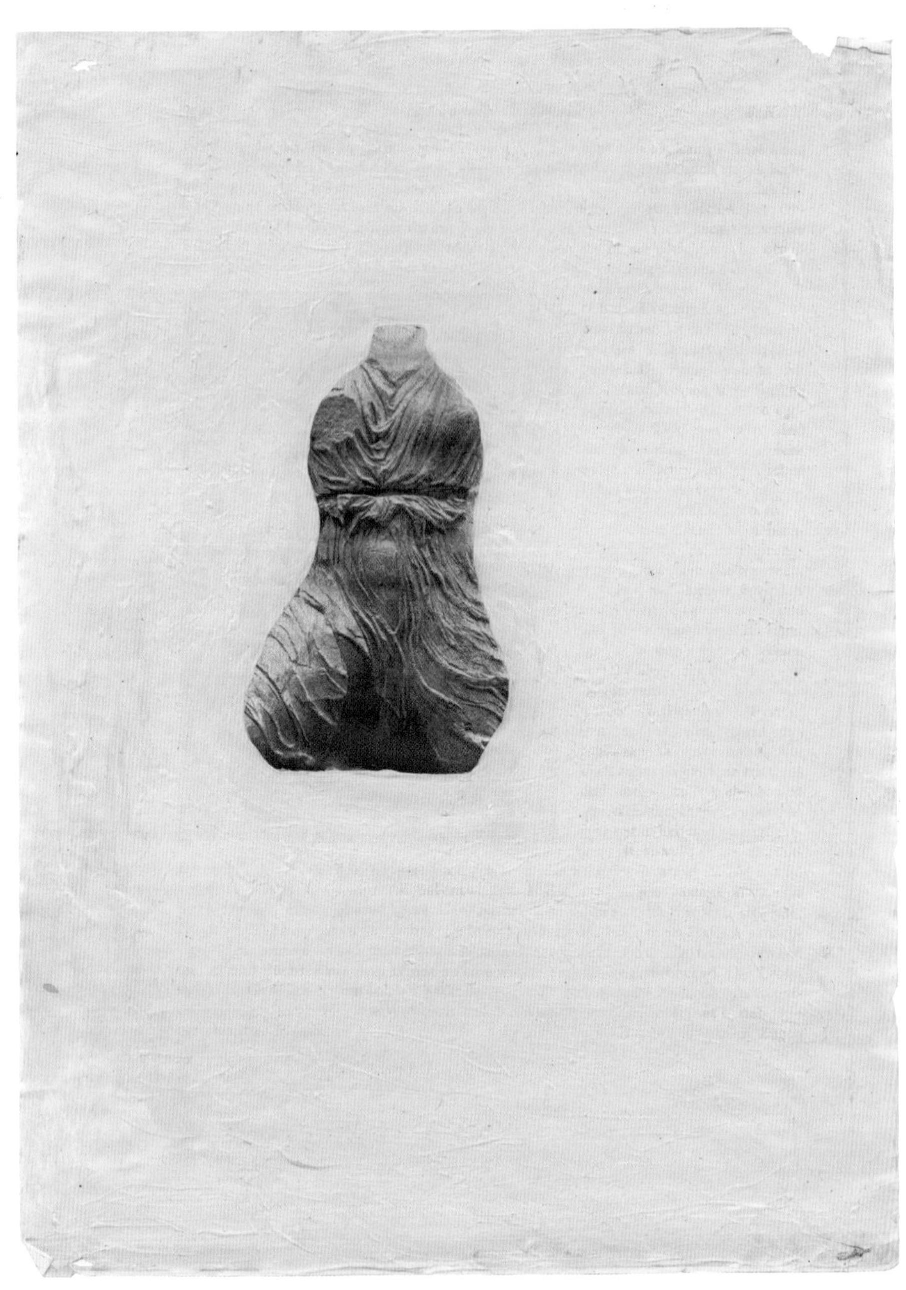

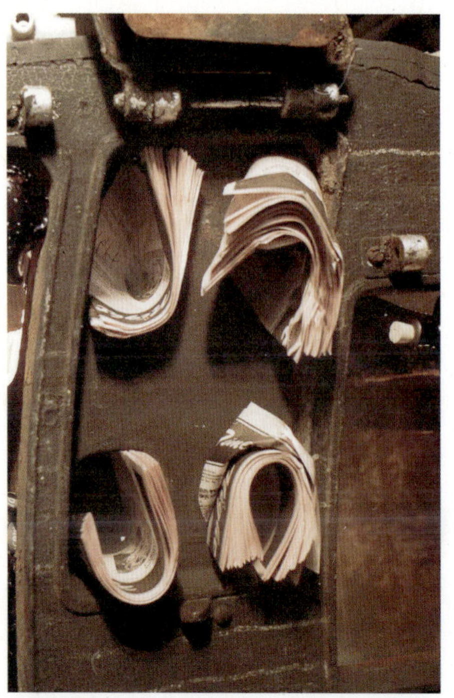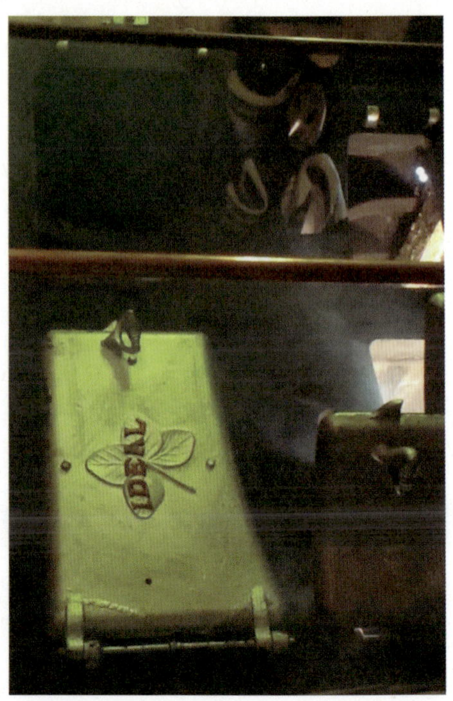

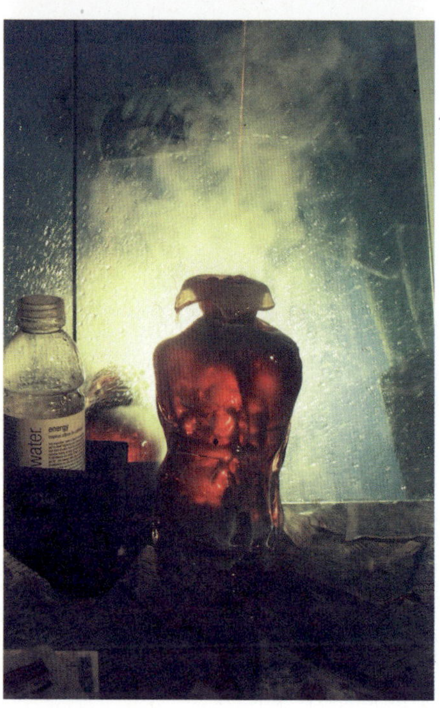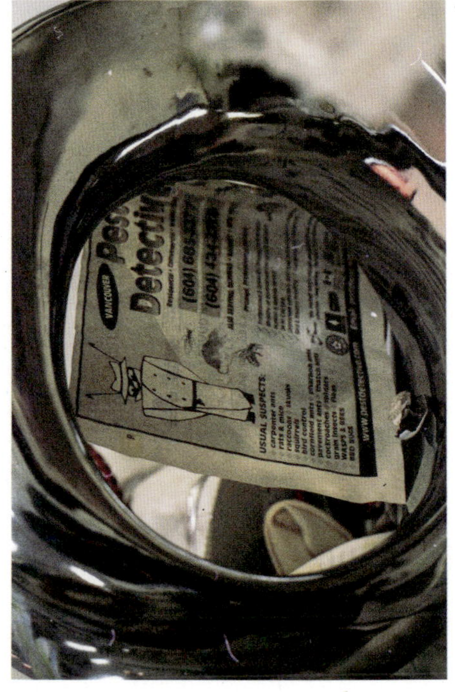
water
energy
VANCOUVER
Pest
Detective
(604) 689-
(604) 4
USUAL SUSPECTS:
www.pestdetective.com

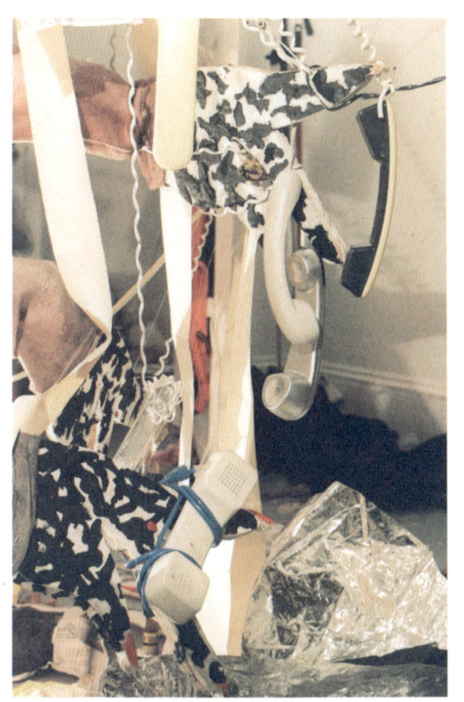
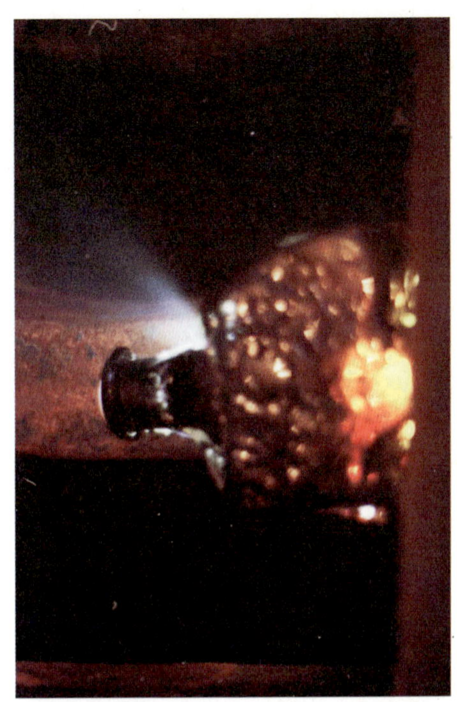
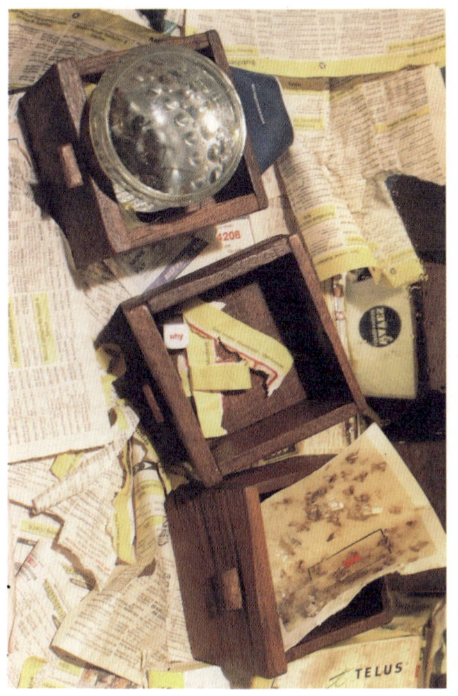
TELUS
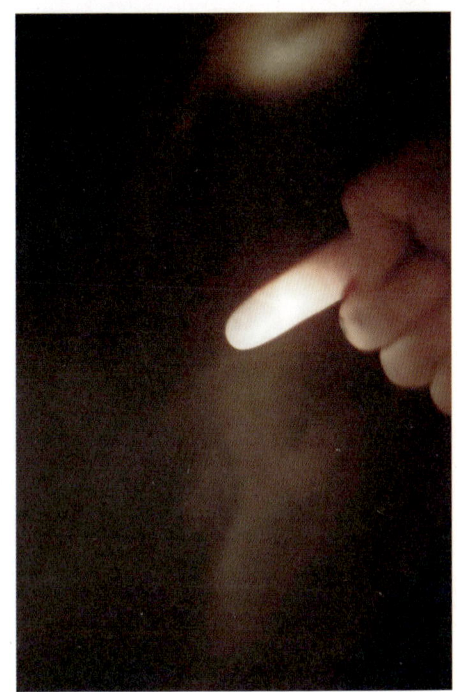

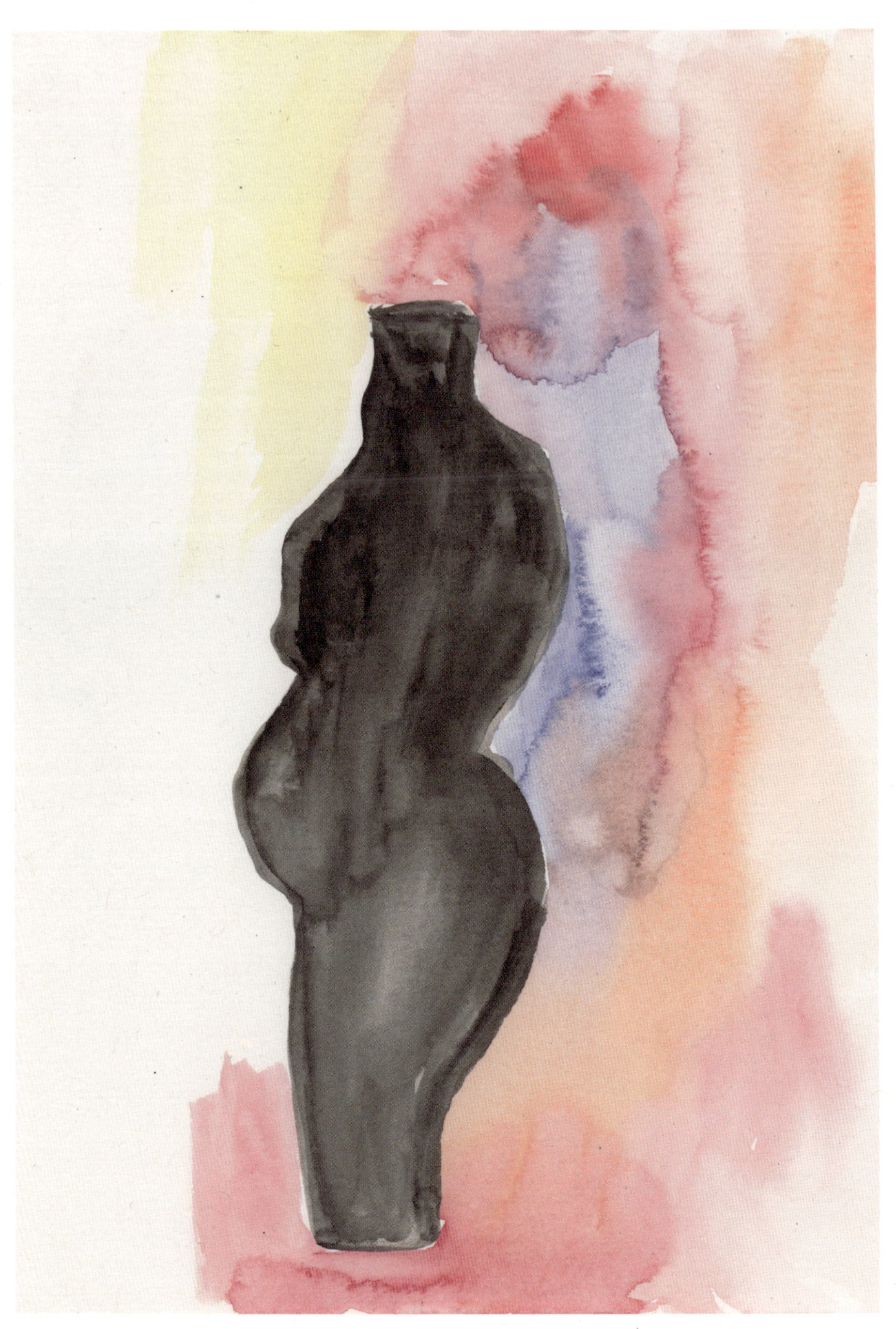

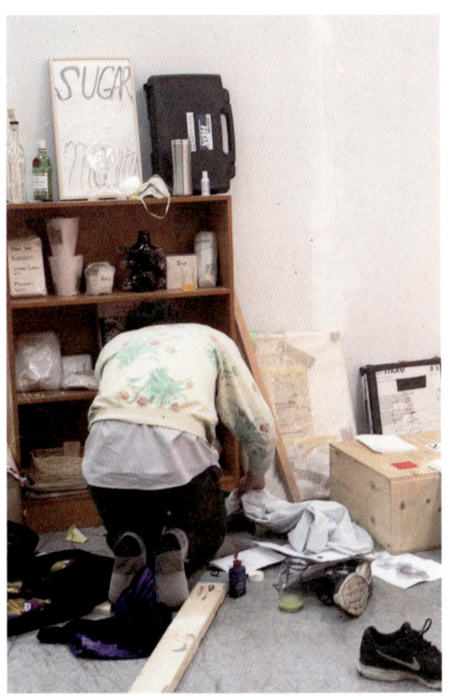

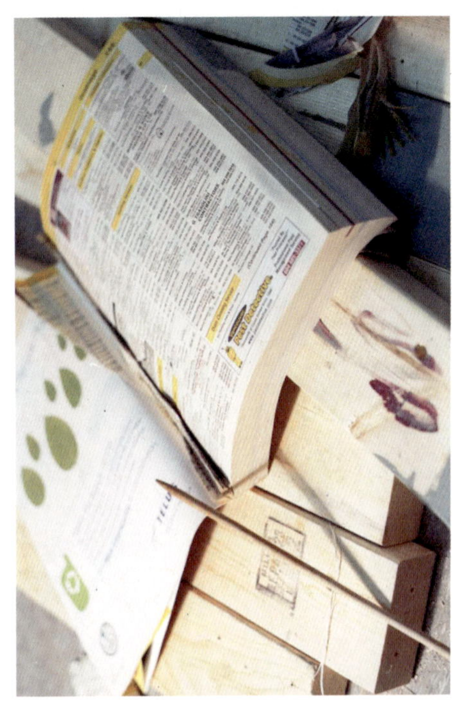

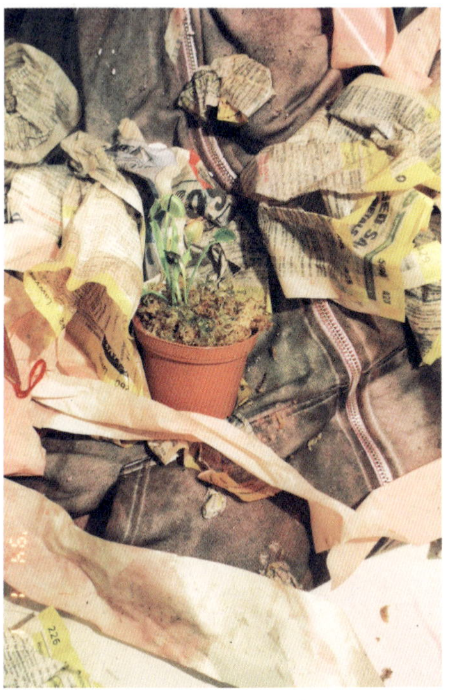

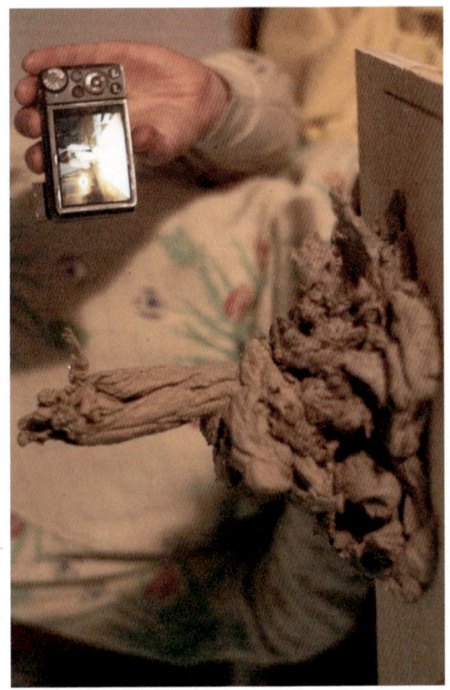

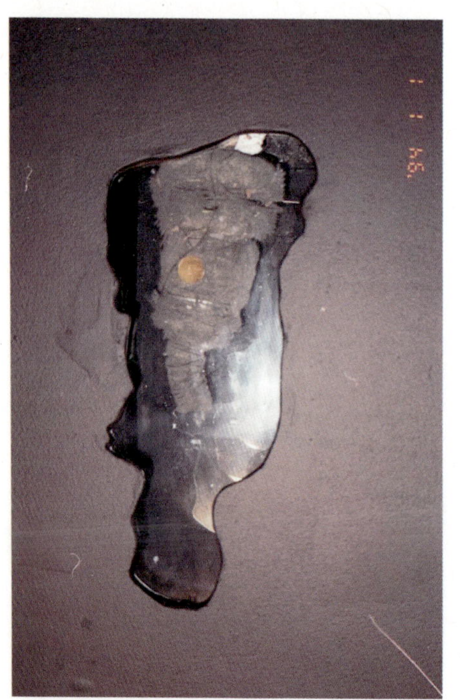
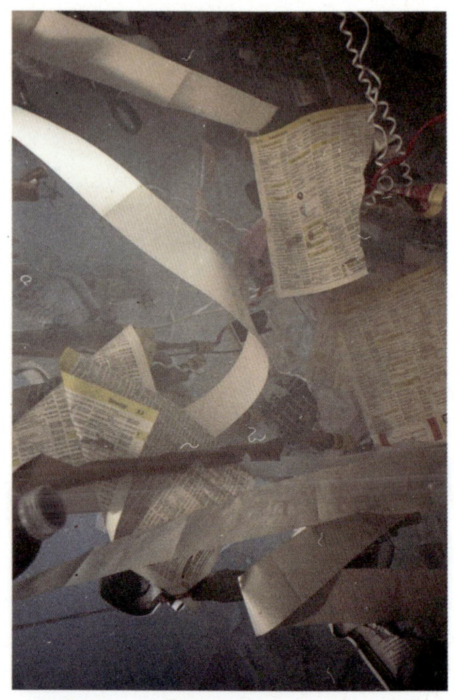
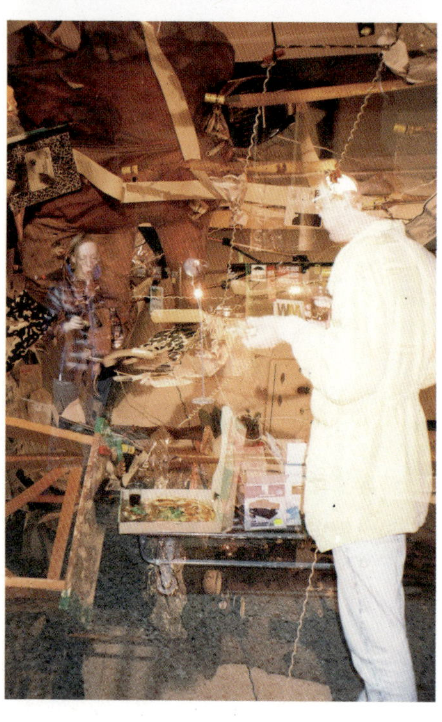
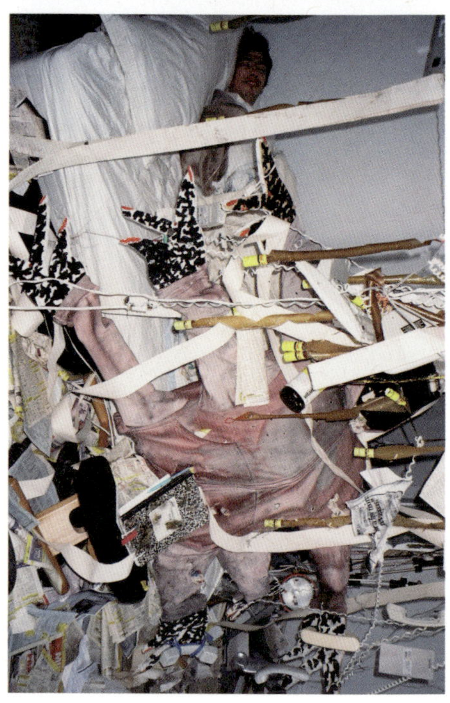

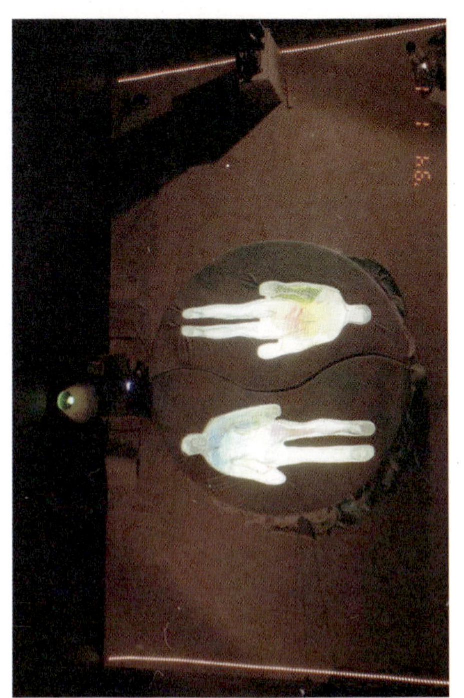

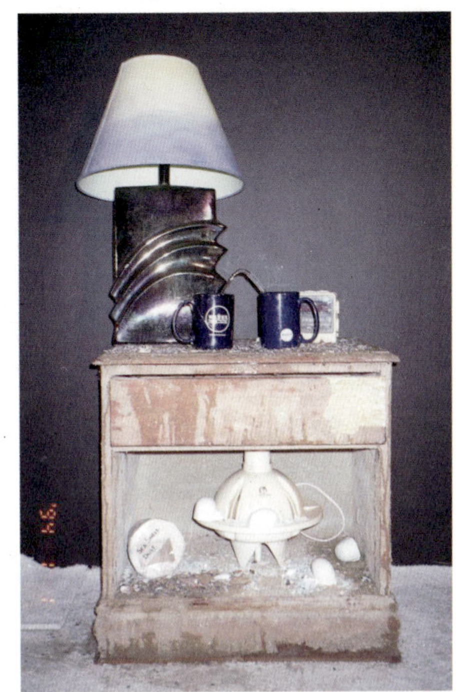

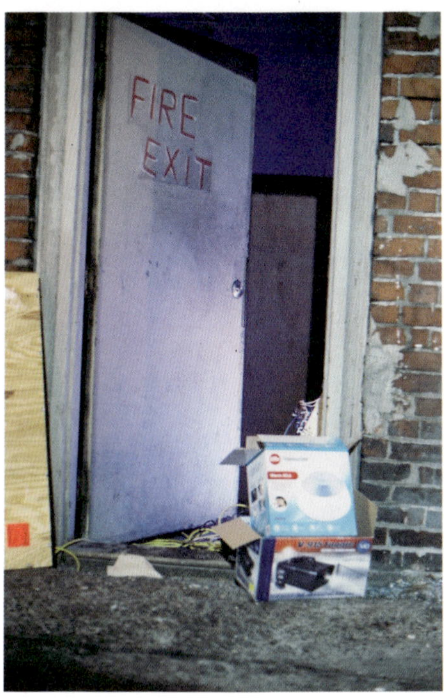
FIRE
EXIT

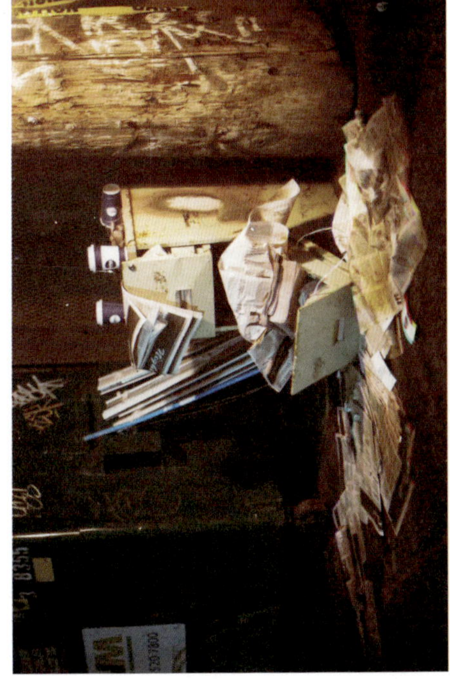

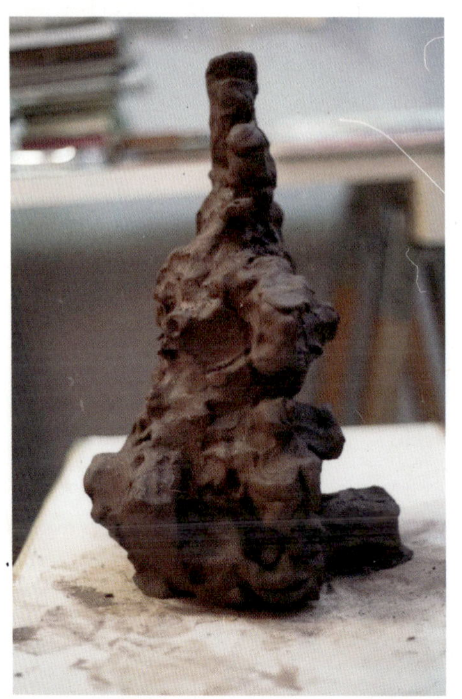

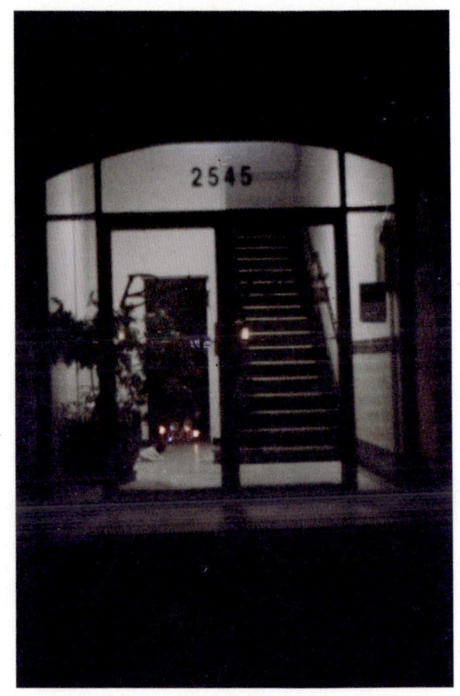

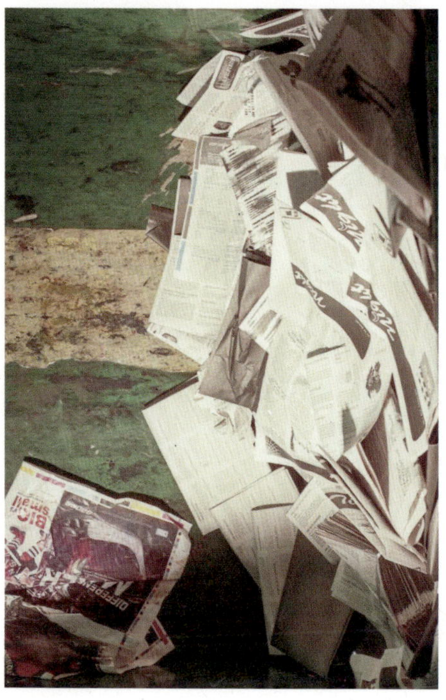

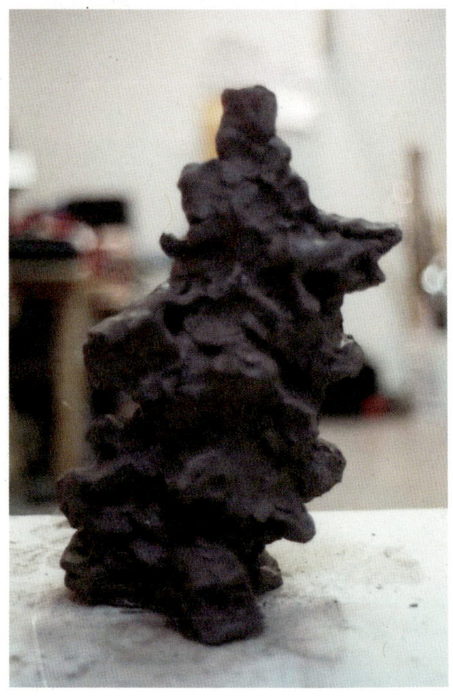

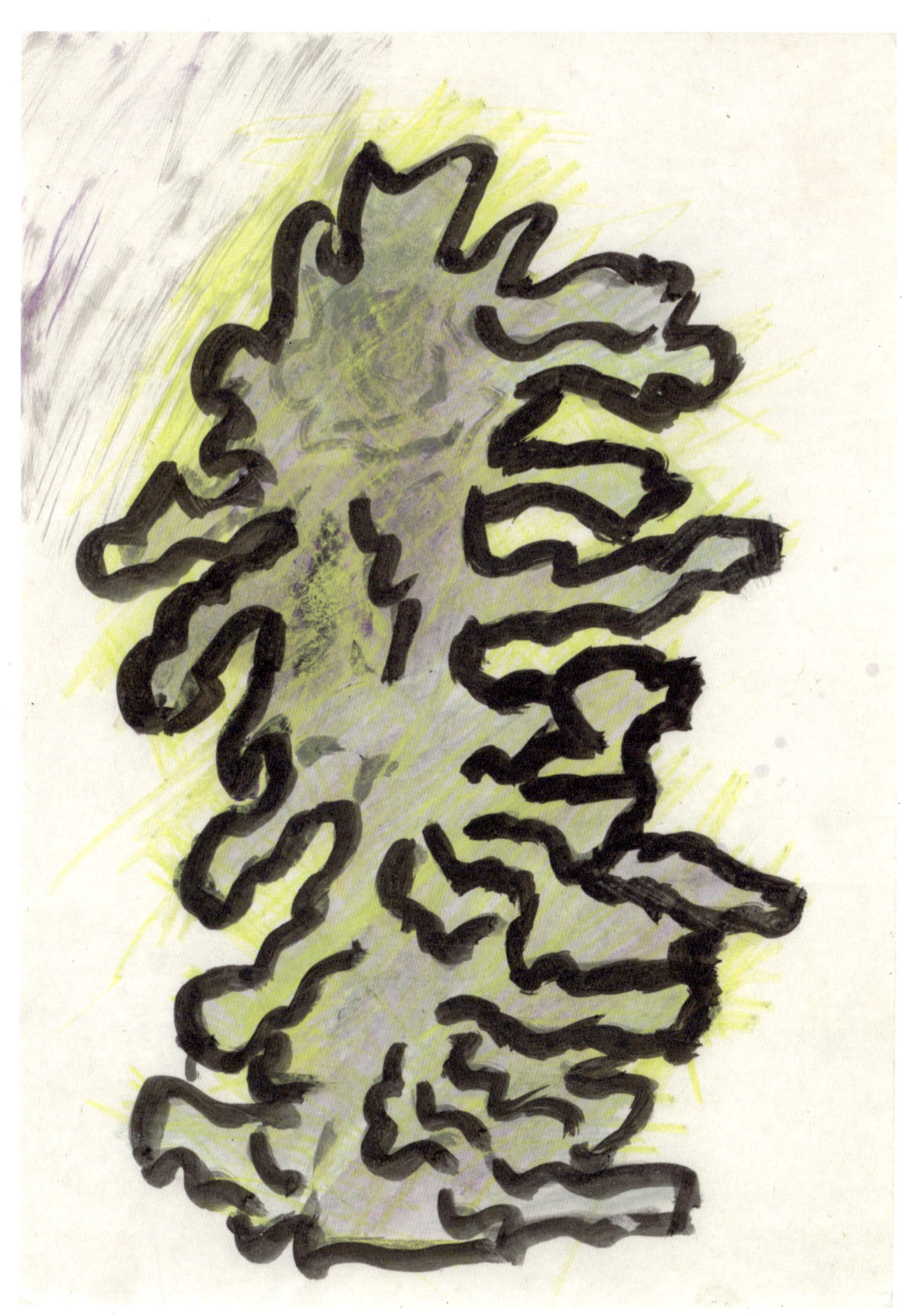

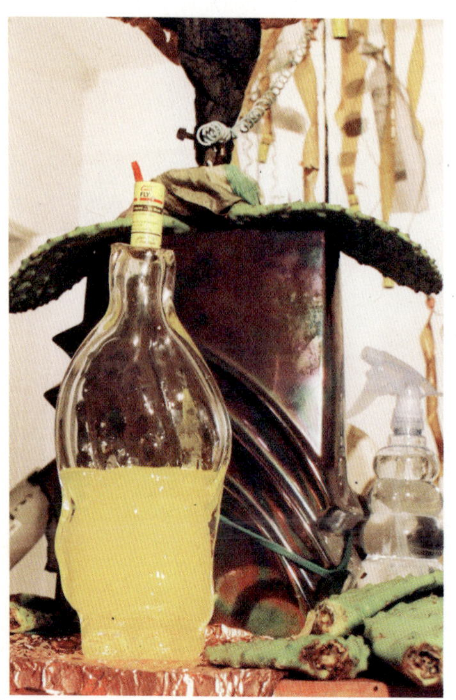
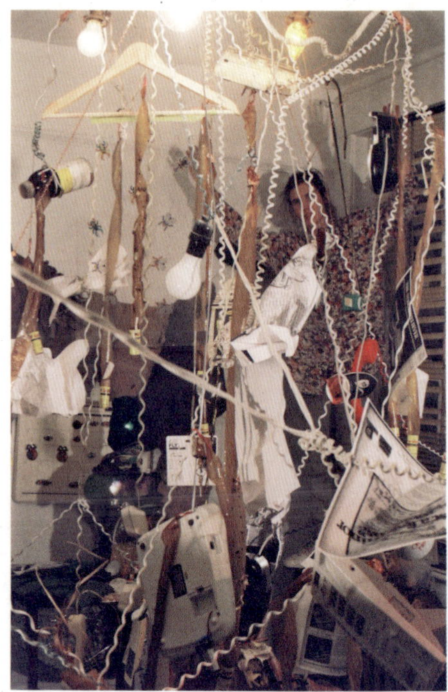
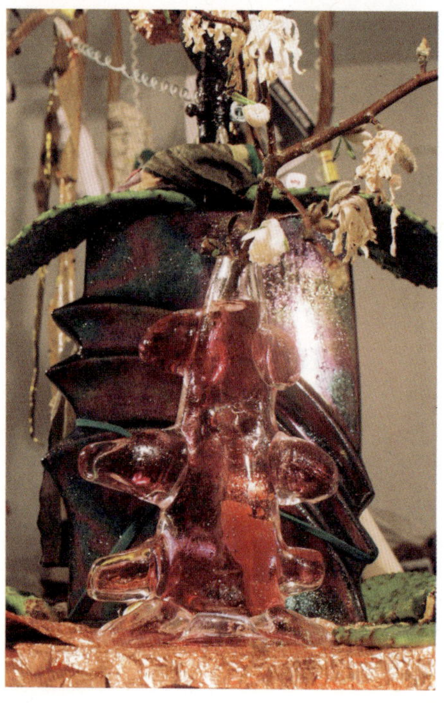
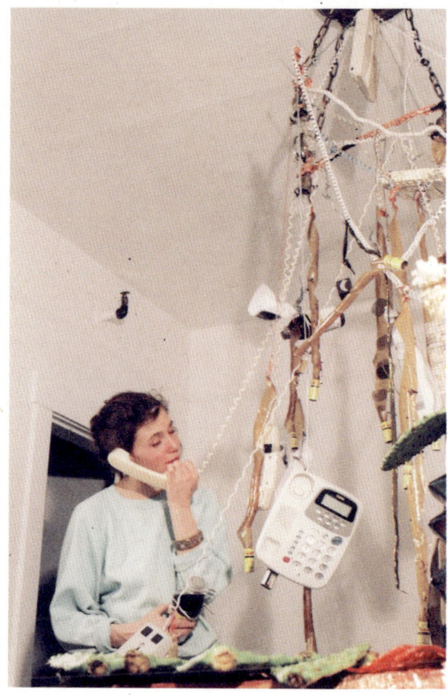

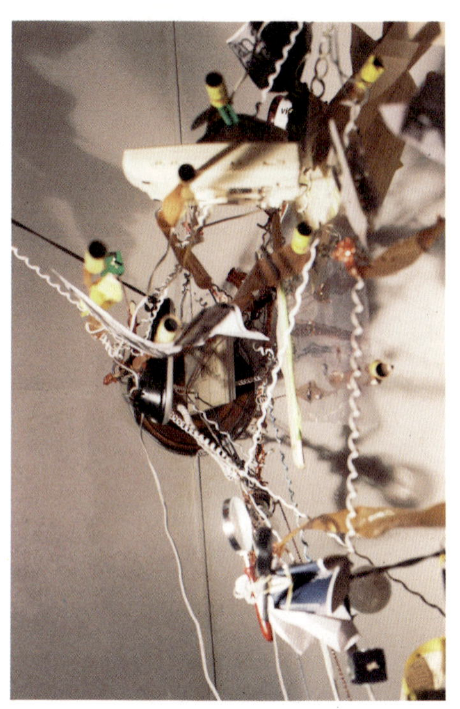

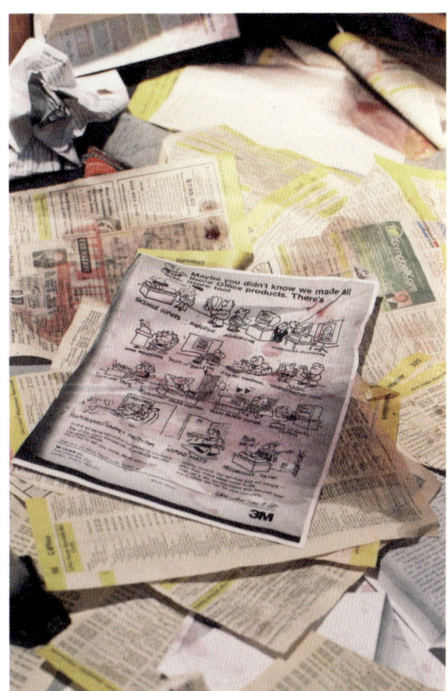

Maybe you didn't know we made all these Office products. There's more too!
3M

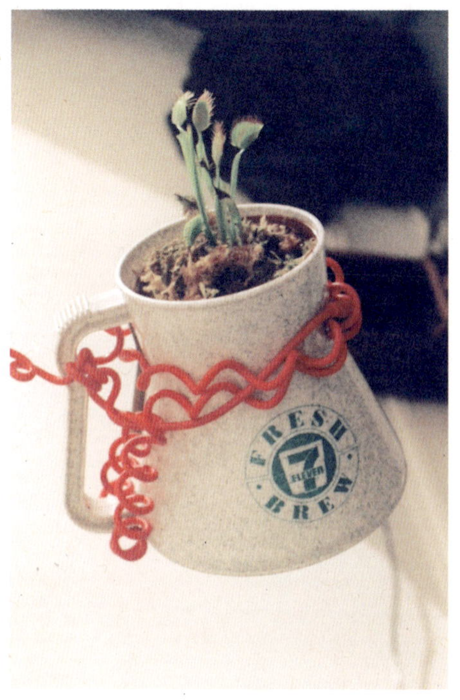

FRESH
7
BREW

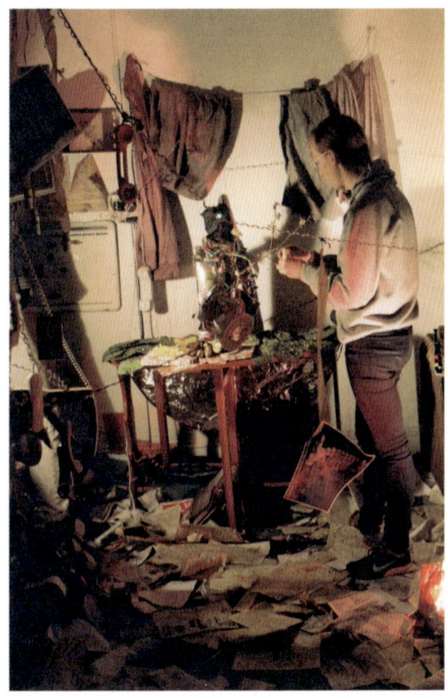

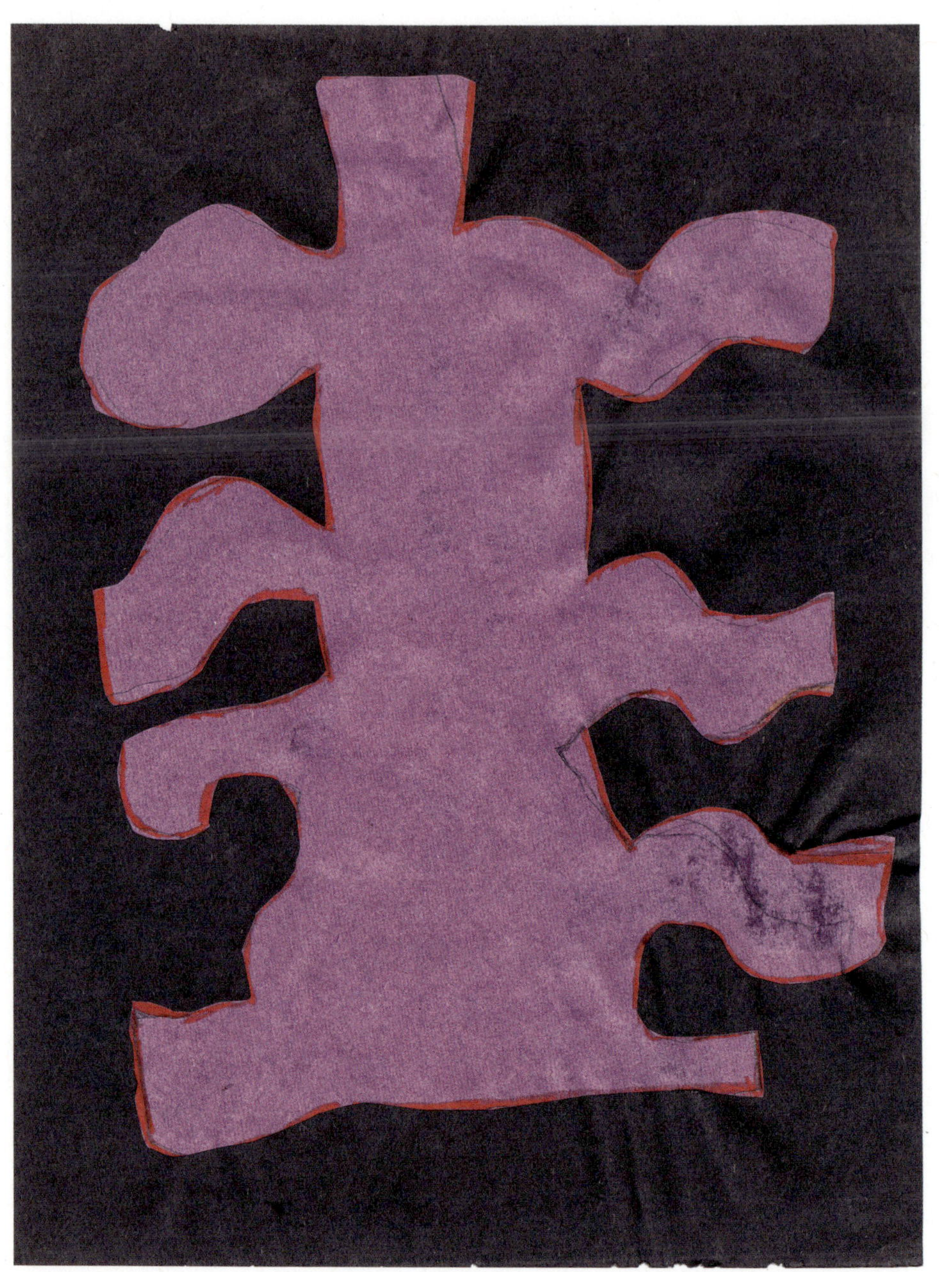

160

Scott Watson

Distant Waves

Julia Feyrer and Tamara Henderson: The Last Waves at the Morris and Helen Belkin Art Gallery is the culmination of an artistic experimentation and the final stage of a three-part exhibition project. The first was initiated in 2013 by curator Jesse McKee for the Walter Phillips Gallery at Banff Centre as *Bottles Under the Influence*. Its second iteration, *Julia Feyrer and Tamara Henderson: Consider the Belvedere*, was curated by Alex Klein and took place in 2015 at the Institute of Contemporary Art, University of Pennsylvania. The exhibition at the Belkin Art Gallery was curated by me and the Belkin staff in 2016, with the third and final film based on *The Last Waves* to be completed in 2019.

The collaborative process of Julia Feyrer and Tamara Henderson is generative, imaginative and intuitive, offering something deeply generous to the world during these times that are dark and troubled. They have careers as individual artists, but working together they create something akin to what Brion Gysin and William S. Burroughs called the "third mind," an agency that consists of both of them and is also independent of them. The automatic, aleatory and clairvoyant practices they deploy give rise to the natural magic that becomes manifest in their work. Dadaists, surrealists, and before them, cubists and cubo-futurists, established bricolage and assemblage as an art practice. Bricolage, the recycling of materials, both man-made and from nature, is a method that is deeply animistic—it breathes new life into old materials and forms. We might even suggest that this new life is also a realization of something latent in the old, something present but occult until the artist, aided by "chance," discloses it.

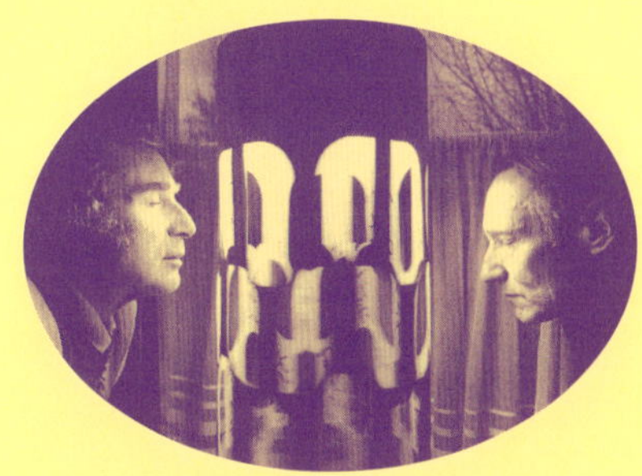

Brion Gysin and William S. Burroughs with the *Dream Machine*, 1972

Assemblage and bricolage have become powerful concepts in new-age magical handbooks like Gilles Deleuze and Felix Guattari's instruction manual for "a sorcerer" (as they describe it), *A Thousand Plateaus* (1980). In more "rational" explorations of "the savage mind," such as Claude Lévi-Strauss's, the concept stands for nothing less than a way of knowing the world. Arguing that there are "two distinct modes of scientific thought," Lévi-Strauss distinguished them:

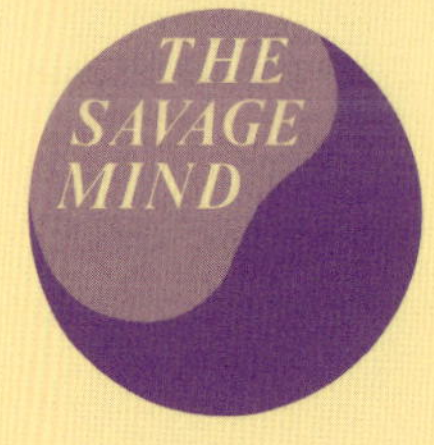

Claude Lévi-Strauss, *The Savage Mind*, 1966

"These are certainly not a function of different stages of development of the human mind but rather of two strategic levels at which nature is accessible to scientific enquiry; one roughly adapted to that of perception and imagination: the other at a remove from it."[1] The bricoleur, Lévi-Strauss's figuration of the former type of enquiry, works with a finite set of what is there, what exists, to forge new knowledge. The second method proposes to create out of nothing. One method is sustainable, the other exploitative. Thus, the bricolage artist today; and in this part of the world that would include, besides Henderson and Feyrer, artists such as Gareth Moore, Geoffrey Farmer and Brian Jungen, and from a previous generation, Jerry Pethick, Al Neil, Jess, George Herms, Bruce Conner, *et al*.

The installation at the Belkin immerses the viewer in a sequence of hallucinatory film sets evoking a bar, a lab and a hotel room, locations made familiar in many film genres. In *The Night Times Press Bar* at the Belvedere Court, an early twentieth-century apartment building at the corner of East 10th Avenue and Main Street in Vancouver, each of the window dioramas represents one of the Belvedere's floors and its inhabitants. Built in 1912, the building's upper-floor apartments provided modest accommodation for women completing their secretarial training at a private academy on the ground level. It is one of the few Edwardian structures left in the city and is known for housing artists, musicians and other creative sorts, a kind of living structure that is rapidly disappearing in Vancouver and symbolic of the current housing crisis that will eventually deprive the city of young people working in the arts. From the mid-1960s onwards, Vancouver's artists and writers saw these crumbling

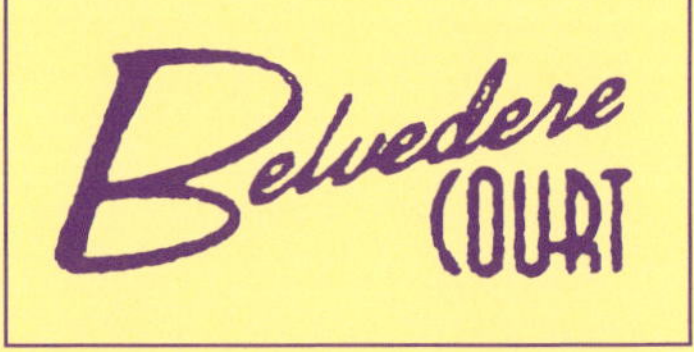

Edwardian buildings as signposts of improvised communal living, a basis for a spatial imagination that informed painting, film, writing and performance. Likewise, Feyrer and Henderson used their own apartments in the Belvedere as sets for the 2015 film, with kitchen cupboards opening onto curiously lit and staged dioramas.

 Scott Watson

Visitors to the bar, which was painstakingly built at ICA and moved across the continent for the Belkin's exhibition, can linger over a copy of *The Night Times News* that records and categorizes the artists' dreams—or record their own, using an ergonomic keyboard that projects their writing into the Gallery to flicker for a moment before disappearing. This deployment of dreams sets the mood for the whole installation. We are reminded of the emphasis on dreams not only by Freud and the surrealists, but also by outsider psychoanalyst Rolf Loehrich, who believed that things that happened in the "dreamsphere" announced events in the outside environment.[2] Accordingly, the installations and films of Feyrer

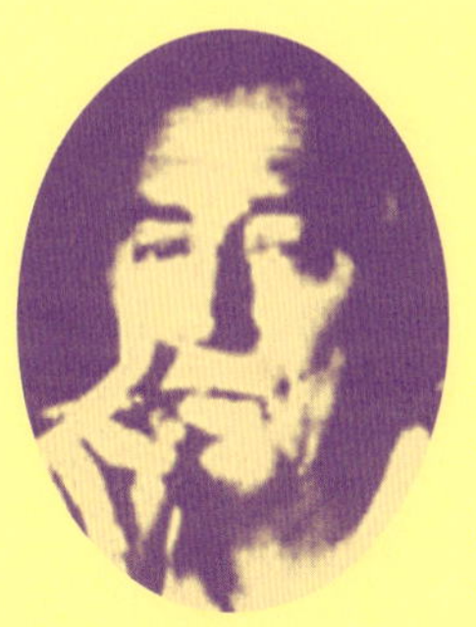

Rolf Loehrich

and Henderson are "peopled" by entities that themselves arose from "dreams and chances." These entities, none of them quite human, drive the narrative potential that animates the set. The *WAVES* installation reimagines the coffee shop that was located on Main Street across the street from the Belvedere, which is also the location for the opening and closing scenes of the film *Consider the Belvedere* (2015). Earlier research into the collection of the Historical Museum of Wines and Spirits in

Stockholm inspired and provoked such elements as a drinking song for women and the film *Bottles Under the Influence* (2012), in which glass bottles are featured as characters. These "vessels," with coven-like names like *The Old Hag*, subtly unhinge the pairing of psychosis and female sexuality, instead pulling focus to the potent, transformative hypnagogic states between sleeping and waking explored by the surrealists and writers like Proust and Joyce.

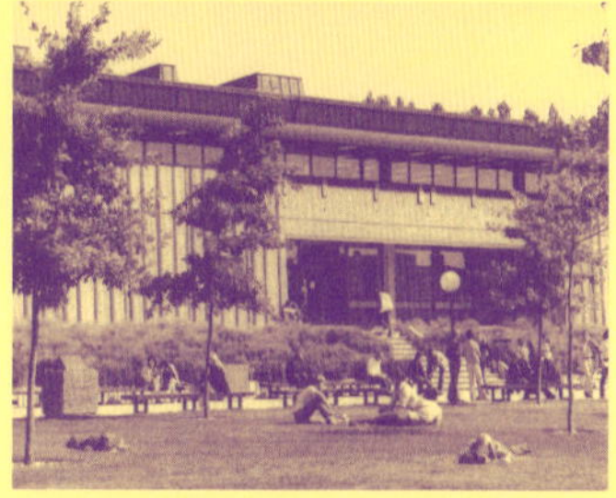

UBC Student Union Building (SUB), completed in 1968

Feyrer and Henderson's work is influenced by the artists' location, with traces of their environment ending up in their installations. In the Belkin's exhibition, the artists culled furniture and fixtures from the old Student Union Building on campus—which was slated for renovation immediately following the exhibit—including the reception desk in the hotel, the tables in the lab and the display cases of *WAVES* coffee bar. The *Bug of the Month Calendar* affixed to the hotel wall was borrowed from the Beaty Biodiversity Museum. Feyrer and Henderson worked closely with Brian Ditchburn from the UBC Chemistry Department's glassblowing studio to create *Communicating Vessels*, situated in the lab, for the Belkin's exhibition. The artists likened Ditchburn's ability to "heal" the broken piles of chemistry glass to the protagonist in Philip K. Dick's 1969 sci-fi novel *Galactic Pot-Healer*, in which the central character is called to different planets to heal broken ceramic pots. *Communicating Vessels* sits next to the original bottles from the exhibition at Banff Centre—*Blind*, *Pest Detective*, *Old Hag*, *Newspaper* and *Chance Bottles*—with corresponding tables that radiate outwards. The table that radiates from *Blind Bottle*, for instance, includes the hardened clay forms that Feyrer and Henderson moulded while blindfolded during the installation of the exhibition, along with other bottles made from the lenses of melted 3D movie glasses.

This installation alters the space of the Gallery to a site of production as well as presentation. The individual works, which include the accumulated effects of experimentation across a number of years, become the spaces for the set of a third film to be shot at the end of the exhibit. During the course of the exhibition, a viewer is invited to interact, record a dream, eavesdrop on murmurings from a hotel room or visit a laboratory.

At the end of the exhibition at the Belkin, the set for the lab was acquired by the Vancouver Art Gallery for its permanent collection, while the *Night Times Bar* was received by Plaza Projects, an artist-run centre located in a suburban mall, to be re-activated at openings. But it is the films themselves that will become the final documents of the shows at Banff Centre, ICA and the Belkin, as many of the components that Feyrer and Henderson create for each iteration do not survive the exhibitions.

1
Claude Lévi-Strauss, *The Savage Mind* (Chicago: University of Chicago Press, 1966), 15.

2
See for example Rolf Loehrich, *Oneirics and Psychosomatics: An Introductory Treatise Concerning a New Theory of Psychoanalysis, Its Logic and Methodology* (McHenry, IL: Compass Press, 1953).

    Scott Watson

Julia Feyrer (b. 1982, Victoria, BC) and Tamara Henderson (b. 1982, Sackville, NB) have worked together since 2009. They have collaborated on *The Last Waves* at the Morris and Helen Belkin Art Gallery, Vancouver (2016), *Consider the Belvedere* at the ICA, Philadelphia (2015), *Enter the Fog* at The Rooms, St. John's, NL (2016), *Bottles Under the Influence* at Walter Phillips Gallery, Banff Centre (2013) and *Unfinished Corpse Bar* at Jacob Lawrence Gallery, University of Washington, Seattle (2013). They recently participated in residencies at The Rooms, St. John's and at IASPIS in Stockholm, Sweden.

Feyrer's work has been the subject of solo exhibitions, including *Julia Feyrer* at Catriona Jeffries Gallery, Vancouver (2018); *New Pedestrians* at Potts, Alhambra, CA (2017); *Kitchen* at grunt gallery, Vancouver (2014); *Escape Scenes* at Western Front, Vancouver (2014); *Alternatives and Opportunities* at Catriona Jeffries Gallery, Vancouver (2012); and *Irregular Time Signatures* at Johan Berggren Gallery, Malmö, Sweden (2011). She has participated in group exhibitions at museums including the Vancouver Art Gallery; the Morris and Helen Belkin Art Gallery, Vancouver; The Rooms, St. John's; Jewish Museum, New York; Art Gallery of Greater Victoria; Presentation House Gallery, North Vancouver; and Bielefelder Kunstverein, Bielefeld, Germany. She is co-editor of the online *Spoox Audiozine* and author of a series of artist books from Perro Verlag.

Henderson's recent solo exhibitions include *Womb Life* at KW Institute for Contemporary Art, Berlin (2018); *Seasons End: Out of Body* at Oakville Galleries, ON (2017); *Seasons End: Panting Healer* at Rodeo, London (2017) and Red Cat, Los Angeles (2016); *Tate Exchange* at Tate Liverpool (2016); *The Blur Inbetween* at the Art Gallery of Alberta (2016); *Charmer Scripture* at Rodeo, London (2014); *Speaking in Scales* at Andrew Kreps Gallery, New York (2014); *Tapped Out and Spiraling in Stride* at Grazer Kunstverein, Graz, Austria (2014); *Sans Tê te Au Monde* with Santiago Mostyn at Kunsthall Stavanger, Norway (2014); and *Evergreen Minutes of the Phantom Figure* at Kunstverein Nürnberg, Germany (2013). She has participated in group exhibitions at venues such as the Vancouver Art Gallery; the Morris and Helen Belkin Art Gallery, Vancouver; Glasgow International; Toronto Kunstverein; Rodeo, Istanbul; Western Front, Vancouver; Magasin III, Stockholm; and Midway Contemporary Art, Minneapolis. Her work was included in Documenta 13, Kassel, Germany (2012), where she presented *Sloshed Ballot & Anonymous Loan*. Henderson was shortlisted for the 2013 Sobey Art Award.

Alex Klein is the Dorothy and Stephen R. Weber (CHE'60) Curator at the Institute of Contemporary Art, University of Pennsylvania where she has recently worked with artists such as Suki Seokyeong Kang, Nathalie Du Pasquier, Barbara Kasten, Tamara Henderson and Julia Feyrer, Sondra Perry and Ane Graff to produce exhibitions and new commissions. She has lectured widely, and her writing has been published in numerous collections, including *Public Servants: Art and the Crisis of the Common Good* (MIT Press, 2016), *Shannon Ebner: Auto Body Collision* (CMOA, 2015), *The Human Snapshot* (Sternberg Press/ CCS Bard, 2013), *How Soon Is Now?* (LUMA, 2012) and the critical volume on photography *Words Without Pictures* (LACMA/ Aperture, 2010), which she also edited. From 2013 to 2015 she served as an agent in the Carnegie Museum of Art's Hillman Photography Initiative. Before joining the ICA in 2011 she held positions in the Wallis Annenberg Photography Department at the Los Angeles County Museum of Art, the Roski School of Fine Arts at the University of Southern California and The Metropolitan Museum of Art, New York.

Jesse McKee is the Head of Strategy at 221A, Vancouver where he is responsible for leading its research-based programming and aligning all aspects of the organization's work with a strategic plan that develops and sustains self-organized cultural infrastructures. Previously, McKee was the Curator of Walter Phillips Gallery, Banff Centre and the Exhibitions Curator of Western Front, Vancouver. He has developed commissions with the artists Lee Kit, Tamara Henderson and Julia Feyrer, Andrea Büttner and Neïl Beloufa. McKee was recently a curatorial resident with Tranzit.org, Romania and he curated a group exhibition on contemporary depictions of the grotesque, *Stopping the Sun in Its Course*, Ghebaly Gallery, Los Angeles. Along with Daina Augaitis, he was the co-curator of *Vancouver Special: Ambivalent Pleasures*, a major citywide survey exhibition at the Vancouver Art Gallery, from December 2, 2016 to April 17, 2017.

 Contributors

Scott Watson is Director of the
Morris and Helen Belkin Art
Gallery and Professor in the
Department of Art History, Visual
Art and Theory at the University
of British Columbia. A curator
whose career has spanned more
than thirty-five years, Watson is
internationally recognized for his
research and work in curatorial
and exhibition studies, contempo-
rary art and issues, and art theory
and criticism. His distinctions
include the Hnatyshyn Foundation
Award for Curatorial Excellence in
Contemporary Art (2010) and the
Alvin Balkind Award for Creative
Curatorship in BC Arts (2008).
Watson has published extensively
in the areas of contemporary
Canadian and international art.
Recent publications include *Tom
Burrows* (2018); *Letters: Michael
Morris and Concrete Poetry* (2015);
*Thrown: British Columbia's
Apprentices of Bernard Leach and
Their Contemporaries* (2011), a
finalist for the 2012 Roderick Haig-
Brown Regional Prize; "Race,
Wilderness, Territory and the
Origins of the Modern Canadian
Landscape" and "Disfigured
Nature" (in *Beyond Wilderness*,
McGill University Press, 2007);
and "Transmission Difficulties:
Vancouver Painting in the 1960s"
(in *Paint*, Vancouver Art Gallery,
2006).

Contributors

*Grey Smoked Whiskey
Bottle (Night Times
Journalist Bottle)*, 2013
Pyrex and uranium glass

*Yellow Apfelwein Bottle
(Pest Detective Bottle)*, 2013
Pyrex and cobalt glass

*Clear Chance Mixed-Alcohol
Bottle (Chance Bottle)*, 2013
Pyrex glass

*Purple Valerian Bottle
(Old Hag Bottle)*, 2013
Pyrex glass

*Moonshine Bottle
(Blind Bottle)*, 2013
Pyrex glass

The Night Times News, 2013
newsprint

The Night Times News, Feyrer
and Henderson's investiga-
tion into dream journalism,
is a newspaper-style publication presenting journalists'
reportage from the realm
between the waking and dream
worlds. Each issue is printed
offset in a run of five hundred
copies. Offset plates will be produced and printing will occur
locally for each new issue.

Bottles Under the Influence, 2012
16 mm film, colour, optical sound
7 min. 48 sec.

Bottles Under the Influence,
produced in Stockholm, depicts
a collection of found bottles
that simulate bodies, appearing
headless, limbless, mutable
and distorted, becoming a cast
of characters that are staged,
observed, projected on, used
and destroyed.

Bottles at the Round Table, 2013
artist book

Animating this collection
of bottles is Feyrer and
Henderson's artist book,
published by Perro Verlag,
Mayne Island. In a lim-
ited edition of fifty copies,
the book contains several
drinking songs for women,
collected and transformed by
the artists, alongside prelimi-
nary and speculative drawings
of their character bottles.

Consider the Belvedere, 2013
performance
40 min.

During the course of the exhibition, the artists present a
slide show and soundscaped
reading from the script of the
upcoming film, *Consider the
Belvedere*.

 Checklist

The Night Times Press Bar, 2015
bricks made from newspaper,
mortar (genuine Stockholm pine
tar, cochineal, water, newspaper),
Plexiglas, miscellaneous materials
from the Belvedere Suite collection,
tar paper (roofing material), ergonomic gel pads, ergonomic keyboards, windows, lighting, wood,
The Night Times News newspapers, stress mats, projection and
Mac mini

Software programming and
custom keyboard controller
hardware assembly and
programming by Dan Riley

The Night Times News, 2013
newsprint

Bottles Under the Influence, 2012
16 mm film, colour, optical sound
7 min. 48 sec.

Consider the Belvedere, 2015
16 mm film, colour, optical sound
9 min. 28 sec.
Music composed by Johan Björk

Artificial Beach, 2015
recycled plastic pellets, beach
towel body pillow and mirrors

Le Melatonia, 2015
minifridges, lights and bottles,
carpet, LED lighting, wood, paintings, beds and bedside table

Pest Detective Painting, 2015
acrylic, UltraLite fabric and
Yellow Pages

Assassin Painting, 2015
acrylic and newspaper

A Place to Connect, 2015
bedside table with humidifier,
sand, seashells, plaster eggs,
WAVES mugs, alarm clock, lamp
with custom lampshade, acrylic
paint, coloured lights and water

The Aura Readers, 2015
vacuum forms of the artists' bodies
(colours determined through aura
readings that took place at ICA),
polyethylene terephthalate (PET),
water, wood, coloured gels, bed-
sheets and acrylic paint

Boiler Room Bottle, 2015
cast iron and cork containing a
nettle infusion

Chance Bottle, 2015
magnet bottle dragged along
Kitsilano Beach at sunset to
attract magnetic material and
phosphorescent rocks

Blind Bottle 3D, 2015
3D cinema glasses

*Moonshine Bottle
(Blind Bottle)*, 2013
Pyrex glass sculpted while
blindfolded

Checklist

*Yellow Apfelwein Bottle
(Pest Detective Bottle)*, 2013
Pyrex and cobalt glass sculpted
after the image of the Pest Detective

*Purple Valerian Bottle
(Old Hag Bottle)*, 2013
Pyrex glass sculpted after the
image of The Old Hag

*Grey Smoked Whiskey
Bottle (Night Times
Journalist Bottle)*, 2013
Pyrex and uranium glass with text

*Clear Chance Mixed-Alcohol
Bottle (Chance Bottle)*, 2013
Pyrex glass, dimensions selected
using dice

Pest Detective UltraLite, 2015
UltraLite fabric and plastic
water bottle

Secretary Bottle, 2015
polyethylene terephthalate
(PET) containing cochineal,
energy drink and water

Exclusion Cucoloris, 2015
wood, wheels, spray foam,
steel wool, chicken wire and
insulation tile

Secretary Cucoloris, 2015
wood, wheels, *Yellow Pages*,
telephone cords, "hands of the
secretary," WAVES mugs, telephone receivers, fly paper, photocopies from *Canadian Secretary*,
moth trap, vitaminwater bottles,
light bulbs and miscellaneous
materials

Beachcomber's Cucoloris, 2015
Pacific and Atlantic seaweed,
Rockaway Beach detritus, wood,
wheels, fishing line and sweetgrass

Stenographer Ensemble, 2015
custom-made shoes for Jim
Hopper, stenographer: silicon,
cochineal, UltraLite fabric,
stress mat, elastic and shorthand
on fabric, *Yellow Pages* from
Philadelphia and Vancouver, and
mirrors; Stenograph in custom
stenographer holster: wood, stress
mats, vest and steno paper

Les Bouteilles de la Table Ronde,
2015
performance

During the exhibition opening,
bartenders served Magnussonian
Twists to visitors who recorded
their dreams. Stenographer Jim
Hopper recorded the events.
Drinking song libretto by Julia
Feyrer and Tamara Henderson;
score by Tony Solitro; performed
by mezzo-soprano Lauren Pearl
Eberwein

  Checklist

Bottles Under the Influence, 2012
16 mm film, colour, optical sound
7 min. 48 sec.

Bottles Under the Influence, 2013
blown and cast-formed glass,
edition 2 of 2
Commissioned by Walter Phillips
Gallery, Banff Centre
*Grey Smoked Whiskey Bottle
(Night Times Journalist Bottle)*,
Pyrex and uranium glass; *Yellow
Apfelwein Bottle (Pest Detective
Bottle)*, Pyrex and cobalt glass;
*Clear Chance Mixed-Alcohol
Bottle (Chance Bottle)*, Pyrex glass;
*Purple Valerian Bottle (Old Hag
Bottle)*, Pyrex glass; *Moonshine
Bottle (Blind Bottle)*, Pyrex glass

The Night Times News, 2013
newsprint

Newspaper/Boiler Room Table,
2013–16
brick press, paper bricks, *Night
Times* offset plates, glassblower's
newspaper, *Night Times Press Bar*
coasters (2013), *Newspaper Bottle*
extras (2015), ink and indigo

A Place to Connect, 2015
bedside table with humidifier,
sand, seashells, plaster eggs,
WAVES mugs, alarm clock, lamp
with custom lampshade, acrylic
paint, coloured lights and water

Consider the Belvedere, 2015
16 mm film, colour, optical sound
9 min. 28 sec.
Music composed by Johan Björk

Bed Nests, 2015–16
vacuum forms of the artists'
bodies, wood, carpet, lights
and eggshells

Blind Table, 2015–16
clay, 3D glasses and lenses,
Mindfold blindfolds, *Blind
Bottle* extras (2015) and
page flipper

Chance Table, 2015–16
Chance Bottle drawings, rope,
dice, sand, magnets, *Chance Bottle*
(2015), fluorite, kraisslite, chalco-
pyrite and other phosphorescent
geological specimens

Pest Detective Table, 2015–16
seashell dust typewriter, rock,
fruit replicas, *Pest Detective Bottle*
extras (2015), traps, UltraLite
Cubic Tech fabric and steel wool

Receptionists, 2015–16
Plexiglas and colour filters (colours
determined through individual
aura readings that took place at
ICA, Philadelphia)

*Revolving Cucoloris:
Beachcomber's, Exclusion and
Secretary*, 2015–16
Pacific and Atlantic seaweed,
Rockaway Beach detritus, fishing
line and sweetgrass, spray foam,
steel wool, chicken wire and insu-
lation tile, *Yellow Pages*, telephone
cords, "hands of the secretary,"
WAVES mugs, telephone receivers,
fly paper, photocopies from
Canadian Secretary, moth trap,

vitaminwater bottles, light bulbs,
wood and wheels

Secretary/Old Hag Table, 2015–16
stenograph, valerian root, silicone
moulds, keyboard, *Old Hag Bottle*
extras (2015), PET plastic
Secretary Bottle (2015), secretary's clothes, photocopies from
Canadian Secretary and cochineal

The Night Times Press Bar,
2015–16
bricks made from newspaper,
mortar (genuine Stockholm pine
tar, cochineal, water, newspaper),
Plexiglas, miscellaneous materials from the Belvedere Suite
collection, tar paper (roofing
material), ergonomic gel pads,
ergonomic keyboards, windows,
lighting, wood, *The Night Times
News* newspapers, insects from
Panama (bedbug, assassin bug and
cockroach), insects in cargo ships
booklet, projection, Mac mini
running Linux, custom Arduino
and Adafruit Pro Trinket keyboard controller, keyboards and
custom software.

Software programming and custom
keyboard controller hardware
assembly and programming by
Dan Riley. Insects courtesy of the
Spencer Entomological Collection,
Beaty Biodiversity Museum, UBC

The Night Times Press Bar was
originally commissioned and
constructed at the Institute of
Contemporary Art, University
of Pennsylvania as part of
Consider the Belvedere and mod-
ified for its iteration at the Belkin
Art Gallery.

*Communicating Vessels:
Galactic Glass Healer,* 2016
blown glass, water, retort stands,
monkey bars, tubing and stan-
dard tapered joints built by Brian
Ditchburn in the UBC Department
of Chemistry glassblowing studio

Hotel Reception Desk, 2016
desk with collage drawings and
paintings, eggshells, commu-
nicating Bembels (Hessischer
Apfelwein ceramic and carved salt
crystal) and vacationing compo-
sition books; storage cupboards
and drawers with drawings of
Last Waves objects by the Emily
Carr University drawing class of
Tiziana La Melia (aritsts: Clarissa
Chupik, Julia Cundari, Dawn
Ding, Emily Fu, Audrey Halim,
Ye Ji, Mitche Kenworthy, Sky
Kong, Blaire Lee, Rebecca Levy,
Gabriella Li, Lainka Li, Lingjing
Meng, Kristine Suddaby, Freya
Wan, Nancy Yangjingna, Brian
Yeo and Hong Zhou)

WAVES, 2016
indigo-dyed paper and coffee cup
flooring, display cases, stools,
decanters and fountain

*Karen Needham
Bug of the Month Calendar*, 1997
11 specimens, pins and box
Courtesy of the Spencer
Entomological Collection, Beaty
Biodiversity Museum, UBC

*Les Bouteilles de la Table
Ronde*, 2016
performance
Drinking song libretto by Julia
Feyrer and Tamara Henderson;
performed by Kallie Clayton and
Scott Rumble

Page 51: Walter J. Phillips, www.lochgallery.com/artist/walter-joseph-wj-phillips

Page 52: Portrait of *Le Grand Jeu*, www.rogergilbertlecomte.com/le-grand-jeu.html

Page 55: Vincente Minnelli, *On a Clear Day You Can See Forever*, 1970, film still

Page 56: Werner Herzog, *Heart of Glass*, 1976, film still. Courtesy of Deutsche Kinemathek - Werner Herzog Film

Page 57: Werner Herzog on the set of *Heart of Glass*, 1976. Courtesy of Deutsche Kinemathek - Werner Herzog Film

Page 57: Photograph of André Breton by Man Ray, c. 1924, www.wikiart.org/en/man-ray/andré-breton-1930

Page 59: Cesare Ripa, "Allegory of Eternity" from *Iconologia*, 1669

Page 59: Rosalind E. Krauss, from the cover of *Perpetual Inventory*, 2010, reprinted courtesy of MIT Press

Page 59: Gena Rowlands and Peter Falk, *A Woman Under the Influence*, Los Angeles, CA, 1974. Photo: Sam Shaw. © Sam Shaw Inc. licensed by Shaw Family Archives, Ltd.

Page 60: SafeType™ keyboard, © ErgoType BV

Page 60: Belvedere Court, 2545 Main Street, Vancouver. Photo: Karen Magill, 2012, www.karen-magill.blogspot.com/2012/08/belvedere.html

Pages 142–43: Photo by Jean-Baptiste Béranger, courtesy of Bonniers Konsthall, Stockholm

Page 161: Brion Gysin and William S. Burroughs with the *Dream Machine*, 1972. Photo: Charles Gatewood

Page 163: Rolf Loehrich. Photo: Gerry Altman

Page 163: UBC Student Union Building, ca. 1979. Courtesy of the UBC Archives Photograph Collection, 41.1/2299

Wherever possible every effort has been made to provide accurate attribution and to obtain appropriate permissions for images and materials reproduced in this catalogue. Any errors or omissions will be corrected in any future editions.

Julia Feyrer and Tamara Henderson is co-published by the Morris and Helen Belkin Art Gallery, University of British Columbia and the Institute of Contemporary Art, University of Pennsylvania.

Bottles Under the Influence
Walter Phillips Gallery, Banff Centre
Jesse McKee, curator
May 4–June 23, 2013

Julia Feyrer and Tamara Henderson: Consider the Belvedere
Institute of Contemporary Art, University of Pennsylvania
Alex Klein, curator
April 22–August 16, 2015

Julia Feyrer and Tamara Henderson: The Last Waves
Morris and Helen Belkin Art Gallery, University of British Columbia
Scott Watson, curator
September 6–December 4, 2016

Editing
Greg Gibson, Jana Tyner, Scott Watson

Photography
Michael R. Barrick, Morris and Helen Belkin Art Gallery; Constance Mensh, Institute of Contemporary Art; Donald Lee and Rita Taylor (pp. 23, 28, 33, 34, 39, 55), Walter Phillips Gallery

Design
Mark Owens

Type
Basel Medium, Chi-Long Trieu
Times New Roman Seven

Printing
Shapco, Minneapolis

Writing
Alex Klein, Jesse McKee, Scott Watson

Morris and Helen Belkin Art Gallery
University of British Columbia
1825 Main Mall
Vancouver, BC
V6T 1Z2 Canada
www.belkin.ubc.ca

Institute of Contemporary Art
University of Pennsylvania
118 South 36th Street
Philadelphia, PA
19104 USA
www.icaphila.org

ISBN: 978-0-88865-305-5

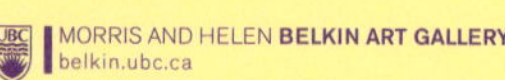

Julia Feyrer and Tamara Henderson: The Last Waves at the Morris and Helen Belkin Art Gallery was made possible with the generous support of the Canada Council for the Arts and our Belkin Curator's Forum members: Audain Foundation, Christopher Foundation, Nicola Flossbach, Henning and Brigitte Freybe, Jane Irwin and Ross Hill, Michael O'Brian Family Foundation, Phil Lind Foundation, and Scott Watson and Hassan El Sherbiny. We gratefully acknowledge the support of the UBC Department of Art History, Visual Art and Theory, the Beaty Biodiversity Museum, the Department of Theatre and Film, the Faculty of Arts, the AMS Student Society and the Department of Chemistry, with special thanks to Brian Ditchburn.

Julia Feyrer and Tamara Henderson: Consider the Belvedere at the Institute of Contemporary Art was supported by Wendy Fisher, Cheri S. and Steven M.

Friedman, Christina Weiss Lurie, Norma and Lawrence S. Reichlin, and by Lori W. and John R. Reinsberg. Related programming was supported by the Christian R. and Mary F. Lindback Foundation. ICA is always Free. For All. Free admission is courtesy of Amanda and Glenn Fuhrman. ICA acknowledges the generous sponsorship of Barbara B. and Theodore R. Aronson for exhibition catalogues. Programming at ICA has been made possible in part by the Emily and Jerry Spiegel Fund to Support Contemporary Culture and Visual Arts and the Lise Spiegel Wilks and Jeffrey Wilks Family Foundation, and by Hilarie L. and Mitchell Morgan. Marketing is supported by Pamela Toub Berkman and David J. Berkman and by Lisa A. and Steven A. Tananbaum. Additional funding has been provided by the Horace W. Goldsmith Foundation, the Overseers Board for the Institute of Contemporary Art, friends and members of ICA, and the University of Pennsylvania. General operating support is provided, in part, by the Philadelphia Cultural Fund. ICA receives state arts funding support through a grant from the Pennsylvania Council on the Arts, a state agency funded by the Commonwealth of Pennsylvania and the National Endowment for the Arts, a federal agency. ICA acknowledges Le Méridien Philadelphia as our official Unlock Art™ partner hotel.

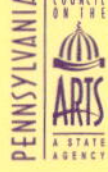

 Colophon